SANDY
McMAHON

& THE EARLY CELTS

First published 2015 by DB Publishing, an imprint of JMD Media Ltd, Nottingham, United Kingdom.

ISBN 9781780914565

SANDY McMAHON

& THE EARLY CELTS

DAVID POTTER

CONTENTS

ACKNOWLEDGEMENTS

I have been very fortunate to receive a great deal of help and encouragement in the writing of this book. First and foremost the Celtic Graves Society were the real inspiration for this book by their hard work in discovering and renovating the grave of 'The Duke' in Dalbeth Cemetery and holding a ceremony of dedication. At this ceremony, it was my pleasure to meet a great many of Sandy's family.

Celtic historiography is huge, probably a lot larger than any other club on earth. It has been my pleasure to read and dip into the works of people like Tom Campbell, Pat Woods, Marie Rowan, Jim Craig, George Sheridan, the late Eugene MacBride and many others to whom I will apologise for forgetting to mention their names.

The Mitchell Library in Glasgow, and to a lesser extent the National Library of Scotland in Edinburgh, has been a great source of information, and their staff were always unfailingly courteous, polite and prompt in answering queries and questions.

Several others deserve a mention. Allan Lugton was very helpful with the Hibs part of Sandy McMahon's life; Heather McMahon sent me a couple of pictures; and various others with the odd word of encouragement kept me going. It has been a long task, but the subject, Sandy McMahon, makes it all worthwhile.

David Potter, Kirkcaldy 2015.

PROLOGUE

There can be little doubt that one of the features that has characterised Celtic over their (almost) 130 years of existence had been a personality goal scorer. Three immediately spring to mind in Jimmy Quinn, Jimmy McGrory and Henrik Larsson. Others of scarcely less value to the club include Jimmy "Sniper" McColl, Joe Cassidy, John McPhail, Billy McPhail, Steve Chalmers, John Hughes, Bobby Lennox, Dixie Deans, Kenny Dalglish, Frank McGarvey and Frank McAvennie, Chris Sutton, John Hartson and one or two others in more recent years on whom the verdict of history awaits.

Several years ago, the author wrote a book on Jimmy Quinn, which was subtitled "Celtic's First Goalscoring Hero". This, I now recognise, was an error for which the McMahon family are due an apology. Jimmy Quinn was indeed great and he was indeed a goalscoring hero. He was not however the first. The first was Sandy McMahon, whose floruit was some ten years earlier than Quinn, but it is no insult to either man to link them together. They both played their part in creating the early Celtic tradition.

SO WHO WAS SANDY MCMAHON?

There was no greater admirer of Sandy McMahon than Willie Maley who both played alongside him and was his manager for a spell. Maley, of course, not without cause described as "The Man Who Made Celtic", was a giant in the Scottish game for 50 years, winning as either manager or player 19 Scottish League Championships and 15 Scottish Cups. Maley's opinion, in *The Story Of The Celtic* therefore, should count for something.

"Sandy McMahon was one of Celtic's earliest stars and certainly one of its brightest, and was regarded as the most marvellous header of the ball of the period. Tall, almost ungainly in appearance, Sandy depended on footwork and the deceptive swerve to beat an opponent. Of speed, he had little. His judgement of the flight of the ball when free or corner-kicks were being taken was simply marvellous, and despite the fact that there were always several opponents set to watch him, at these times he scored a great number of goals with his head. Although he was regarded as a centre forward during the very short time he spent with Hibernians before coming to Parkhead, it was as an inside-left he made his reputation in partnership with Johnny Campbell, who in those days played on the wing".

His sentiments are echoed by James E. Handley, author of *The Celtic Story*, who talks about;

"…one of the greatest of them all, Sandy McMahon – 'The Duke' they called him – who with swerve and head formed with outside-left John Campbell from Benburb one of the most formidable wings in football…His partnership with Campbell was one of perfect understanding. They formed a manoeuvring pair whose accurate passing, as one or other darted forward to receive the ball from his partner or skipped to the rear for a back-heel touch, left defences bewildered. In addition to a gift for mazy manipulations with his toe McMahon was the greatest header of a ball that the Celtic team knew until the arrival of Jimmy McGrory…"

Neither Jim Craig nor Pat Woods are anything like old enough to have seen Sandy McMahon, but in their recent book *Celtic, Pride and Passion*, they describe Sandy thus; " 'The Duke', so called after either the Duke to whom he bore a physical resemblance, or Duc Patrice de Mac-Mahon, the late President of France (take your pick) could be regarded as the first Celtic 'superstar'. He was considered a genius of a player by the *Glasgow Observer* which once profiled him as a player with outstanding heading ability – 'endowed with extraordinary cervical elasticity' – and one who 'danced dances with the sphere at his toe and generally indulged in such mazy gyrations that opposing half-back was prepared to swear McMahon was in three places at once' ".

But as valid a testimony as any was the verdict of a veteran Celtic supporter (my grandfather) who had been there at the start. Before his death in 1950, he, apparently, would talk about Sandy McMahon and would unreservedly put him in the same bracket as Jimmy Quinn and Jimmy McGrory. You cannot really get better than that, can you?

1.

EARLY DAYS, HIBS AND CELTIC

Sandy McMahon was born of Irish stock near Selkirk on 16 October 1870, but at an early age his parents moved to Edinburgh (to find a job, presumably) in Edinburgh's Old Town area commonly known as "Little Ireland". As a generalisation, the Irish who came to the east of Scotland usually arrived earlier than those who settled in the west. There is a tendency to think that the immigration started only after the Potato Famine of 1846. In fact it had been going on since before the rebellion of 1798, and even the term "immigration" is misleading, for after the Act of Union in 1801 and until the violent times of the 1920s, Ireland was all part of Great Britain. Someone moving from Donegal to Edinburgh, for example, was no more an "immigrant" in the 19th century, than someone moving from Edinburgh to Cambridge in the 21st century.

As to whether the McMahon family were Scottish or Irish, they didn't really care, although there were others who did. Religion would normally in these circumstances define the nationality as well. If you were Catholic, you were Irish, and if you were Protestant, you were Scottish. But it was not a matter of huge importance to the McMahon family. "Dual nationality" would have been a label that might have appealed to them.

What was crucial to the McMahons was, of course, education. Two years after Sandy was born, the Gladstone Government passed the Scottish Education Act, compelling the setting up of a school in every town and village, instead of leaving it to the Parish Church, as had been the case previously. This had immediate benefits in an immense and sharp decline in illiteracy well before the turn of the century. In the case of Sandy McMahon, who not only went to school but enjoyed the maximum encouragement from his aspirant parents, education and learning became very much part of his psyche, and it was often said that Sandy was one of the best read football players of his generation with a sound knowledge of the Bible, William Shakespeare and Robert Burns.

Scotland and Ireland, as we have stated, in the 19th century were part of the same country called Great Britain. The Irish were a recognised and accepted unit in the Scottish capital. Not far away from where the McMahons lived, in the Grassmarket in Edinburgh resided the family of James Connolly, the great Socialist and one of the leaders of the Irish Rebellion of 1916. He was the man who was infamously put into a chair to be shot by the British at Kilmainham Gaol, Dublin, that historic morning in May 1916, and is arguably the greatest Irish rebel of them all, not least because of his trade union and socialist activities which were seen as subversive.

> *They told me James Connolly was shot in a chair*
> *His wounds from the fighting all bleeding and bare*
> *His fine body twisted all battered and lame*
> *They soon made me part of the Patriot Game.*

Connolly, of course, was not just a hero of Ireland. He was also a hero of the working class, and his socialism came from having had the same background as Sandy McMahon – bright, well educated and with the ability to look around at the social conditions in his environment, and realise that there was something wrong with this!

We do not know for certain whether Connolly and McMahon ever met (Connolly was four years older than McMahon) but they would have heard of each other, certainly by the 1890s and the 1900s when the both of them made their mark on the world. Each would have followed the other's career with interest. Connolly was a football fan, with a love of Hibs (it is claimed) and McMahon was certainly interested in the wider world of politics.

Sandy grew to be a tall, athletic boy, and began to play football for Leith Harp. Football was of course the great occupation of working class youths in Scotland in the 1880s. At the start of that decade, Scotland had beaten England at football five years in a row, and the boost given to the game by those five years of success was enormous. For a game of football, all you really need is a ball, and about thirty lads can be kept happy with that, so there was little surprise in its popularity with the working classes. And of course Edinburgh had the wide-open spaces like the Meadows where the game could be played!

The young McMahon

Street football, of one kind or another, had of course been played for centuries in Scotland. But now since about 1867 with the foundation of the Queen's Park Football Club, and perhaps more significantly, the playing of an annual International match between Scotland and England from 1872 onwards, the game began to become a lot more organised and formalised with rules, referees etc. It is impossible to state with any degree of accuracy when football was actually born. It basically evolved and was certainly burgeoning when Sandy came to live in Edinburgh.

It was perhaps a little strange that the poorer sections of Scottish society, especially the Irish enclave in Edinburgh, found it possible to identify with the middle class, snooty and rather exclusive Queen's Park who supplied the bulk of the players for the Scottish team. But Scotland was, then as now, definitely a country, if not in the political sense since 1707, certainly in the cultural, social and now sporting sense. So a Scotsman, irrespective of social class or ethnic origin would certainly support Scotland in everything. And of course, within this concept of being Scottish, the McMahons were also Irish as well.

In Edinburgh since 1875, the Irish had had their own team – the Hibernian – the unashamed team of the Irishmen, (the Latin name for Ireland is "Hibernia") and every Irish lad (and there were many, although by the 1880s possibly second or even third generation) would love the Hibs. They had their ready-made opponents in the Hearts, the Heart of Midlothian, a more obviously Scottish organization. They were a club formed originally for dancing, rather than football, it was said, and founded a year earlier than Hibs in 1874. There was also the team from Stockbridge called St Bernard's.

Leith Harp were recognised as one of the feeder teams for Hibernian. The Hibs management committee noticed this young lad called McMahon there, and on Saturday 7 November 1885, Sandy played at left-back, it is claimed by Alan Lugton in his excellent *The Making Of The Hibernian*, in a 4–1 win over St Mirren. If this story is true – and we have no reason to believe otherwise, although there is a possibility that this was another Alexander McMahon, for McMahon was a common enough name in the Irish community – then Sandy was only 14 when he made his debut in senior football! He played again on 27 February 1886 when Hibs defeated Dumbarton in a game that was marked by the debut of another Hibs and future

Celtic player – Willie Groves, commonly known as "Darlin' Willie". The Scottish League had not yet been formed, so, with the exception of the Scottish Cup and a few local competitions, most games were so called "friendlies". Often, they were anything but!

Sandy was still a reserve with Hibs (and presumably attended Hampden Park as a spectator and supporter) on that iconoclastic day of 12 February 1887 when Hibs won the Scottish Cup, beating Dumbarton 2–1 in the Final with his friend "Darlin' Willie" scoring one of the goals. Hibs thus became the first east of Scotland team to win the Scottish Cup, and in so doing; put an idea or two into the head of people like Brother Walfrid. Surely an Irish football team in Glasgow (where Irish immigration, much more noticeable in Glasgow than Edinburgh, meant that there would be a huge support) might be a very good idea, and that whatever the Edinburgh Irish did, the Glasgow Irish could do as well – and even better.

McMahon was over six feet in height, considerably taller than the average person in those unhealthy, consumptive days of the late 19th century, and left-back did look like the best place for him to play. But when his friend Willie Groves decided to become the darling of Glasgow rather than Edinburgh and left for the new Celtic team in summer 1888, Sandy was tried in the Hibernian forward line, and after a few indifferent performances, suddenly struck form on 19 January 1889 at Beechwood Park, Glasgow against Glasgow Thistle, when this tall figure with no teeth (apparently) and a drooping moustache who looked more like a schoolteacher or a bank clerk suddenly hit form and scored an individual goal after a long, mazy run. He was still 18 months short of his 20th birthday.

By this time he was said to be working in a printer's firm in Edinburgh. He was said to have played a few games for a team called Darlington St Augustine's (presumably having gone to Darlington to further his career as a printer) but if he did, he did not stay there long and soon returned to Scotland. A Hibs source tells us that he was, "big, awkward, ungainly and gawky with a shambling gait, but when he put on that Hibs jersey he was transformed, all ease and grace, Sandy could take out a whole defence with just one swerve of his body. When he got the ball he hunched over it with arms outspread and weaved his way past desperate defenders with eel-like grace. And nobody could score goals like him, especially with his head. It was one of his many specialities."

But by 1890, Hibs were beginning to struggle. Heart of Midlothian would soon overtake them as the major team in Edinburgh and would join the inaugural Scottish League in that year and would win the Scottish Cup in 1891. Already denuded of many of their best players by the more obviously ambitious Irish outfit in the west (which had already reached the Scottish Cup Final in their first year of existence and were telling everyone of their plans to build a massive new stadium to house the Scotland v England International as well as provide a home for a team that intended to change world football), Hibs were still bogged down in internecine strife with a pronounced lack of vision or ambition, and a reluctance to open their doors to anyone of a non-Irish or non-Catholic background.

This new team in Glasgow called the Celtic and sometimes pronounced the Keltic had deliberately chosen their name to indicate that they were to be both Scottish and Irish. There was to be no narrow religious discrimination. Although the support were, at least at the outset, more or less 100% Irish and Catholic, and all lived in the Glasgow area, the way ahead lay in bringing the best players to the club, irrespective of their ethnic origins or religious background.

Meanwhile back in Edinburgh, Hibs had lost their ground in Bothwell Street, and were virtually in abeyance when the energetic Celtic committee in late 1890 made an approach for Sandy McMahon and Jimmy McGhee. In McMahon, they clearly saw possibilities. McMahon, although loyal to Hibs, began to question the future of his first love and slowly began to see that the new Celtic team were the ones that were going to make the Irish challenge on Scottish football.

There also exists the possibility and perhaps even the probability, although rigorously denied at the time, that a little money (possibly a lot of money) was offered. Professional football was legalised in England in 1886, but would not be officially recognised in Scotland until 1893. One would have had to be incredibly naïve however to believe that the new Celtic club were able to persuade so many stars to join them without some money being offered. In particular, very few people doubted that James Kelly had left the village team Renton for the metropolis of Glasgow for any reason other than money.

A few wealthy Catholic (and, oddly enough, Jewish) sponsors were behind Celtic. The gates that the team attracted were nothing short of phenomenal for the time, helped by the fact that the team almost immediately had some sort of success, and there was also the steely determination on the part of men like John H. McLaughlin and John Glass that the Irish in Scotland were going to have something to be proud of. The way of the Fenians with their bombs and botched assassination attempts would achieve little; success in this new game of football which had bewitched Scotland for the past 20 years or so, would surely do far more to gain respectability for the immigrant Irish. Paying football players was seen as little more than a stepping-stone for this lofty ideal.

It would also, more mundanely, in the long term generate a lot more money for the club. It was as true in the 1890s as it is true in the 21st century that although football allegiances are defined by a variety of circumstances like ethnicity, culture and family pressures, the decision whether or not to attend a game and pay money at the gate is determined by the possibility or actuality of success. Everyone likes to be identified with success, and if this meant that the Celtic club had to invest in a few players, then so be it. The long-term gains would outweigh any short-term loss.

The club had of course been formed with the honourable intentions of providing soup kitchens for poor children. This tradition, one would like to think, has not been entirely lost even to this day, but the hard headed founders of the club soon realised that to be successful in their game of football, one had to be ruthless as well, and if this meant "poaching" players from other clubs, even the club in Edinburgh with which there would seem to be a lot in common, then that would have to be what happened. What was important was that the Glasgow Irish would have a team to be proud of!

Sandy McMahon, "late of Hibernian" as *The Glasgow Herald* puts it, played his debut game for Celtic in a friendly played at Old Celtic Park on 1 January 1891 before a crowd of 15,000 against Dumbarton. The result was a 1–1 draw. "The game throughout was fast and exciting, at times brilliant," says the report. Celtic scored first when Willie Maley "headed through". The reporter annoyingly does not tell us who scored for Dumbarton but says that the Sons of the Rock deserve credit for playing so well after left-back Stewart was injured early on. Nothing is said about McMahon's performance, but a newspaper serialisation of the *History of Celtic* in 1931 talks about McMahon apropos of this game in a bizarre way saying that he played "arms held high, ostrich-style, head down, body bent forward". What that actually means is hard to imagine, but he seemed to have played well enough not to be immediately rejected. Indeed the very fact that his unusual style of playing was even noticed is itself an indication of how well he played.

The crowd of 15,000 is much commented upon. For the time, it was a huge crowd and showed yet again that the ambitious club from the East End might well have to move to new premises soon, for there was evidence of crushing as the crowd left the ground. It being New Year's Day, the crowd was in good humour, full of enthusiasm for "the bould Celts" with their green and white vertical stripes and looking forward to the day when Celtic would land a major trophy.

Celtic, however, were already out of the Scottish Cup that season, having been defeated 3–0 by the same Dumbarton at Boghead on a pitch that was far from suitable. Celtic had wanted the game to be played as a friendly, but were overruled by the referee. Some of the travelling Celtic support (a surprising amount had travelled by train from Glasgow to see this game) had not reacted well to the defeat, with a few beer bottles and stones being thrown. The Celtic committee, embarrassed by such disorderly activity, were therefore quite relieved on New Year's Day that their crowd had behaved and that the team had, to a certain extent at least, redeemed themselves after their Scottish Cup exit. As for young McMahon, who had recently arrived from the east, he was worth another game.

McMahon played in another friendly on 17 January (a 1–3 defeat by Clyde) before on 24 January making his competitive debut. 1890–91 was, of course, the first season of the Scottish League, an alien concept to many in the game. Celtic, ambitious and forward looking, were all in favour. In fact it had been one of their founding fathers John H. McLaughlin who had driven the idea. It was not so much the idea that every team had to play every other twice for points (two for a win and one for a draw) that caused such angst. It was the codification and the strict application of rules. The "gentlemen's agreement" ideal had gone. Celtic, for example, were deducted four points for playing goalkeeper Jamie Bell whom they had signed and then played in too much of a hurry; Cowlairs and Third Lanark would suffer similar penalties and Renton would be expelled altogether for playing in a friendly against a club (St Bernard's of Edinburgh) which was unashamedly and openly professional.

Professionalism was of course a hot topic in 1891. As we have already stated, it is difficult to believe that McMahon and others joined Celtic without some financial enticement, and one of the reasons why Queen's Park refused to join the Scottish League was because they felt (correctly, as it turned out) that the Scottish League would inevitably compel the legalisation of professionalism. Professionalism eventually came to pass in 1893, but all that 1893 really achieved was an official recognition of something that had been going on for a long time, and something to which the middle-class Queen's Park were, and remain, irrevocably opposed, even though the odd whiff of hypocrisy has been detected throughout the years. Stories of the odd coin or two or pound note being found in a player's shoes at the end of a game, have emerged from time to time! Their motto however remains *ludere causa ludendi* – to play for the sake of playing.

Images of the Celtic team that Sandy was joining

Be that as it may, McMahon (whether amateur, professional or "shamateur") made his League debut for Celtic on 24 January 1891 at Millburn Park, Alexandria against Vale of Leven. That Celtic, however far-seeing and perspicacious, were not yet the finished article in having a proper attitude to the game was seen in the fact that they had to play with only ten men! Mick McKeown, the talented but turbulent left-back failed to appear. The reason officially given was that he "missed his train". In fact it was well known that Mick had a drink problem and was probably on one of his periodic "benders".

One could ask two questions of the Celtic committee here. Why did they persist with Mick? And why did they not take an extra man with them? As it was, Sandy McMahon, nominally down as centre-forward, was in fact playing his debut at left-back, (he had of course played there for Hibs) as Celtic opted to play with four forwards. Hardly surprisingly then, that although Johnny Campbell, a man with whom Sandy had already struck up a friendship, scored first for Celtic, the team went down 1–3 to the men of Alexandria, and what little chance Celtic might have had of winning the first ever Scottish League possibly evaporated that day. In the event it would be shared between Rangers and Dumbarton

For McMahon, just turned 20 years old, although *The Glasgow Herald* says he "put in some fine work while at left-back", it was a terrible start to his official Celtic career, but he was wise enough to realise that he would have to bide his time. He also grew to understand that the opinions of men like right-half Willie Maley and centre-half James Kelly were worth listening to. He could learn from them.

McMahon was now out of the team for a spell, and he thus missed Celtic's first ever major trophy win. This was the Glasgow Cup, won in an emphatic 4–0 win before a large 10,000 crowd over Third Lanark at Hampden Park on 14 February 1891. The game was won in a devastating spell in the second half with a goal from Peter Dowds and two from Johnny Campbell after Celtic had gone in 1–0 up at half time through an own goal. Celtic Reserves beat a team called Carrington 10–0 in the North-Eastern Reserve Cup that day and it would have been a reasonable assumption that Sandy was playing and indeed scoring a few goals.

He possibly was invited to the meal at the Alexandra Hotel in Bath Street to celebrate the winning of the Glasgow Cup. If so, he would have witnessed and indeed joined in the lavish festivities. He would have seen the hordes outside, cheering and clapping their team who had now won a Cup at last. There was the occasional "outburst of singing" of openly subversive Irish rebel songs like *A Nation Once Again, The Wearing O' The Green* and *God Save Ireland* as well as a few Glasgow Music Hall favourites like *Clementine*.

It was at moments like this that the wiser elements of the committee and the players may have realised the breathtaking potential of this organization, who had now played football for less than three seasons, but had already made such a huge impact on the game and their many supporters who, God knows, had little else to make them happy. McMahon would have noticed this and accepted that, although there was no lack of support for the Hibs in Edinburgh, the adulation and enthusiasm for this club in Glasgow was something different!

A week later the Celtic Crusaders (as the Reserves were called) won the Second XI Cup by winning 13–1 over the St Mirren Strollers, but there is no sign of McMahon playing in that game. But he was given a game for the first XI at Whitefield Park, Cambuslang on 7 March. We are told that the Celtic team drove out to the village in a horse-drawn brake, and we can imagine the thrill that that in itself gave the youngster, to sit along with such great names and to be part of "the Celtic". The game however was no great success, for the team went down 1–3. McMahon was listed at inside-right, but late in the game was brought across to the inside-left position (he was more naturally a left sided player) where he teamed up for the first time with Johnny Campbell.

He then missed the game against Cowlairs the following week, but the week after that, we find McMahon and Campbell listed on the left wing for the Scottish League game against Rangers at Old Celtic Park. Rangers of course had been established in 1873, and although they had not yet won the Scottish Cup (nor would they do so until two years after Celtic did) they were recognised as being one of the more successful and permanent of the many Glasgow sides.

This was a big game, but it is important to realise that this was not necessarily the special occasion that it would become later, – they were not yet called the "Old Firm", nor had Rangers as yet identified themselves with the despicable sectarianism that would befoul their reputation from the 1920s onwards – but it was still a Glasgow derby between two well-supported sides with clear ambitions for the future. There was indeed, even in Celtic circles, a special kind of affection for Rangers who, from the start, had been very supportive and helpful to the fledgling Celts. If anyone had asked a Celtic supporter in 1891 who the big rivals were in the city, he would certainly have said "Queen's Park" rather than "Rangers".

Most sources say that the result at Celtic Park on 21 March 21 was 2–2 although *The Glasgow Herald* seems convinced that it was 1–1! It is important, however, not to be too judgemental about the quality of newspaper reporting in the 1890s. The "reporter" simply stood in the crowd, wrote something down and gave it to a boy who would cycle into town to the office. The reporter would not necessarily even be anyone who knew very much about the game! And sometimes some important games were simply ignored by some newspapers, while others of less significance were highlighted!

Everyone agrees however that the left wing partnership of McMahon and Campbell worked well. Indeed, it never looked back. Following a successful tour of the north of England at Easter, and a few games against English teams at Celtic Park when giants like Bolton Wanderers and Preston North End (winners of the English League and Cup double in 1889 and rightly called "proud Preston") were put to the sword, Celtic hit a rich vein of form. It was too late for Celtic to win the League themselves, and indeed a few games were lost in any case, but they took points off both the League challengers, Rangers and Dumbarton.

Sometimes McMahon was listed as left-winger with Campbell inside, (in the same way as in the late 1960s, sometimes it was "Lennox and Auld" – other times "Auld and Lennox") but whatever combination it was, Celtic produced the goods. On 2 May at Ibrox, McMahon inspired Celtic to stage a late fight back to beat Rangers 2–1. He was, late in the game, "cheered for a grand run but was grassed as he was about to shoot". Then a few days later McMahon scored a hat-trick in a 9–1 demolition of Vale of Leven, and the first League season ended with McMahon scoring in a 2–0 win over the Paisley side Abercorn. The Celtic side had a new hero.

Hopes were high in Celtic circles for the Charity Cup (called in 1891 the League Charity Cup rather than the Glasgow Charity Cup because Dumbarton and a few other League teams were invited to join, leaving the non-League teams like Queen's Park to play in another Glasgow Charity Cup, which the Queen's won 9–1 by beating Northern). Third Lanark were twice beaten, a second game being necessary because Third Lanark for some obscure reason protested after their 8–1 hammering the first time (McMahon scoring a hat-trick). Protests and replays were by no means unusual in Victorian football, but in this case it availed Third Lanark little, for they lost 6–1 the second time with McMahon scoring twice. Indeed it looks like an attempt to make more money, admittedly in this case of the Glasgow Charity Cup, for a good cause.

But the Final was lost to joint League Champions Dumbarton at Cathkin on the late date of 10 June 1891 in sweltering heat. Dumbarton were a good side (joint champions of course of the first ever Scottish League spoke for itself) and there was no disgrace in the defeat. Yet the Celtic fans felt that their team was improving. The Glasgow Cup triumph in February was tangible proof that the team could win things. Their dealings with English teams showed that they could live with the best. Now with their new left wing partnership of McMahon and Campbell showing promise, there was hope that the team could do even more. There was already much talk in Glasgow about "the Celtic", "the Celts" or "the bould Celts" as more and more supporters began to flock to see the green and white vertical stripes.

2.

1891–92 – THE FIRST SCOTTISH CUP

Season 1891–92 can almost be put in the same category as 1907–08 and 1966–67 as one of the truly great seasons in the history of the club. One says "almost" because the glaring omission of the trophies landed was the Scottish League, won that year by Dumbarton. But the other three trophies were all won, the Glasgow Cup and the Glasgow Charity Cup, and of course the greatest trophy of them all, the Scottish Cup. All this occurred when their new stadium was being built as well! If Willie Maley was "the man who made Celtic", 1891–2 was, "the season which made Celtic" and of course Sandy McMahon played a glorious part in that momentous year. It was a tremendous occasion on which to win one's spurs. To the astonishment of the footballing world and the amazement of their fans, Celtic, by 1892, were clearly here to stay, unlike so many other clubs who rose and fell in the 1880s and 1890s.

The Celtic success was purchased to a large extent by the (temporary) downfall of Hibs – something that might have caused McMahon a little distress. Hibs would of course come back and in 10 years time they would win the Scottish Cup and a year after that, the Scottish League. But for the mean time, there was in the Irish in Edinburgh a certain jealousy, irrational but sharp and residual, about the achievements of the Celts, and McMahon and his family (some of whom still lived in Edinburgh) may well have felt uncomfortable about all that. Those of the Hibernian persuasion who were able to take a broader view of things would have seen that Celtic's great season of 1892 meant that the Irish were here to stay in Scottish football, and that Celtic, with their broad-based selection policy were indeed pointing the way to others.

Willie Maley's *The Story Of The Celtic* is an invaluable book for the early history of Celtic. Published in 1939 when Maley was past his 70th birthday, it has a few errors caused by Maley's failing memory and occasionally by his desire to hide something or give something else undue prominence, but it remains excellent source material, and of course can be called a "primary source" for Maley himself took part in the events about which he writes. Not unnaturally, he is consistently fulsome in the praise of McMahon, but makes a strange statement about the 1891–92 season when he says that, "The League results during the early months of 1891–92 gave no indication that the season was to be a memorable one in the history of the new club…"

This is not true. Maley is probably confusing this season with 1898–99 when the Scottish Cup was indeed won in April 1899, but League form in the autumn of 1898 had been dreadful. Although the opening League game in 1891–92 was a disappointing 1–3 defeat to last year's Scottish Cup winners Hearts, the rest of the calendar year of 1891 saw a 100% Scottish League record with a settled forward line of McCallum, Brady, Madden, McMahon and Campbell. Sandy fitted perfectly with Johnny Campbell, and behind them were a fine half-back line of Maley, Kelly and Dowds with full back the charismatic Jerry Reynolds and Dan Doyle, that brilliant enigma of British Victorian football. Rangers, Dumbarton and Hearts were all defeated with McMahon scoring in all three games, and detached observers like the leader writer of *The Glasgow Herald* compelled to come to the conclusion that the "green devils" were as good as anyone in Scotland, or even Britain.

In the game against Rangers on 22 August, a very impressive 3–0 win, McMahon opened the scoring with an "amazing screw-kick", and the team never looked back. That McMahon was beginning to sparkle for Celtic was indicated by the unofficial "cap" awarded to him on 3 October 1891 when he was invited to play for Scotland against the Canadian-Americans. They were a touring team called "Canada" for short, but they were hardly representative of their country, and they were patronisingly described by *The Glasgow Herald* as having "but a dim idea" of how the game should be played. In particular they made "free use of their hands" both in handling the ball and in holding men back. It was thus an unofficial International, but it was still a great honour for the young McMahon to be asked to play for Scotland. For someone of even the most distant of Irish origins, it was yet another sign of acceptance into the Scottish community.

The game was played at Ibrox before a sparse attendance with "the gate not exceeding £70". Willie Maley was also playing that day, and although McMahon didn't score, he is described by the Press as teaming up well with Jack Bell of Dumbarton (with whom he would play in the future for Celtic) to make a "thrusting left wing" for Scotland in their very easy 5–1 victory. The 5–1 score line was sadly in tune with the other results of the Canadians, most of whom were of Scottish origin in any case, and in later years were able to boast about having played against men like Willie Maley and Sandy McMahon. On occasion on their tour, it was not unknown for a man who had lived in Great Britain for a long time but claimed some vague connection with Canada, making himself known to them and finding himself in the team for the next game! Indeed Maley himself might have done this, for his mother was Canadian!

*Scotland v Canada 3 October 1891. McMahon is at the
front with his arms clasped round his knees*

In the meantime, things were progressing at Celtic Park. While the
New Celtic Park was being built, Old Celtic Park saw some marvellous football being played. Concrete proof of the rise of this Celtic
side and of the emergence of McMahon's career came on 12 December 1891 at Cathkin when Celtic won the Glasgow Cup for the
second time in the calendar year. The score was 7–1 against Clyde
and the football was in tune with the way Celtic had played against
other teams on the way to the Final. Admittedly, the opposition was
not always great, but the goalscoring and general attacking football
ensured that Celtic very soon became the best supported team in the
country, if they had not been so originally. Attacking football thus, at
a very early stage, became a Celtic concept and tradition, and in this
McMahon played a full part.

Very early do we find contemporary reports of the effectiveness
of McMahon and Campbell. One account in the *Scottish Sport* of a
game against Cambuslang says, "With machine-like accuracy Sandy
passed the ball to Campbell, darted forward for the return, skipped
to the rear with a cute back-heel touch, danced dances with the

sphere at his toe and generally indulged in such mazy gyrations that the opposing half-back was prepared to say that McMahon was in three places at once". Those of us who can recall the second goal of the 1965 Scottish Cup Final involving Bertie Auld and Bobby Lennox might have some idea of how well McMahon and Campbell read each other.

Sadly, the Glasgow Cup final on 12 December 1891 attracted a crowd of only 4,000. This was because the game was played in heavy rain and sleet, which occasionally turned to heavy snow and rendered play difficult and visibility virtually impossible from time to time. Rumours had circulated Glasgow all morning that the game would be off, and in spite of men with sandwich boards wandering around Buchanan Street and Sauchiehall Street assuring people that the game was still on, the attendance was poor. But the Glasgow FA were determined that the game would go ahead – they had even commissioned goal nets (a rare luxury for 1891) – and referee Mr Hay from Dumfries, who presumably might not have been paid if the game had been off, agreed that play was possible. The game started on time at 2.15 pm. The teams were;

Celtic: Cullen; Reynolds and Doyle; Maley, Kelly and Dowds; McCallum, Brady, Madden, McMahon and Campbell.

Clyde: Fortune; A. Sawers and Maxwell; Bowie, Cherrie and McLaren; McIntosh, Harvie, W. Sawers, Johnstone and McInnes.

Celtic led 2–0 at half-time, Clyde came back into it for a spell and pulled a goal back but then Celtic "sweeping through all opposition" scored three goals (McMahon scoring the first of these three) and as the snow gradually eased, Johnny Campbell picked up two through balls from McMahon to score two late goals. McMahon and Madden are singled out for praise by *The Glasgow Herald,* and McMahon would have enjoyed his tea that night at the Alexandra Hotel.

There was considerably less exuberance from the fans outside because of the weather, but there were still a few, cheering and singing Irish songs mingled with the occasional Scottish one and indeed a few, incongruous ditties from the music hall. But Sandy sat back, enjoying his whisky and thinking how warm it was in here, compared to the afternoon. Yet he listened to the Celtic fans who had braved the elements in the afternoon and were braving them again at night. There was surely here a very special club.

He looked round at the genial Maley, the serious but kindly Kelly, the quixotic Doyle and his own special friend John Campbell. They were personal friends as well as business friends – the football business! – and Sandy knew that a great future beckoned. 1892 promised a great deal, and what a tremendous thing it would be for all these underfed and ill clad supporters (some of them stood in the snow without any kind of jacket or coat at Cathkin today!) if only their beloved Celtic could win one of the major Scottish trophies, the League or the Cup. What a signal that would send out to the whole country! The team had only been going for three and a half years… but his thoughts were cut short. It was his turn to do his party piece for the players of Celtic and Clyde (some nice chaps there as well, including ex-Celt James McLaren "the Ould Giniral" – affable and sociable now that the game was over!) and the august, forbidding, wealthy but now mellowingly pleasant fellows of the Glasgow FA. A Burns song maybe, or in view of the weather, what about a rendition of Tam O'Shanter? McMahon excelled in such things, and he had a wide choice, drawing on the family tradition of education and oral culture.

Apparently (and surprisingly) the Glasgow Cup was not presented that night, but it mattered little, for the Cup remained in the possession of Celtic who had won it in February as well. Celtic had thus won the Glasgow Cup twice in the same calendar year! (They would in 1969 perform a similar feat with the Scottish League Cup). Midwinter was spent well by McMahon and his friends, but New Year's Day 1892 brought things to earth with a sudden and rather dramatic thud. Following the Glasgow Cup triumph, important progress was made towards the elusive and much cherished Scottish Cup with a fine 3–0 victory over a team called Kilmarnock Athletic, (not Kilmarnock FC as we know them, but another team) then Boxing Day saw a good 2–0 win over St Mirren in the Scottish League.

Thus 1891 finished with Celtic and their fans in a huge state of optimism that their team could open the new stadium (already much progress could be seen) as "grand slammers" by winning both Scottish trophies and both Glasgow competitions. Little wonder that volunteers turned up in large numbers every Sunday to do some labouring, for the building of the new ground which was to be the best in the world and would have the best team in the world! Working on a Sunday, even for nothing, still horrified Presbyterian Scotland, of course, but it did show the world that something remarkable was happening in Glasgow's East End!

It was also another subtle, and socially acceptable, way of the Irish taking over, or at least making their mark on, Scotland! The new stadium could hold a crowd about six or seven times the size of the average Celtic home gate, and there was little doubt that the new stadium was being built to host the biggest game of the era, the biennial visit of England to Scotland for "the" International. Now, if this ground could be bigger and better than Hampden, Ibrox, Cathkin or anywhere else, and could thus host the Scotland v England game, what a coup that would be for the Irish in Scotland!

It is of course to the eternal credit of Celtic's founding fathers that they realised that there was no need for the Irish in Glasgow to remain a self-pitying ghetto enclave. That was what had happened to

Hibs, and they barely existed at the moment, being more or less in abeyance, but men like McLaughlin and Glass realised that the Irish had talent. They had a great deal to contribute to Scottish society. They were, as a distinguished Irishman, Patrick Pearse, would put it a quarter of a century later, "august despite their chains". Their football team was to be their vehicle in Scotland. It could achieve far more than Fenian violence.

No official game had been arranged for New Year's Day, but Celtic invited League Champions Dumbarton for a friendly at Old Celtic Park. (The League programme was already well advanced and Dumbarton, last year's joint winners with Rangers, were doing well). There may have been financial advantage in all this, but in footballing terms it turned out to be an embarrasing mistake. The players, it appeared did not take the game seriously enough and quite a few of them, McMahon included perhaps, decided to celebrate the arrival of the New Year in the traditional Scottish way. Dumbarton clearly thought otherwise, and their players were noticeably fitter than Celtic's. Some interest was raised by the deployment for the first time at Celtic Park of goal nets. They would get a good hanselling that day, although not in the way that Celtic would have liked. To help the holiday mood, the game was kicked-off by Colonel Burke of Buffalo Bill's Wild West Show.

A huge crowd of 20,000 turned up. Celtic were without James Kelly and borrowed a man called John Cherrie from Clyde as centre–half. He did not have a good game, to put it mildly (he had hardly distinguished himself in Clyde's 1–7 defeat to Celtic in the Glasgow Cup final three weeks earlier) – but neither did Jerry Reynolds and Dan Doyle the full-backs – but the main focus fell on the performance of goalkeeper Tommy Duff. "Focus" was the operative word, for Duff himself seemed to find it difficult to pay attention to the game, and by half-time Celtic, to the horror of their fans, were 0–5 down. They rallied a little in the second half and restricted the incredulous Dumbarton side to only another three and the game finished with "boos and catcalls" at Celtic 0 Dumbarton 8.

Neither Cherrie nor Duff ever played again for Celtic. In Duff's case there was the added factor that he was reputed to have Orange sympathies. Some thought that he deliberately played badly for that reason, but that cannot be substantiated. It is unlikely, in any case, for Orangeism, although it certainly existed in the 1890s, had not yet accumulated its evil momentum of the 1920s, and was, at this stage, but a marginal aspect of Scottish society. Indeed the story of Duff's political sympathies sounds like a later attempt to explain away an embarrassing defeat.

Sandy McMahon said later that Duff had it in him to be a great goalkeeper but did not apply himself enough. That sounds like Sandy being tactful, and reminds one of euphemisms that one uses to describe, for example, an entertainer who fails to turn up for his concert thanks to some alcoholic over-indulgence. He is "unwell" or suffering from "overwork"!

For Celtic themselves, it was "no end of a lesson" about under-estimating opponents and over-celebrating the New Year. For men like McMahon it was a chastening experience to sink in the space of three short weeks from "heroes" (after the Glasgow Cup Final) to "zeroes", and have to be the butt of all the jokes such as the one that the players all went out on the town, drank plenty but ate (eight) nothing! The word "duff" meaning "useless" enjoyed a great boom in early 1892 as well! *The Glasgow Observer,* the unashamedly Catholic newspaper, which, admittedly, did not always report football in detail in 1891–92 is appropriately silent and embarrassed about this game. It was a shocking way to start the calendar year of 1892, which promised and (in the event) yielded so much.

McMahon (and indeed the rest of the team who played on that terrible day) may or may not at this stage of his life have been a "professional footballer" in the sense that he received money (illegally) for playing – we suspect he did – but in any case he was totally "professional" in his attitude. He hated losing and a defeat of that magnitude would have hurt inwardly. He may have been able to laugh it off as "one of those things" or "just a friendly", be he was very sore inside, and all the more determined that, on his watch, such things were never to happen again. As he walked off the field, he saw the looks of incredulity on some of the team's supporters. He would make sure it never happened again.

To a certain extent the team redeemed themselves with wins over Third Lanark and then Rangers in friendlies and then when the serious football resumed towards the end of the month, they consolidated their progress towards the Scottish Cup and the Scottish League with wins over Cowlairs and Cambuslang, thus regaining some of the respect of their supporters who were now willing to put aside the memories of the New Year debacle. McMahon was prominent in both victories.

Saturday 6 February 1892 saw the semi-final of the Scottish Cup against Rangers. Surprisingly, the crowd was only 11,000 and the causes given were the heavy rain (there was of course no shelter at Old Celtic Park) but also the fact that Renton had opted to play their replay from the previous round against Hearts at Hampden, rather than in their own village. That game attracted, amazingly, 14,000 including many "capitalists" (supporters from Edinburgh who found Hampden easier to reach than Renton) and Glasgow people with an affection for Renton. Thus the Celtic v Rangers game played second fiddle. It is hard to imagine that happening today!

It does perhaps also hint at something else, which does not happen today. There is seldom in the 21st century such a thing as a "football fan" per se. Normally a "football fan" is someone with a passionate commitment, irrational, ingrained, endogenous and inherited, towards a particular club. When his team is not involved, he will possibly watch a game on TV but if his wife wants instead to watch a soap opera or *Strictly Come Dancing*, he will not object. He is not really therefore a fan of the sport. It was different long ago. Teams always had their supporters, but there was also a large body of people who would choose on a given Saturday what was the best game to go and see. Even so, it is hard to explain why in 1892, more people chose to watch Renton v Hearts than Celtic v Rangers!

The 11,000 who braved the elements that miserable day at Old Celtic Park saw a remarkable game, which ended 5–3 for the green and white vertical stripes of Celtic. Celtic were absolutely brilliant in the first half, scoring four goals including one from McMahon who, "had not been seen in such grand form this year" as *The Glasgow Herald* put it, and when they scored again early in the second half, the game looked over. Indeed it was, but not before Rangers gave them a timely warning with three goals as they staged a late and determined, but ultimately futile rally. "A high class genuine display of football" was how it was described by the correspondent of *The Glasgow Herald* who was clearly impressed by Rangers late rally, which showed "gallantry and pluck". But it was Celtic who were in the Final to await the winners of Queen's Park v Renton, "the villagers" having defeated "the capitalists" that day at Hampden.

Later that month, McMahon scored a "handsome brace of goals" as the team notched an important League victory against Third Lanark, but by this time excitement was growing at Celtic Park about the opening of the lavish new ground, and, naturally, the Scottish Cup Final scheduled for Ibrox against Queen's Park on 12 March. The dream of course would have been to win the Cup on 12 March, then open the new stadium before the game against Clyde on 19 March. It didn't quite work out that way, for the Scottish Cup Final had to be declared a draw because of dreadful crowd problems, not through any malice or bad behaviour, but simply because of the exuberance and enthusiasm of the Celtic crowd.

In any case the new ground was not yet quite ready for 19 March.

Nevertheless the opening ceremony went ahead with prominent Irish nationalist politician Michael Davitt, one time convicted Fenian and violent extremist, but now involved with more respectable organisations for Irish Home Rule, invited to plant shamrocks on the centre spot at the new Celtic Park before walking the short distance to Old Celtic Park to kick-off at the old ground in the Celtic v Clyde League game.

McMahon would have relished the Scottish Cup Final on 12 March, which meant so much to the infant club and their massive band of supporters. The Celtic crowd amazed all the other clubs, whose income was so much enhanced when they were playing Celtic. But on this occasion, the Scottish Cup Final of 1892, the Celtic crowd would count to the club's detriment, for there were just too many of them for the as yet fairly primitive Ibrox ground. Friday 11 March had seen heavy snow all over Glasgow and it was widely believed that the game could not be played. Things, however, improved on the Saturday, so that the Govan Cleansing Department was able to clear the pitch of snow and spread sand and, of all things, dry seaweed all over the playing area, to give the players a grip.

By midday on the Saturday, it was confirmed that the game was on, but by that time, in any case, the snow was visibly beginning to melt. Confusingly, tickets were sold but cash admission was also allowed. By 3.00 pm, an hour before the 4.00 start, the ground was full and the decision was taken to close the gates, thus leaving thousands, including some who had tickets, outside. Not unnaturally, this decision did not go down very well and the gates were rushed, so that hundreds more got in before the police restored some kind of order. Those still denied admission stayed outside, a sullen, unhappy mob whose misery was alleviated to a large extent by their ability to judge the progress of the game by the roars of the crowd.

It must be stressed that the crowd was not violent, and that their only desire was to see the game, particularly in the case of the Celtic fans who made up about three-quarters of the crowd and who craved victory in the Scottish Cup more than anything else in life. *The Glasgow Herald* intones gravely and melodramatically that, "nothing like this has ever been seen before in the history of the game" and their reporter was generally very impressed, and one suspects, more than a little frightened, by the noise and intensity of the crowd. It was an awesome indication of the potential of the Celtic team to pull in the crowds.

Rangers had erected a couple of temporary stands, but they were totally inadequate for the huge crowd, and starting from the very moment that Bob Smellie of Queen's Park and James Kelly of Celtic led their teams onto the field, the crowd kept encroaching on the playing area, simply because there was no room for them anywhere else and there was real danger of them being crushed to death. After about 20 minutes of constant interruptions, both sides agreed to play this game as a friendly.

Ironically after this, the crowd settled and they saw a good game, not necessarily aware that they were watching a friendly, not the Scottish Cup Final. The nature of the crowd is indicated in the following quote that, "Choral singing was one of the diversions of the afternoon, several choirs going ahead at one time". McMahon is well reported in accounts of the game and Johnny Campbell's goal in the second half won the game for Celtic, although the disappointment of the game only being a friendly must have been intense. The players apparently were not officially told until full-time. The game was quietly re-arranged for 9 April, and to deter such a huge crowd from re-appearing, the prices were doubled from one shilling to two shillings!

To our modern eyes, this seems to be an appalling piece of pocket lining, but that complaint was never seriously made, apparently, in 1892. Yet it did penalise the Celtic crowd more than the Queen's Park one, for the Irish in Glasgow at that time were a lot less able to afford two shillings for a football match than their well-heeled Queen's Park counterparts! It is difficult to assess how much this was in modern terms, but there were 20 shillings in a pound and a labourer would seldom earn anything like a pound per week in 1892. We are surprised to discover a distinct lack of contemporary criticism of the doubling of the charges on these discriminatory grounds, but some newspapers pointed put an amazing coincidence. 1892 was of course Celtic's second Scottish Cup Final, and in 1889 something similar had happened when the game against Third Lanark had been declared a friendly because of heavy snow. Perhaps they are hinting at something there.

The Scottish Cup was thus in abeyance, as it were, when Michael Davitt arrived a week later on 19 March. McMahon would have been thrilled to meet the Irish patriot with the one arm, but behind all the pomp and ceremony, Celtic and McMahon must have taken their eye off the ball, for a vital League point was lost at Old Celtic Park that afternoon when Celtic and Clyde played out a 0–0 draw. The left wing of McMahon and Campbell is praised but they were unable to break down the Clyde defence who had clearly learned a few lessons since their Glasgow Cup Final pasting last December.

Nevertheless, Davitt, who could not watch all the game because he had another political meeting and who probably was not a football fan in any case, returned to the Pinkerton's Hall, Main Street, Bridgeton where he spoke at length, wished the "Keltic" (sic) all the best and then (oddly) accepted the Glasgow Cup (won last December) on behalf of the Celtic club from Mr Geake of the Glasgow Football Association. It was a great occasion for the club, and McMahon would have now realised, if he hadn't before, what a mighty organisation this was, and was going to be in the future.

There is a surprising lack of criticism in the Scottish press about the employment of Michael Davitt for this purpose. Normally, the Victorian Press does not hold back if there is something that it is not happy about, and we might have expected a few questions raised about why Celtic did not invite someone Scottish, like the Chairman of the SFA, or if they had to stress their Irish roots, someone like the Roman Catholic Archbishop of Glasgow, for example. But the fact that it was Davitt, possibly the best-known Irish Home Ruler after the disgrace and death of Charles Stewart Parnell, did not disturb anyone. Indeed *The Glasgow Herald* does a very complimentary feature on the great Irish patriot, and talks about the "great ovation" he received from the crowd. Earlier in his life, he would have been classed as dangerous Fenian.

But something else happened for Sandy McMahon very soon. Rather to his surprise and delight, one feels, he found himself chosen to play for Scotland against England at Ibrox on 2 April! This was of course a great honour for anyone, and particularly for those of Irish extraction, even though, as in Sandy's case, the Irish connection was somewhat distant. It was a great token of acceptance of the Irish community in Scotland, and Sandy and his family were rightly proud of his being selected along with two other Celtic players Dan Doyle and James Kelly.

In McMahon's case it was also an indication of how far he had travelled in season 1891–92. He had only been in the Celtic team for little more than a year, and now here he was playing for Scotland against England. It was often the policy of Scotland to "blood" players by giving them a game against Ireland and Wales, opposition that they frequently outclassed, but on this occasion, Sandy was fast-tracked straight into the team for the England game. Whether this was a wise decision by the Scottish selectors is open to question, but he certainly, in the midst of all else that was happening in spring 1892, was very happy, as indeed were Celtic themselves who provided three players, second only to Queen's Park's four.

They would have had a lot less reason to be happy about the game itself, for Scotland, never recovering from a very early goal, lost 1–4 to a very talented English side, jeered at in the Scottish Press for being "professionals" at a time when Scottish football was, theoretically at least, amateur. The 20,000 crowd (considerably fewer than at the aborted Scottish Cup Final of three weeks previously at the same ground) were seen to "evaporate" in the second half in disgust at the rather inept performance of the Scottish team, but *The Glasgow Herald* has this to say about Sandy McMahon, "McMahon did many clever things, and with the exception of being, on one or two occasions, a little selfish, he, more particularly in the second half, was a success".

McMahon in middle of middle row proudly wearing his Scottish cap.
Standing on McMahon's right is Dan Doyle

That was at least something for Sandy, but it was a sad day for Scotland to whom defeat from "the white Rose" sat ill. International defeats to England were taken very seriously at that time, and all newspapers went into serious introspective analysis of what went wrong. They occasionally even came up with one or two suggestions about the game in general with a somewhat modern ring about them like "youngsters need better training" and "at lower levels, things are not quite right". The truth was, however, on this occasion at least that England simply had a better team. The referee Dr John Smith, who had himself played with distinction for Queen's Park and Scotland, remarked years later when he was practising medicine in Kirkcaldy, that 1892 was the worst Scottish team there had ever been.

Ibrox looked well that day with the pavilion decorated in the colours of crimson and orange, and the crowd being well entertained by a band from the Dumfries Industrial School before the start and with a Highland fling exhibition at half-time. Sandy must have been beginning to feel at home at Ibrox, for he knew that he would be back next Saturday for a piece of unfinished business in the Scottish Cup Final. It would be the game that would be one of the most significant in Celtic's history up to that point, and would remain so for a very long time after.

Celtic's founding father and now Chairman John Glass said unashamedly that this was the best day of his life. For 9 April 1892 was the first time that Celtic won the Scottish Cup, and thus Cullen; Reynolds and Doyle; Maley, Kelly and Gallagher; McCallum, Brady, Dowds, McMahon and Campbell became Celtic's first ever Cup winning team when they beat Queen's Park 5–1 on a dry but windy day at Ibrox. But these bland and anodyne statements cannot begin to do credit to the celebrations and joy that the triumph released in the East End of Glasgow and in other parts of Scotland where already a small Celtic community was beginning to emerge. Stories are told of brass bands, flute bands (yes, flute bands, for that instrument was not necessarily identified with Orangeism at that time!), impromptu singing and dancing in the streets as the Celtic heartlands saw such celebrations as they would seldom see again (to such an extent, at any rate) in their lifetime.

Clearly the new Celtic club had started something. Little else went right for those people, but now they had something to cheer about. Home Rule for Ireland was now confidently predicted by the illogical, and now there was at least some pay back for the landlords, the gombeen men, the British Army, the coffin ships and the potato famine. There was at least one part of the world in the ever growing Irish diaspora, where the wearing of the green would be something associated with pride and achievement.

Willie Maley himself played in the game and would often say that the scenes that he saw that day as the Scottish Cup was brought back in the horse-drawn charabanc from the Alexandra Hotel in Bath Street to the Calton in the East End changed his life and made him decide that from now on he would dedicate himself to the cause of this great club. He saw the destitute, the paupers, the children with no shoes, the beggars – he had seen all this before – but this time they had smiles on their faces, and he had helped to put the smiles there. "Our Bhoys Have Won The Cup" was the cry. They were "the risen people".

As for the effect that this victory had on Celtic's supporters, we, of course, have the account of Willie Maley about how impressed he was that those "urchins" had something to cheer about, and also this brilliantly graphic description from *The Scottish Referee* of the celebrations in the streets of the Celtic heartland that night. "Even the women lent a hand, and helped in no small measure to make the rejoicings hearty. But it was when the boys came marching home from the aristocratic Ibrox that the fun began in earnest… Bands? You ought to have seen them. They perambulated the whole district until well on in the evening… Truly the East End was a perfect turmoil until the very early hours of the Sunday, and many of the crowd won't be able to get over the rejoicing racket for days to come."

Perhaps the only modern parallel to this would be 1967. Those of us who recall the homecoming on Friday 26 May 1967 when the bus came along London Road, big Jock famously emerged with the big Cup, then a lorry (!) took the players round the ground to show off the beautifully ugly trophy to the huge appreciative crowd. This was, once again, "the risen people", and the euphoric glow lasted for months. Tellingly so many people now began to say, "Of course, I have always been a Celtic supporter…" when the facts of their past life did not really support such a contention.

Sandy McMahon, in 1892, was as much a hero as any. Conventional Celtic historiography says that Jimmy Quinn in 1904 was the first man to score a hat-trick in a Scottish Cup Final, and that Dixie Deans came next in 1972. There is however a distinct possibility that Sandy McMahon scored a Scottish Cup Final hat-trick before Jimmy Quinn, although the evidence is inconclusive, and the truth is that this is something that will never be proved.

The SFA fearing that the controversially inflated prices would result in a miniscule crowd, (and influenced no doubt by the jokes now beginning to appear in various newspapers about money making with reference to the alliterative names of the Queen's Park full-backs called Sillars and Sellar!) suddenly on Friday 8 April decided that the admission charge would, after all, be one shilling, not two, and inserted an advertisement in various newspapers to that effect. As a result, a crowd of about 26,000 appeared – huge for 1892 and bigger than last week's Scotland v England International, although still considerably smaller than the first game. The crowd was well policed with some 200 officers there, including a detachment of 30 mounted police. Following the unfortunate events of last month, no chances would be taken. The teams were;

Celtic: Cullen; Reynolds and Doyle; Maley, Kelly and Gallagher; McCallum, Brady, Dowds, McMahon and Campbell.

Queen's Park: Baird; Sillars and Sellar; Gillespie, Robertson and Stewart; Gulliland, Waddell, Hamilton, J. Lambie and W. Lambie.

Referee: Mr G Sneddon SFA.

Celtic were without "the rooter" Johnny Madden, out with an injury, and it was feared that they would suffer as a result, but with McMahon and Campbell on song, even a great player like Madden was hardly missed. The facts of the game are simple enough. Queen's Park, with the advantage of the gale blowing from the west (a constant theme apparently at Ibrox Cup Finals, for it happened again in 1900 and 1912) scored in the first half, but then Celtic, with McMahon and Campbell rampant, scored five times in the second half. The crowd is described as "sympathising with the Spiders rather than the Celts", but Celtic had a large contingent, and at the full time whistle in the pleasant April sunshine made their feelings plain with their cries of jubilations at the triumph of their team. Certainly the reporter of *The Scotsman* was very impressed by their exuberance, enthusiasm and the sheer noise that they made.

The question of whether or not McMahon scored a hat-trick lies in the scoring of the first two goals. Sandy definitely scored the third and the fifth – the third according to Willie Maley's *The Story of The Celtic* "McMahon indulging in one of his mazy runs – head down arms outstretched – simply walked through the Amateurs' defence to register the third goal", and the fifth a glorious headed goal from a corner kick of the sort that McGrory and McNeill would score in later years. The fourth goal is generally agreed to be an own goal, but the first two are both described as scrimmages, although Maley gives the pair of these goals to Johnny Campbell.

The Scotsman however gives the first goal to McMahon, which would indeed give him a hat-trick, and in later years, McMahon himself would claim that, "I scored goals one, three and five". *The Glasgow Herald* however gives both the first and the second goals to Campbell, as indeed do the majority of papers. *The Glasgow Observer* says something else again, or appears to. *The Glasgow Observer* in later years reports on Celtic avidly and passionately, but in 1892 does not usually talk too much about football. An exception however is made for the 1892 Scottish Cup Final, which must have affected the lives of more or less every one of their readers! "The Celts equalised in four minutes out of a scrimmage and in two minutes more McMahon scored a second point for Celtic...McMahon scored a third goal for the Celtic...with fifteen minutes to go, Kelly scored from a kick...scoring another, the Celtic won by five goals to one..." This seems to say that McMahon scored number two and three, and they decline to mention who scored the fifth.

There is thus the possibility that Sandy scored a Scottish Cup Final hat-trick for Celtic before Jimmy Quinn did in 1904, (John Smith of Queen's Park – the man who refereed the International of last week – had already reputedly scored one in the 1881 Scottish Cup Final against Dumbarton, although that too is disputed), but the honest and impartial historian would have to say that it is only a possibility. *The Glasgow Observer* however leaves no dubiety in the minds of its readers about the value of Sandy McMahon and Johnny Campbell to the cause. "Forward, the left wing were the best pair on the field. They were splendidly effective in the second half when most of the goals resulted from their efforts. McMahon was the more prominent and much of the credit of the victory was due to his efforts." Then by way of bathos almost, it talks about the large crowd and "In the park adjoining, three or four improvised wheel of fortune stands were surrounded after the game was over, and one at least did a roaring trade". Is there a hint of disapproval here in a Roman Catholic newspaper about gambling? Possibly, but there is total sanctification and blessing of Sandy McMahon.

But the team generally earned all the plaudits. An anonymous commentator, quoted in James E. Handley's *The Celtic Story* says. "The crowd are treated to many fine touches, bits of trickery begotten only by infinite practice. From McMahon to Cullen, there was unmistakable evidence of a course of hard training in a school, which is peculiar to the Celts and from which those who have undergone a course of teaching emerge hallmarked, jewelled in nine holes". Another is quoted as asking, "what can a defence do with players who pass the ball from toe to toe with a precision somewhat akin to musical drill?" Another concludes that Celtic's skill and teamwork is all to do with "association with the prince of dribblers, Sandy McMahon". Another encomium of Sandy McMahon is found in *Scottish Sport* magazine, which says that he was, "so deft in the manipulation of the ball. He patted and pirouetted with it in the manner of a premier danseuse".

Sandy is wearing his Scotland cap in this Celtic picture.
Behind him and to the right is Willie Maley

This is indeed striking imagery when one considers that the very culture of football in the 1890s was as far removed from any idea of ballet dancing that one could get. Football was tough, injuries were frequent and there was still the idea that if you were hurt; you tried not to show it. Still less did you appeal to the referee to sort out the bully. Yet here we have, in the middle of this unashamedly virile and brutal sport a comparison between one of its best exponents and a ballerina! One wonders what Sandy himself made of it all!

Sandy had little time to rest on his laurels after this great triumph, for on the day after, he and another three victorious Celts were on the train to Pike's Lane, Bolton to play in the first ever Inter-League match, the Monday being chosen because it was a Lancashire holiday. This was not quite an International, but it was considered to be almost as good, and it was another great opportunity for the young McMahon, along with Doyle, Maley and McCallum to travel with players from other Scottish clubs to play against England's finest. *The Glasgow Herald;* "Some of the works closed early to allow the hands to get to the game in time" and that there were special trains from many parts. All this resulted in a splendid crowd, for Lancashire in the 1890s, of 9,500.

In fine spring weather, the game was a 2–2 draw. McMahon acquitted himself well, scoring a good goal for "the Caledonians" just after half time when he picked up a through ball from Willie Maley. This made the score 1–1, and then Taylor of Dumbarton put the Scottish League ahead before the English League equalized more or less on the stroke of time. Following the cataclysmic Scottish defeat at Ibrox nine days earlier, some sort of honour had been restored to Scotland.

In the meantime, on a more mundane and domestic level, Celtic's challenge for the Scottish League began to falter. On the day of the Scotland v England international, the weakened Celtic had dropped a point at Vale of Leven, and now injuries began to play a part. Johnny Madden "genial Johnny" as he was called or "the rooter" (so called, allegedly, for his ability to knock over goalposts with his shooting) had missed the Cup Final, as we have noticed, and now in the League game against Cambuslang on 16 April (when the Scottish Cup was on display, heavily guarded, to the meagre support on a foul day) Celtic, albeit without Madden, won 3–1, but at the cost of a nasty injury to the influential Willie Maley.

Celtic then travelled to Bank Park, Leith on the Monday for a game arranged for the Edinburgh Holiday weekend. But they did so without Peter Dowds, who for some reason travelled to the capital on a different train from the rest of the party. This train was late, and then Dowds, unaware of where Leith Athletic played, went to the wrong ground and missed the game altogether! As a result, Celtic were compelled to play the half fit Alec Brady at right-half in place of Maley and to bring back prematurely Johnny Madden to the forward line. Madden was indeed recovering but he was not yet match fit. The 5,000 crowd (a good turnout in spite of inclement weather with not a little unseasonal snow) saw Leith defeat Celtic 2–1 with only a Sandy McMahon goal in the second half for consolation.

Celtic now had to beat Dumbarton at Boghead on 23 April if they were to retain any interest in the League. Special trains from Glasgow brought a huge crowd of 15,000 to Boghead, leading to the caustic and envious comment in the Press that there is, "no team like Celtic for drawing the cash". *The Glasgow Herald* is impressed and says that, "the trees round Boghead were covered with eager partisans", but the massive Celtic crowd were disappointed to see their side go down to a 0–1 defeat in a very even game. On two occasions, one in each half, McMahon hit the post, but in spite of Celtic having the balance of the pressure, it was Dumbarton with a late goal who won the day when the referee called for the "cessation of hostilities".

Dumbarton duly won the second Scottish League (they had shared it with Rangers last year) but the season was not yet over for Celtic and McMahon. McMahon kept getting the goals and frequently we find references like, "for the Celts, McMahon shone like a beacon", "McMahon was the best forward afield" and "Celtic are never defeated as long as they have their devastating left flankers, McMahon and Campbell". There was still another trophy to be played for, of course, in the shape of the Glasgow Charity Cup, but the team were still high after their Scottish Cup win, and of course with the new stadium now nearing completion, the future looked bright.

But on 5 May, McMahon and others received a severe blow when the SFA again voted down professionalism. To a large extent this was a victory for Queen's Park against Celtic, for it was Celtic under their energetic committee man John H. McLaughlin who were pushing for the legalisation of professionalism, arguing that football should be a means of allowing poor but talented boys to earn some money from the huge crowds that could be persuaded to come and watch them. Besides, in any case, was it not obvious that the paying of players was going on anyway?

But amateurism won the day, and this decision would have a major effect on young Sandy later in the summer, as we shall see. But in the meantime, there was still a chance for Celtic to win an unprecedented third Cup in a season. As late as 21 May, Celtic got their revenge on Dumbarton by beating them 3–1 in the semi-final of the Glasgow Charity Cup (Dumbarton, being the League Champions, were invited to perform in the tournament). The game was of course Scottish Cup winners versus Scottish League champions and therefore attracted a very large crowd of around 15,000 to Ibrox.

As often seemed to happen in those days, Ibrox was subject to a fierce wind, although the overhead conditions were generally good in spite of the occasional shower. Playing with the wind, Dumbarton scored first, but then in the second half, the pressure applied to their defence by the left wing combination of McMahon and Campbell (the "wizard left wing pair" as Maley calls them) began to tell, as even the full-backs like Reynolds and Doyle began to push forward. It was McMahon who "squeezed in" the equalizer, and then a minute later, with Celtic clearly in the ascendancy, Neil McCallum put Celtic ahead from a "beautiful corner" taken by Johnny Campbell. Ten minutes later, virtually the same thing happened, and the game finished with Celtic well on top.

This meant that Celtic were through to the Final, and their opponents were Rangers. Both teams agreed to play the game on Old Celtic Park, as it was likely to be the last game ever played there. There was a genuine affection for the old ground – "the old claypit", as it was sometimes unkindly called, for there had been a great deal of good football played there at the birth of the mighty Celtic. But now after four years of phenomenal success in terms of crowds and achievement, it was time to move on to the huge new arena a little to the south-west. Such was the ambition of men like Glass and McLaughlin, and it was an ambition that permeated down to players like Maley, Kelly and McMahon.

The final was played in the evening of Wednesday 1 June. It was a glorious day at Epsom for the Derby won by Sir Hugo at the astonishing odds of 40/1, but the weather was less good in Glasgow. There had been heavy rain throughout the day, and puddles could be seen on the pitch, but a wind had sprung up, the weather took a distinct turn for the better and a fine night attracted a crowd of 8,000, thus swelling the coffers of the various Glasgow charities by an estimated £300. Celtic won 2–0 with two second half headers from Johnny Campbell, although some newspapers say Johnny Madden for the second, but McMahon is frequently singled out for praise. "Celtic's forward play was superior with McCallum, McMahon and Campbell being the most prominent," says *The Glasgow Herald* and Maley's *The Story of The Celtic* gives a graphic account of how the first goal was scored.

"Sandy McMahon, however, was a crafty player. Realizing that

direct methods were not going to be profitable against such a tac-
tician as Gow (Rangers' right-back), he wandered over to the right
and getting the defenders where he wanted them suddenly screwed
the ball over to Campbell who, lying unmarked, headed past Haddow fifteen minutes after the restart". The teams were:

Celtic: Cullen; Reynolds and Doyle; Maley, Kelly and Gallagher;
McCallum, Brady, Madden, McMahon and Campbell.

Rangers: Haddow; Gow and Dunbar; Marshall, McCreadie and
Muir; Kerr, McInnes, Gibb, Turnbull and McPherson.

Referee: Mr T Park, Cambuslang.

The full-time whistle at the end of a very sporting contest between
"two teams who always got on well together" brought great scenes of
rejoicing among Celtic players, supporters and committee men with
Rangers fulsome in their praise and appreciation for the team which
had created history by winning three cups in the one season. Regret
was expressed by some of course that the Scottish League was not
won as well, but clean sweeps would come later in the infant club's
history. The Cups were put on show in various public houses and
barber's shops in the East End, all bedecked with green and white
favours, and committee man Ned McGinn, so the story went, sent
a letter to the Vatican asking for candles to be lit. The request was
either turned down or simply ignored, one presumes.

It was a great time for the new and vibrant club who had revo-
lutionised Scottish football in their short period of existence. Their
supporters walked about the East End with their shoulders back
and their heads held high, looking forward in anticipation for the
next season and the real opening of the new ground, which would
become the greatest and most famous on earth.

For McMahon, it was a wonderful summer, as everyone nudged each other and said, "Hello, Sandy" as "big McMann" or simply "the big yin" passed. Sandy himself, always modest and sociable, would respond. Even in Edinburgh, where his family still lived, the name of McMahon was slowly becoming a famous one. Fame and celebrity thus came to McMahon, and he enjoyed that, but there was still a fly in the ointment. He, like the rest of the Celtic team would have loved to be paid for the job – officially. But he was only 21 and a great future beckoned.

3.

1892–93 – KIDNAPPED AND
THE FIRST LEAGUE CHAMPIONSHIP

Before the start of the 1892–93 season, McMahon was involved in a remarkable affair. It has been called by some historians "Kidnapped" after the novel of Robert Louis Stevenson (written only six years earlier and still in 1892 the talk of the literary world), and it shows the extent to which the infant Celtic club, notionally amateur, were prepared to go in order to protect and keep the man whom they saw as their prize asset. Maley in his *The Story of The Celtic* in a curious oxymoron calls the club "paid amateur" – a contradiction in terms to most of us, except to those who have had some involvement in Scottish cricket, where one also gets, incidentally, another paradoxical juxtaposition in "unpaid professional"!

The origin lay of course in the refusal in May of 1892 of the SFA to sanction professionalism. Professionalism had been legal in England since 1886. This meant that all of Celtic's fine side ("Scotland's best side in our lifetime" according to the less that totally impartial *Glasgow Observer*) could go to whatever club they wanted to, and not for the first or last time in footballing history, English teams began to offer tempting bait in the shape of a good wage. Celtic's Scottish Cup Final triumph in April had been extensively reported in the English press, and indeed representatives of various clubs had been at Ibrox that day, returning impressed with what they had seen.

In August 1892 when the club had other matters to deal with, notably the opening of the new stadium (and the associated teething problems) at the start of the new season, Chairman John Glass, already aware that Johnny Madden and Alec Brady were tinkering with an invitation from one of the Sheffield teams, received a tip-off from a contact that Neil McCallum and Sandy McMahon were heading for Nottingham Forest. This was bad news. The loss of McCallum could be coped with, but the young, bright starlet Sandy McMahon was another matter altogether.

What then happened was dramatic, although possibly a little less so than some historians would like to imply. But there was treachery, espionage, clandestine conversations, sudden changes of mind etc. The problem is that it sounds exactly like what happened in Victorian novels and melodramas of the time, – the only things lacking were the fair maiden and her wicked stepfather – and the wise student would do well to bear that in mind! It was probably a lot less exciting than what we have been led to believe – but it is a good tale nevertheless!

McMahon and McCallum suddenly finding themselves whisked away to Nottingham, were amazed to discover that they were being kept hidden in "safe houses" in the Sherwood Forest, (Robin Hood even enters this melodrama!) and then latterly in the Curtis Hotel. This was because Nottingham Forest had been informed that a Celtic rescue party had been mobilised. This information came from Celtic's trainer, one Joe Anderson who was promptly sacked for this selling of vital information, but Celtic's committee man David Meikleham and Sandy's elder brother (James?) were already on their way, while Michael Dunbar and John Glass went to Sheffield to bring back the other absconding Celts, Brady and Madden.

At this point Notts COUNTY (not FOREST) entered the affair. They did not of course want Forest to get such good players and, just as treacherous as Celtic's trainer, they gave the Celtic party exact information as to the whereabouts of McMahon and McCallum. Meikleham shaved off his beard, lest anyone recognise him, (was there any limit to what those early Celts would do for the club they loved?) and then he and the elder McMahon hung about the railway station until the two Celts arrived from their secret hideouts, with a couple of "escorts" or "minders" with them.

Sandy of course recognised his brother and may have recognised the now beardless Meikleham as well, but pretended not to as the two Celtic men walked a discreet distance behind them to a hotel. Once in the lounge of the hotel, the two Celtic men came up to the Nottingham Forest party and began to talk to them about general things, particularly the progress of Nottinghamshire Cricket Club, (who would finish second that year to Surrey in the County Championship) and expatiating at length about current Notts cricket stars like Arthur Shrewsbury and William Attewell.

Somehow or other, Sandy managed to say that he would be happy to return to Celtic in a coded manner to his brother and Meikleham, whilst Meikleham, for his part, may well have hinted that some more illegal money might be on offer. Suddenly, the two McMahons and Meikleham departed. Stories of them alarming other guests and knocking over tables sound fanciful, but they hailed a cab which took them to the railway station with another cab containing the Nottingham Forest men in hot pursuit, we are told. At the station, the Celtic party jumped into the first train they saw, and from wherever that took them, they got a train back to Glasgow, having sent a wire about their successful coup! But even then, the melodrama did not stop, for they disembarked from the train at Eglinton Street, rather than Glasgow Central Station where there might be spies or secret agents from Nottingham! They were clearly enjoying themselves.

This story, although widely believed and much spread about Glasgow by Celtic themselves at the time, strains our credulity to a certain extent. For one thing, Sandy McMahon was still, apparently not having signed any contract, a free agent. Great Britain, moreover, in 1892 was still, in spite of many other things going wrong with it, a free country! The absence of subsequent legal action makes one think that he had not signed anything, and Sandy probably was a little homesick, generally overwhelmed by the whole situation, and had a genuine change of heart, particularly when he saw his brother. Maley would later say patronisingly that "McMahon was too young to know his own mind", and that was probably true. He may have been one of the best football players in the United Kingdom, but he was still in his early 20s.

In any case, the Celtic committee had less success with Neil McCallum, who stayed on with Nottingham Forest. McCallum played for a variety of English clubs, but like loads of ex-Celts, never so well as he had done for Celtic. Celtic and their supporters tend not to like those who leave them to play elsewhere, and for a spell McCallum became a hate figure at Parkhead, but in 1905, out of his luck and his career now finished, he was given employment as an odd job man at Celtic Park. He has his special niche in Celtic history for being the scorer of the first ever goal for the club.

As far as those who went to Sheffield were concerned, there was a parallel development. Madden came back, but Brady didn't. In the case of Brady, there are similar tales of him being hidden by Sheffield Wednesday to keep Glass and the Celtic committee at bay, but he went on to became a legend for the Owls, winning the English Cup with them, "The Wednesday" as they called themselves, in 1896. He thus has the honour of winning both a Scottish and an English Cup medal with teams on their first winning of the trophy. In addition, he had at an earlier stage in his life been with Everton when they won the English League for the first time!

Celtic themselves of course were not above the melodramatic kidnapping of players from time to time. Soon after the Nottingham and Sheffield episodes, Jimmy Blessington, a talented inside forward of Hibs but now somewhat disillusioned with the feckless management of the Edinburgh Irishmen disappeared from his home in Edinburgh. It was no secret that he had moved to Glasgow, but

Celtic had the problem of persuading the authorities that "no undue pressure" had been put on Blessington to join Celtic, by which it was clearly meant that no financial inducement had been made. Sandy McMahon, a friend of Blessington, was persuaded to appear before the SFA and to tell them that Blessington had always wanted to play for Celtic. It was an interesting prototype of "the only team I ever wanted to play for" and "a dream come true" sort of cant that one tends to hear on transfer deadline day in the 21st century, but the young McMahon already had sufficient standing and respectability in the game that his word was accepted.

McMahon's escapades in England meant that, sadly for his family and future historians, he missed the first ever official Scottish League game at New Celtic Park on August 20 1892. The reporter of *The Evening Times* says that it is something that "no fellah can understand" i.e. that McMahon and others could even contemplate not wanting to play at such a magnificent stadium as New Celtic Park. Johnnie Madden was back however, but may well have wished that he too had stayed in England, for he was sent off for fighting by referee Mr Higgie of Hearts along with McQuilkie of Renton in a 4–3 win, in which an understrength Celtic team (described eccentrically by *The Glasgow Herald* as a "nebulous hypothesis") struggled to beat a team whom they should easily have disposed of. They were greatly indebted to Johnny Campbell for all four goals.

But McMahon was back for the visit to Tynecastle the next week. He would have enjoyed the prospect of returning to Edinburgh again, even though he could hardly have expected a warm welcome from Hearts fans in view of his earlier link with Hibs. A huge crowd of 20,000, probably Tynecastle's biggest ever crowd up to that time, assembled to see this game, but Celtic after a bright start against the sun and the wind, faded badly and lost 1–3 in front of some very excited supporters. There then followed a tour of northern England with mixed fortunes in which they beat Middlesbrough and

Newcastle East End (soon to become Newcastle United) but lost to Sheffield United and Sunderland. The Newcastle game on 3 September marked the opening of St James' Park.

A poster advertising Celtic and showing
what McMahon would have worn

But all this time, a good team was slowly developing and in Scotland at least, defeat and McMahon would be strangers for some time. But Sunderland came to Celtic Park on Thursday 6 October to play a "friendly", a description that turned out to be a total misnomer for this game. Sunderland, last year's winner of the English League, had already beaten Celtic at their ground in Newcastle Road a month previously, and also won this game 3–0 but only after McMahon had been carried off in the first half, his leg in splints, with what had looked like a broken leg. It wasn't as bad as that, as it turned out, but Sandy was out for well over a month, returning on 19 November to score two goals as Celtic beat Partick Thistle 8–0 in a replayed Glasgow Cup tie.

Bad weather with frozen pitches became a problem this winter, and progress in the Scottish League was halting and slow, because apart from the weather, Cup ties were given priority, but by February, Celtic found themselves in two Cup Finals, the Glasgow Cup against Rangers and the Scottish Cup against Queen's Park. They had beaten teams like Linthouse and the King's Royal Volunteers to progress in the Scottish Cup before the turn of the year, and then in early January they had beaten Third Lanark twice in back-to-back games, a Glasgow Cup semi-final and then a Scottish Cup quarter-final.

The Glasgow Cup game in fact was the third attempt, two previous attempts on Christmas Eve and Hogmanay having both been declared a "friendly" because of a frozen pitch. When this game was eventually played on 7 January, the weather was little better but 3,000 huddled together in intermittent snow at Celtic Park to see Celtic win 5–2. *The Glasgow Herald* says that Celtic were, "in active trim all round, the attack being carried out in brisk, concerted style" and at another point describes that as being, "as active as cats and fairly hemmed in their opponents" as they took a five goal lead of which McMahon scored one and had a hand in all the other four with his left wing partnership with Johnny Campbell coming in for repeated praise. Thirds scored two near the end, but it was a fine day for McMahon and for Celtic.

Celtic and Third Lanark were due to meet again in the Scottish Cup quarter-final a week later again at Celtic Park, but this time the weather was just too bad to contemplate any kind of football, even a friendly. Conditions improved the following week however to allow 8,000 people to see another fine Celtic performance in a 5–1 victory, in which McMahon "dazzled" as he scored a hat-trick and laid on a couple more for the grossly under-rated Tom Towie, on loan from Renton.

But February was a bad month for Celtic, after a good first game in which they beat St Bernard's of Edinburgh 5–0 in the Scottish Cup semi-final. After that, they lost to Abercorn in the League at Paisley, then went down to Rangers 1–3 in the Glasgow Cup Final on 18 February at Cathkin, with Sandy McMahon's consolation goal coming too late, although he had come close earlier in the game; in the words of Maley "McMahon with his head failed by inches to convert a corner taken by his partner". The teams were:

Celtic: Cullen; Reynolds and Doyle; Maley, Kelly and Dunbar; Towie, Blessington, Madden, McMahon and Campbell.

Rangers: Haddow; Hay and Drummond; Marshall, A. McCreadie and Mitchell; H. McCreadie, Davie, Kerr, McPherson and Barker.

Referee: Mr Hay, Dumfries.

The after match banquet had an interesting exchange of views at the speeches when Baillie John Ure Primrose of Rangers, after congratulating Celtic on being "plucky and sporting losers," said, "I imagine that there is no club other than themselves whom Celtic would rather see winning the Cup than Rangers". John Glass, for Celtic, in reply commented on the very good relationship that the two teams had always had, and agreed with the sentiments. He had of course little cause for Celtic to feel jealous of Rangers, for apart from their sharing of the League Championship with Dumbarton in 1891, Rangers had won nothing since the Glasgow Charity Cup of 1879. It was also (incredibly) almost five years after Celtic's first game, the first time that Rangers had ever beaten Celtic!

Willie Maley seems to have enjoyed this game, even though it ended up badly for Celtic. "It was a tremendously hard fought and at times brilliant game, although Rangers were fortunate to win". Haddow the Rangers goalkeeper had a tremendous game, but quite apart from that, "Celtic were most unfortunate, experiencing very hard lines on many occasions." Still the attitude of Maley and McMahon at this stage of their careers was that the loss of the Glasgow Cup, although disappointing to Celtic, meant that their friends Rangers were able to enjoy their first success in the competition. It would not be a sentiment that was replicated very often in the future!

Celtic would be considerably less magnanimous about their defeat in the Scottish Cup Final to Queen's Park, a team with whom they were now beginning to enjoy less happy relationships in 1893 than they did with Rangers. As was often the case in these days (like 1889 and 1892) the first "Scottish Cup Final", played the week after the Glasgow Cup Final, was in fact a friendly, in this case because of the bone hard pitch.

Celtic actually won that game 1–0 and some of their supporters departed Ibrox that day under the not unreasonable apprehension (in the absence of any announcement) that Tom Towie's goal had actually won the Cup. Indeed no official announcement was made, although *The Glasgow Herald* tells us that at half-time the secret "eked out" that it was a friendly.

There is the suspicion that the decision was deliberately kept quiet. The authorities suspected, not without cause, that there might be a little crowd trouble if any official announcement was made. Certainly any announcement at the end of the game to the Celtic supporters that they had not in fact won the Scottish Cup as they thought they had, would have been courting disaster.

The pitch was indeed hard, but by no means unplayable in the opinion of several of those who were there. It was only the Sunday morning or even as late as the Monday before some Celtic supporters realised for certain that they had not in fact won the Scottish Cup for two years in a row! They might however have expected that the game was in fact a friendly because of the demeanour of the players who showed no exuberant celebrations at the full-time whistle but merely shook hands with the Queen's Park players and trotted off.

Whether or not one agrees with referee Mr Harrison's opinion of the state of the Ibrox pitch, there is certainly a question that must be asked of the authorities and that is why they did not tell the fans at the start? As it was, they persuaded 23,000 people to part with their money under false pretences. If the game was declared a friendly, then surely free admission should have been the order of the day. These events did nothing to dispel all the talk about the authorities, and the teams themselves, being guilty of duplicity and greed.

The real Scottish Cup Final was re-arranged for 11 March, before a fairly small crowd (for a Scottish Cup Final) of 13,239. One might have expected another 10,000 at least but there is a certain amount of evidence, gleaned from newspaper reports, some of which were experts at innuendo, that the fans were making a point about being taken for a ride at what they thought was the real Cup Final a fortnight previously. The feeling was growing that a replayed Scottish Cup Final was happening just a little too frequently! Celtic had now been in three Scottish Cup Finals, and every one of them had been declared a "friendly" the first time round! Was it any coincidence that the three replayed Finals all involved the team that had the biggest support and drawing power?

The game itself was contentious, to put it mildly. The final was once again at the rather primitive Ibrox and once again there was a gale, which would play a significant part in the play. For some reason (allegedly Queen's Park vetoed the idea) goal nets were not used and this would have a crucial effect on the outcome of the game.

It was not one of McMahon's better games for the club – indeed he had not had a great game on the Glasgow Cup Final either – but Celtic had reason to feel hard done by. Willie Maley in *The Story Of*

The Celtic starts off his account of the game by saying (irrelevantly), "Then, of course, Celtic, to put it very plainly, were looked upon as interlopers and not too welcome at that, but although they were regarded with feelings amounting to hatred in many quarters, their success and unquestioned talent were responsible for an increasing respect for their progress". Maley is here showing a little paranoia, and Celtic being looked upon as interlopers simply does not bear scrutiny when one considers that it was under the leadership of John H. McLaughlin that the Scottish League was formed (he himself, Maley, would become an office bearer in that institution in later years) and that McLaughlin would soon persuade the SFA to accept professionalism. Maley might have done better to focus on this particular Cup Final if he wanted a chance to prove that the authorities were against Celtic.

Maley himself was badly injured (and had to retire for attention for a key spell in the first half) when he took a ball in the face, Reynolds was also injured and goalkeeper Joe Cullen took a real battering from the charges of the Queen's Park forwards. Meanwhile at the other end, McMahon, not without cause considered Celtic's "main man" after his successes last year was well marked and policed, and made little impact on the game.

Sellar scored for Queen's who were playing with the wind in the early stages of the game, and then towards the end of the first half when Celtic were still struggling with injuries, the Spiders scored one of the most contentious goals in Scottish Cup Final history. Seller shot for goal and Dan Doyle diverted it past his post, deeming it wiser to concede a corner kick if necessary rather than leave the ball for the still injured Joe Cullen to save. James Handley in *The Celtic Story* gives a slightly different story when he says that, "Maley headed out the ball but the referee adjudged that in its flight to the goal, it had crossed the line". Maley himself is emphatic that it was Doyle, for he himself ("W. Maley" as he coyly describes himself) was not even on the field. He "had sustained a facial injury during the siege previous to the award, and was now forced to retire".

Whoever it was who chose to concede the corner kick does not matter. Whether it was Maley or Doyle, he then with the rest of the Celtic defence turned to defend the corner-kick. To their amazement, Queen's Park started claiming a goal. There were of course, as we have said, no goal nets, and the referee Mr Harrison from Kilmarnock could not really adjudicate as to which side of the post the ball had gone. Anyone who has ever refereed a schoolboy game or an amateur game on a public park with no goal nets will sympathise with the predicament of Mr Harrison. But Queen's Park persisted in their claims of "It's a goal, Mr Harrison! Honest!" And the referee, thinking perhaps that Queen's Park, being amateurs and gentlemen, would not tell lies, gave into their pressure, and awarded a goal to the astonishment of Dan Doyle, the rest of the Celtic team and most of the crowd. Maley says there was "general amazement" and "protests were of no avail". *The Glasgow Herald* concedes that many people thought that it wasn't a goal.

This did little to defuse the suspicion that referees were all in the pay of Queen's Park, (the saying went that they didn't pay their players, had loads of money, so they paid referees instead!) but there was still a game to be won. Celtic, now 2–0 down, in the second half had the benefit of the wind, and when Jimmy Blessington pulled one back, their support began to take over and to out-shout their Queen's Park counterparts. This was now Sandy McMahon's big chance to repeat last year's triumph, but this time Queen's Park's defence was a little more successful, occasionally using rough tactics which earned them the annoyance of the Celtic crowd and crippled a few of the Celtic players, but they did enough to keep out the eager Celts.

In addition, McMahon and Madden had little luck – both hitting the woodwork, and fluffing chances through excitement. Even Dan Doyle joined the attack in the last few desperate attempts to gain an equalizer, but it was not to be, with *The Glasgow Herald* questioning the wisdom of such a move, and saying that Doyle's "directness" did not work to the advantage of the Celtic team, who, might through the more subtle approach of McMahon, have saved the day. Those who can recall the 1961 Scottish Cup Final against Dunfermline will have an idea of what 1893 was like in terms of pressure bringing no reward, but this time with the added piece of gall that a feeling of injustice brings. In more modern times, this feeling can be paralleled in the Cup Finals of 1970 and 1984, both against Aberdeen, when refereeing decisions played a major part in Celtic's downfall. The teams were:

Celtic: Cullen; Reynolds and Doyle; Maley, Kelly and Dunbar; Towie, Blessington, Madden, McMahon and Campbell.

Queen's Park: Baird; Sillars and Smellie; Gillespie, McFarlane and Stewart; Gulliland, Waddell, Hamilton, Lambie and Sellar.

Referee: Mr Harrison, Kilmarnock.

With the considerable benefit of 120 years of hindsight, the whole Scottish Cup Final does lead one to suspect that a few questions need to be answered by the amateurs. Celtic had at least three reasons to feel ill done by. In the first place, they had already won the Scottish Cup as they thought on February 25 1–0 only to discover that it was declared a friendly. Then there was the goal that never was, and finally the rough tactics of Queen's Park condoned by the referee Mr Harrison who became the first in the Celtic demonology of referees – to be joined in later years by Bobby Davidson, Bob Valentine, Hugh Dallas and a few others.

Maley quotes *The Glasgow Herald,* which is very laudatory of Queen's Park, whom it loves, but also talks about, "the splendid way in which they (Celtic) contested the game and the sporting manner in which they accepted defeat". So much for the establishment, *Glasgow Herald,* way of looking at things. Maley then perhaps reveals his own feelings when he says that the writer of the newspaper fails to take account of Celtic's many injuries and hints darkly at something more sinister when he says, "this great struggle in which they were fighting against the odds from the moment they set foot on the pitch".

For a long time after this, relations between Celtic and Queen's Park took a dip. It was, of course, more than one Scottish Cup at stake. With the continuing debate about professionalism, it was about the direction in which Scottish football was going. In later years Celtic would repair bridges with Queen's Park, but for the next few years there was more than a little bitterness between the teams.

McMahon had every reason to be despondent about that 1893 Cup Final, but his season was by no means over. He felt that, although his form had shaded a little, he had a chance of winning an International cap, and he also felt that Celtic had a chance of winning the Scottish League, a competition, of course, that they had never won. Celtic were lagging behind Rangers – in fact they were fourth – but they had only played 10 games out of 18 thanks to the bad winter and their commitments in the Scottish Cup and the Glasgow Cup. Most of the games were rescheduled for the month of May when the pitches might be drier. This did not upset McMahon. He reckoned that a good player should be able to play on all conditions – in fact, in Scotland, you were likely to get all conditions, sometimes all within one month!

In 1893, Internationals were played only against Wales, Ireland and England and they tended to be held in the spring, in March or April. It was assumed in the 1890s that Scotland would easily defeat Wales and Ireland, but the game that really mattered was the game against England, called simply "the International". The Wales and Ireland games were often used to give promising youngsters a chance to show their value. McMahon did not play against Wales at Wrexham (but Scotland won 8–0 in any case) but found himself in the team, along with Maley, Kelly and Campbell, to play against Ireland. The reason for the fielding of four Celts in this particular game seemed to have a lot to do with the fact that the game was at Celtic Park (the new ground's first International) and Celtic players in the team would draw in the crowd. As it happened, 12,000 people saw Scotland win 6–1, and McMahon scored one of the goals.

In the meantime, Celtic had taken two important steps towards their first League championship. McMahon played at centre-forward (Johnny Madden was playing for Scotland in Wales) in the game against Dumbarton on 18 March as the team took out its frustration for the previous week's Scottish Cup Final by beating the Sons Of The Rock 5–1. Then, when the Scotland v Ireland game was played at Celtic Park, a somewhat understrength Celtic team travelled to Tontine Park to beat Renton 2–0.

But then on the Monday, the International team was announced for the England game and the four Celts who had played against Ireland – Maley, Kelly, McMahon and Campbell – found themselves in the team, along with five men from Queen's Park and one each from Rangers and Renton to play against England in London. Crystal Palace and Wembley had not yet been built, so the game was to be played at the Richmond Athletic ground – and it would be graced with royalty for Princess May of Teck would be in attendance.

Princess May would of course in time become Queen Mary. She would marry George, the grandson of Queen Victoria later that summer, having already been engaged to Prince George's older brother, the louche and dreadful Prince Eddy. When Eddy died, Princess May, nothing daunted, settled for his younger brother instead, a course of action which attracted surprisingly little criticism from the Press and the Church. Indeed, it was a rather narrow field for Prince

George, given that non-royalty, poor people (even middle class people with respectable trades and professions!) and Roman Catholics were excluded, so the British establishment were probably glad to settle for anyone!

Princess May of Teck shook hands with James Kelly, captain of Scotland, (in later years, Maley would try to imply that she shook hands with him as well!) then watched the game in which Scotland lost 5–2, but the Press universally declared that Scotland had been unlucky to lose, an offside goal being given by referee Mr Clegg at a key juncture. It was only in the last quarter of an hour that Scotland began to lose control for at one point they were 2–1 up with both goals scored by Willie Sellar of Queen's Park. McMahon is consistently praised by *The Glasgow Herald* for his "grand runs" and his "pretty play" (particularly in conjunction with John Campbell) while another newspaper talks of his "plucky, albeit unsuccessful shooting". Sadly, however, the English forwards overran the Scottish defence towards the end of the game.

It was a great experience for McMahon to travel to London (a venture in itself in 1893) to play in this game. The team arrived in London on the Friday, did some sight-seeing on that day, then travelled to Richmond early on the Saturday well in time for the 3.30 pm kick-off. It was a beautiful sight. A temporary stand had been erected between the pavilion and the main stand, and it was occupied by Scottish supporters who had clearly a wide knowledge of Burns songs for *Rantin' Robin*, *Ye Banks and Braes* and then the more stirring and aggressive *Scots Wha Hae* were "bellowed forth with a lung power which showed stamina" from what *The Glasgow Herald* describes as "Scotch Corner". Then, in a sentence, which would bring a tear to the heart of any Unionist, "It fairly surprised the Englishmen who loudly shouted their approval of the Northern songsters and the Scotch concert (sic) was loudly appreciated".

The weather was good, and there were many ladies in attendance, dressed in fine hats and carrying the obligatory umbrella. Behaviour or overcrowding did not seem to be a problem (both of these things currently caused increasing concern in Scottish domestic football) and we are told that the President of the SFA "danced with delight" as McMahon, Waddell and Sellar teamed up together to score the first goal. The one bad thing about the ground was the facilities for the Press who were given benches to sit on, but people were allowed to walk in front of these benches, thereby blocking the view of the reporters. Not only that but the telegraphic arrangements were defective, thereby seriously delaying the sending of news to Scotland, where almost every town had a group of supporters hanging around newspaper offices or Post Offices waiting for news.

McMahon was impressed by the amount of Scottish supporters there (most of them were Scotsmen who now lived in London, although McMahon had seen a few travel down on the same train as the team) but he was now painfully aware that he had played two games for Scotland against England and lost the pair of them. The teams were:

England: Gay; Harrison and Holmes; Reynolds, Holt and Kinsey; Bassett, Gosling, Cotterril, Chadwick and Spicksley.

Scotland: Lindsay; Arnott and Smellie; Maley, Kelly and Mitchell; Sellar, Waddell, Hamilton, McMahon and Campbell

Yet McMahon was no failure, for he was chosen the following week to play for the Scottish League against the English League at Celtic Park. This was a very close game before a large crowd of 30,000. McMahon scored, fed Taylor and Madden for other goals and had hard luck when a shot of his skimmed the bar near the end, but in a very exciting finish the English League edged home 4–3. Press reports talk highly of McMahon and Campbell using phrases like "very tricky" and "a good edge about their play". McMahon would say later that he felt very unlucky to be on the losing side to England in two successive weeks, but most sources agree that he had little to reproach himself for the way in which he played in either game.

The League programme was eventually resumed after a long, enforced break (for various reasons) on 22 April. It was a fine spring day, and a wonderful day for Celtic and Sandy McMahon who scored a hat-trick as Celtic beat Third Lanark 6–0 at Cathkin. Thirds were "outclassed for effectiveness" and McMahon became the talk of Glasgow that night. Blessington, Mulvey and Campbell scored the other goals but it was McMahon's hat-trick that was "outstanding in its value". Although he was playing at centre-forward (Johnny Madden still being injured), his teamwork with Campbell was once again a joy to behold – for example he passed to Campbell for the fourth goal, then a couple of minutes later Campbell returned the compliment by passing to him for the fifth, before McMahon scored the sixth with a wonderful solo run. The "goodly crowd" were much impressed, and then just as the triumphant Celtic team were leaving Cathkin, a "wire" arrived from Dumbarton to the effect that Dumbarton had beaten Rangers 3–0.

This effectively gave Celtic the initiative, for Rangers had now played 16 games for 26 points (two points for a win, one for a draw in the 18 game League), but Celtic, although still behind with 21 points had only played 13 games, and it did not take a genius to work out that the game on Saturday 29 April at Parkhead against Rangers would be vital.

But Celtic were now on fire. Having beaten Everton in a friendly on Tuesday night, they then proceeded to beat Rangers 3–0 on Saturday 29 April. The crowd is given as 14,000 but we suspect there might have been a few more than that for such an important game. We are told that Celtic began playing to what is now the Lisbon Lions end of the ground and were two goals up before half-time with a fine strike from James Kelly, then one on the stroke of half time from Johnny Campbell. They then had to face the wind in the second half, but remained on top and Sandy McMahon scored a third near the end. This meant that Celtic now needed only six points from four games to guarantee their first ever Championship.

And it all happened on three glorious days in May. There was nothing glorious however about the weather on Tuesday 2 May when heavy rain deterred many people from attending the game at Parkhead against St Mirren which Celtic won very comfortably 4–1 with Campbell and McMahon scoring two goals each. McMahon was still in the centre of the field even though Madden was playing. McMahon indeed had pushed him to outside-right. As the small crowd trudged homewards through the wet streets with the weather still cold for early spring, there was the growing feeling that Celtic might be on the verge of their first Championship.

It was not the only piece of good news that night for Celtic. That very evening (John H. McLaughlin had left Celtic Park early to present the case) Celtic at last won the argument at the SFA that professionalism should be legalised, enough clubs having seen the strength of Celtic's arguments as distinct from those of Queen's Park. From now on, Sandy McMahon would be able legally to earn a wage (and a decent one) playing for the team that he loved, and there would be no more Nottingham or Sheffield adventures like last summer. It also marked a shift in the hegemony of Scottish football from Queen's Park to Celtic.

It was no accident that for the next few years, the "England" international would now be played at Celtic Park. And as an added bonus for Celtic, with the events of the Scottish Cup Final in mind, McLaughlin was able to win with his motion of goal nets for big games. Not every team could afford these expensive items however, so it was not yet made universal, but all in all it represented a very good AGM for Celtic and that shrewd administrator John H. McLaughlin!

Possibly at this stage we should consider the constant carping about "the world being against us" in the writings of Willie Maley. Maley seems to have had some sort of paranoia, a condition by no means uncommon in Celtic circles today whereby he believes that Celtic were hated and despised by everyone. Frankly, the facts in 1893 do not bear this out. Yes, they had bad luck through a refereeing decision in the Scottish Cup Final, but in other respects they were leading the way in Scottish football in at least two respects – one was the winning of the professionalism argument, and the other was the building of the New Celtic Park stadium which would host the Scotland v England International in 1892, 1894, 1896, 1898 and 1900, and was clearly, in the opinion of most English journalists, the most commodious best appointed ground in the world.

Saturday 6 May saw Celtic at Barrowfield to play Clyde while Rangers played their final League game of the season at Ibrox against Hearts. With Celtic one point behind, and two games in hand, supporters were able to work out that Celtic could actually win the League that day if results went in their favour. In the event, both Celtic and Rangers won 2–1 and both had to work very hard for their points. Clyde scored first at Barrowfield, and until half-time gave as good as they got. But Celtic kept pressing and soon after half-time McMahon "headed through" for Celtic to make the scores level before Jimmy Blessington added what turned out to be the winner. Celtic were the likelier of the two teams to add to the tally with McMahon shooting again and again but being denied by Clyde's inspiring goalkeeper McCorkindale. When full time came, Celtic were relieved but could not yet celebrate, for they had heard the news from Ibrox.

The celebrations were only delayed, however. On Tuesday 9 May before a crowd of 4,000 (there would surely have been more if it had been a Saturday), Celtic beat Leith Athletic 3–1 to win the Championship. McMahon did not score, and he may have been injured in this game, for he did not play in any of the remaining games that season. The team left the field to a polite round of applause and a little cheering with the celebrations noticeably a lot less raucous than the Scottish Cup winning celebration of the previous year. There were several reasons for this. One was that it was indeed a Tuesday night before a fairly small crowd, but there was the bigger factor that the Scottish League was not yet the major tournament that it would become. It was certainly diminished by the reluctance of Queen's Park to enter, and would for many years be considered of inferior value to the Scottish Cup.

The Glasgow Herald gives an account of this game, for example, but fails to mention that, in winning this game, Celtic had also won the Scottish League! But then again, *The Glasgow Herald,* unashamedly pro-Queen's Park, possibly considers the Scottish League to be decidedly infra dig. But, "facts are chiels that winnae ding," says Robert Burns (and no doubt Sandy MacMahon would delight in telling everyone that!) and Celtic had now won their first League Championship, albeit in a somewhat anti-climactic sort of a way.

Be that as it may, McMahon, in two seasons and a half, had now won every one of the four major trophies that Celtic entered. Celtic themselves, without the injured McMahon would win the Glasgow Charity Cup at the end of May, and they would certainly feel that progress had been made and would continue to be made in their new stadium. For McMahon there were a couple of extra factors in his International recognition for the second successive year, even though both appearances had been disappointments. There was also the cult status that he was beginning to earn among the Celtic faithful. He had begun to hear himself referred to as "The Duke" after a French President, but it also had connotations of the Duke of Wellington, the hero of Waterloo in 1815, to whom he was said to have a slight facial resemblance. It was in any case a highly flattering nickname. The youngster from Selkirk had come far.

Eugene MacBride in his mighty work *An Alphabet of the Celts* claims that it was Tom Maley who gave him the name "The Duke" after the French President the Duc de Mac-Mahon. He also then goes on to tell the story about how, when the said French President died on 17 October 1893, a Glasgow paper boy trying to sell his papers at the railway stations cried out "McMahon's Deid! Whit'll the Cel'ic dae noo?" In fact Sandy's career still had a long way to run.

4.

1893–94

The 1893–94 season was almost an exact replica of the previous season as far as Celtic were concerned. The Scottish League and the Glasgow Charity Cup were retained, whereas the Glasgow Cup and the Scottish Cup weren't won back. Once again there was a heartbreaking defeat in the Scottish Cup Final, this time to Rangers, and it was probably from this season onwards that Rangers started to be more and more identified as the main challengers to Celtic. There was a good reason for this as well. It was called professionalism.

The Celtic handbook for the start of the new season is jubilant. "A new era is entered upon – professional. To the Celtic lies the credit of bringing about this honest avowal of what had existed long before our inception, aye and in clubs too that had the audacity to pose as purists on the amateur question". Celtic clearly had no bashfulness about claiming credit for what had happened, and that last part of that quotation is an obvious dig at Queen's Park. It also seems to imply that Celtic themselves were not above playing "professional" football players as amateurs even before 1893. But everyone knew that anyway, and one would have been naïve in the extreme to believe that Sandy McMahon, for example, was a total amateur.

Now that professionalism was legally recognised ("It was like trying to stem Niagara with a kitchen chair" in the immortal words of John H. McLaughlin) Queen's Park who remain rigidly amateur to this day, and who refused to enter the Scottish League even after 1893, slowly became more and more of an irrelevance. They still had a few years left in them yet, but by the turn of the century, it was clear that they were no longer the force that they once were.

Mother Nature of course, they say, abhors a vacuum, and some team had to arise to challenge Celtic in Glasgow, and that of course was the ambitious team from the west of the city who also had a large ground and a potentially big support from the shipyard workers, called Rangers.

It is important to recognise and stress however that at this stage, and indeed up to and including the Great War, there was nothing (or very little) sectarian about Rangers. They were quite simply a football team. But because Celtic, in spite of the broad based nature of their team selection in which non-Catholics were always welcome, were perceived as Irish and Catholic, supporters of a non-Catholic background, particularly the descendants of those who had arrived in Glasgow because of the Highland Clearances, tended to gravitate towards a non-Catholic team. Snooty, middle-class Queen's Park were hard for working class shipbuilders on the Clyde to identify with, Partick Thistle, Third Lanark and Clyde were simply not good enough, so it had to be Rangers.

Geography also was on the side of Rangers. One way or another, the River Clyde was a huge employer of men, and as Ibrox was within sight of quite a few shipyards and other related industries, it was natural for the people who worked in the shipyards to try to find a house that was tolerably near there as well. If your house or flat or "single end" was within sight of a football ground, it was natural that you would support the local team.

There are those who say that Scotland, in any case, since the days of the arch-bigot John Knox was a profoundly Protestant country. This is undeniably true, but to what extent this reflected any deep-seated religious prejudice in Glasgow at the time of the 1890s towards anyone of a different persuasion, one cannot be sure. No doubt prejudice did exist, and there are certainly many anecdotal stories of men going to look for a job and finding a notice that said "No Catholics Need Apply", but the picture is patchy, and there were many examples as well of Roman Catholics integrating well into Scottish society.

Willie Maley, for example, occasionally gives in to his paranoia about persecution, but his own life testifies the opposite. It was not until the 1920s with the arrival of shipbuilders from Ulster with their hymns of hate and ridiculous beliefs that anti-Catholicism became a huge problem, encouraged one has to admit by the prickly and insecure Church of Scotland, already under pressure because of the insidious rise of Socialism. Such prejudice was generally ignored by the Labour Party (with one or two honourable exceptions like Jimmy Maxton), and that party took a long time before it realised that it ought to take a firm line against the bigots.

Celtic players, as early as the 1890s, would indeed hear things like "Papist" and "Fenian" shouted at them by the ignorant, but such Neanderthal behaviour was by no means confined to Rangers sup-porters. Supporters of teams like Morton and St Mirren were also identified by Maley as not liking Celtic, but it has to be stressed that the clubs themselves were highly appreciative of Celtic and the big crowds they brought. They were also shrewd enough not to minimise the differences, lest they killed a goose that laid a golden egg. If a few cretins in their support chose to shout absurdities at opponents, providing they paid their money to do so, what was the problem?

The Irish community in Glasgow however was now becoming far more interested in football that anything else. Home Rule for Ireland was of course a live issue and would continue to be so for the next twenty years and more, but there are frequent complaints in letters to *The Glasgow Observer* that the Irish in Glasgow are now far more interested in McMahon and Doyle than they are about going to Mass every Sunday. Still less are they concerned about how the now aged Gladstone is ever going to do what he has wanted to do all his life and provide self-government for Ireland.

Other letters welcome this change, and say that the Irish have now been in Glasgow for more than a generation and their interest in the Scottish game of football allied to their passion for a team that pays "a lot more than lip service to their country of origin" is an ideal marrying of two cultures. Readers are frequently reminded that the word "Celtic" covers both Scotland and Ireland, and sometimes, in an ill-disguised dig at the Irish in Edinburgh, are told that Hibernian can only mean a man of Ireland.

On the other side of the city Rangers' progress in the football field had been a great deal more gradual than that of Celtic. Season 1893–94 was Rangers' best season so far, for it was the year in which they first won the Scottish Cup, something that had eluded them for the past 20 years. It was a well-known jibe from Celtic supporters that although Rangers were fifteen years older than Celtic, Celtic nevertheless won the Scottish Cup before they did!

But another trend that was becoming evident in Scottish football was that it slowly became recognised that the best team in the land was the team that won the Scottish League rather than the Scottish Cup. The Scottish Cup was full of excitement and glamour, and a victory in the Final usually triggered excessive and lavish celebrations, but the team that won the Scottish League was the team that did best over the season against everyone else in all weathers including the relentless rain of November, the gripping frost of January, the winds of March and April and the occasional roastingly hot day when the season started in August.

For McMahon, 1893–94 was also another very good season. He had the occasional injury and a bout of illness which cost him a Glasgow Charity Cup medal, and to a certain extent had an identity crisis about whether he was a better inside-left or centre-forward, but the appearance of Joe Cassidy (not to be confused with the later and more famous Joe Cassidy of the 1920s) from Newton Heath (now better known as Manchester United) to take the centre-forward position settled that issue. The forward line of Madden, Blessington,

Cassidy, McMahon and Campbell was a formidable one, and in the Scottish League, after a couple of early disappointments, Celtic swept all before them.

The Scottish League had now expanded, and teams like Dundee and St Bernard's (from Stockbridge in Edinburgh) were now incorporated as the League made an attempt to get away from being merely "Glasgow and District" as the sneering words of the rest of Scotland would describe it. Hearts of course had been there from the start, but Hibs were still struggling, not least because of having had many of their players (including Sandy McMahon) stolen from them (as they would bitterly allege) by the more business-like Celtic organization.

McMahon, now almost 23, was at the peak of his physical powers. He was aware that he had a great deal to learn about the game which continued to fascinate him in its complexities and skills, but being taller than most men, well built, agile, active, he had all the potentialities. But there was also the mental attitude. He may not have been a Glaswegian by nature (and would still admit to having a slight sympathy for Hibs) but he had also fallen in love with Celtic and their supporters, if not yet the officials who ran the club and all the political dealings that went on behind the scenes. He did not know an awful lot about that side of the team, but what he did know, occasionally disturbed him. But his main issue was of course playing the game and continuing to score the goals, which delighted the fans.

Celtic's second game that season on 19 August 1893 was on the distant field of West Craigie Park, Dundee when the local side and their supporters were treated to a display of Celtic at their best. McMahon scored twice as Celtic won 4–1, and the traditionally pro-Celtic feelings of the city of Dundee (which have repeatedly permeated local MPs, Councillors and the local press, even the arch-Tory *Dundee Courier*!) possibly date from this day. The green and white vertical stripes turned on the style to the obvious delight of the sizeable Irish enclave of Lochee and other parts of the city and surrounding areas. Until Dundee United rose in the early 1960s, the Dundee Irish identified with Glasgow Celtic.

McMahon's value to the team was demonstrated when the team visited Ibrox at the beginning of September. He and Willie Maley were missing, McMahon having picked up a knock in the 0–0 draw against Dumbarton the week before, and *The Glasgow Herald* states pointedly that "Celtic missed McMahon very much". Indeed, they did, for they appalled their supporters who had made the journey across the city to Ibrox, by losing 0–5.

McMahon was still out the next week, but this time, the team did better, winning 4–2 against Hearts at Tynecastle. Celtic had someone called Montgomery playing for them. This fellow played at right-half and had an astonishing resemblance to Willie Maley. Indeed, it was he! Maley was working at the moment for an accountancy firm in Glasgow who, he feared, might have taken a dim view of him playing professional football for Celtic. So to prevent his name being spotted in the newspapers, he used his mother's maiden name! It is not clear whether it was playing professional football per se that might have concerned Maley's employers, or whether it was because of the team called Celtic. Maley doesn't say, but either way it seems a rather unnecessary and even melodramatic ploy.

With McMahon back in the picture, the team's form picked up with goals aplenty. If Sandy wasn't scoring them himself, (as, for example, in his hat-trick against St Bernard's on 14 October) he was foraging and spraying passes for the two men on either side of him, Johnny Campbell and Joe Cassidy, and the team was well on its way to fulfilling its dream of fast, entertaining attacking football. Certainly the crowds thought so. The average home game was often in excess of 10,000 – which was huge for the standards of the 1890s – and every away game would see plenty of Celtic supporters, sometimes outnumbering the home support, particularly for games inside Glasgow or those not too far away.

Train travel was of course still an exciting thing for people in the late Victorian age. Third class fares were not too expensive and, with a little sensible budgeting, a few trips to places like Edinburgh or Dumbarton were within the financial compass of quite a few working men. And another phenomenon began to be noticed more and more at railway stations throughout this autumn of 1893, and that was the amount of out-of-town supporters that arrived in Glasgow to see Celtic home games, attracted by the play of this fine Celtic forward line, with youngsters in particular with their rattles and crawmills, painted green and white in honour of "the bould Celts" while their owners talked excitedly about getting to see someone called "The Duke".

The team had only one hiccup before the New Year, but it was a bad one – a defeat by this season's nemesis, Rangers, 1–0 at Ibrox, and it was an important occasion – the semi-final of the Glasgow Cup on 18 November 1893. The weather was dry, but that was about all that one could say in its favour, for there was a very strong wind and the conditions are described as "exceedingly cold". From our vantage point of the twenty-first century, it is very easy for us to undervalue the effect that the wind can have on a game. In our modern grounds, the stands, certainly at Parkhead, break the wind, and it is seldom that it can be said that the wind has a major adverse effect on the game. But in more exposed grounds, it can be a potent factor.

On this day there was a bitter wind blowing diagonally across the field at Ibrox from the north-east, (usually Ibrox is subject to the milder but wetter west winds) and the play was spoiled with the really talented players like McMahon finding it difficult to control the ball. The 14,000 crowd (it surely would have been a lot more on a more clement or milder day) saw Celtic play against the wind in the first half, and when half-time was reached with no goals scored, things began to look good for Celtic. But playing with this blast was no easier and the game seemed to heading to a 0–0 draw, (although McMahon "all but scored" on one occasion), and a replay on a better day. But then, after Celtic conceded a free-kick with five minutes left "in the environs of their goal", Jock McPherson scored for Rangers through a scrimmage of players.

Celtic were stunned by this, and hard though they tried in the last few minutes, the wind caused them to over kick the ball, and Mr Hay of Dumfries sounded for full-time with Rangers still 1–0 up. This was a major disappointment to Celtic and their many followers at Ibrox that day, for the Glasgow Cup was a very important trophy. The fact that someone won the game at the first attempt did however put a spoke in the wheels of those who believed that the first game would be a draw for financial reasons. Rangers went on to win the Glasgow Cup three weeks later, beating Cowlairs 1–0 in the Final on a snowy day while Celtic beat Queen's Park in a friendly. Thus Rangers' capture of the Glasgow Cup strengthened the impression that Rangers were displacing Queen's Park as Celtic's main challengers.

Celtic however were not set back by this reverse as far as other competitions were concerned and the turn of the year was reached with progress made in the Scottish League and the Scottish Cup. There was one particularly exciting game on 23 December against Dumbarton at Boghead in which, with the scores tied at 4–4, McMahon scored the winning goal at the end. It was a dull midwinter's day and the decision was taken that the half-time interval had to be drastically shortened, otherwise the game would not be finished in daylight. Even then the large crowd (Dumbarton v Celtic games were always well attended in the 1890s and this one had "well over 8,000, without an inch of dubiety") were having to strain their eyes in the "crepuscular penumbra" when McMahon "banged on a fifth point for the Celtic" after Celtic had attacked down the right and Madden had crossed for him.

McMahon then took part in a bizarre experiment on Christmas Night 1893 when Celtic tried out their electric lights for a primitive form of floodlighting in a game against Clyde. The covered stand (on the North side of the ground) was lighted by a row of gas jets the whole length of the field, but there were also poles on the other side of the field with electric lights on strings all the way across, but sadly not really high enough to avoid the ball which kept hitting them with distressing frequency. It was a foggy night, and when the ball did go high and avoided the lights, it was lost to view and no one, neither the players nor the 3,000 crowd, had any idea where or indeed when the ball was going to come down!

There had been half-hearted attempts at floodlighting by other teams before but this was a brave effort, showing the forward thinking nature of the Celtic committee. The crowd were intrigued and the ground was christened "Madden's shipyard" (for shipyards on the River Clyde had this form of lighting as well) but the Press is damning with faint praise. *The Glasgow Herald* says it was "fairly successful" and *The Glasgow Observer,* while impressed with the initiative of those who ran Celtic, has to say that it was "not a pronounced success". For the record, the game was a 1–1 draw, but the experiment was not repeated, and early in the New Year, after a Scottish Cup game against St Bernard's in which the away side unsuccessfully appealed against a 1–8 defeat on the grounds that the ball kept hitting the light fittings (which had been left there with a view to further experiments), the whole idea was dispensed with and not resurrected again for more than 60 years.

On Saturday 30 December at Cathkin Park, Celtic took a big stride towards regaining the League flag with an excellent 3–1 win over Third Lanark. McMahon played a part in all three goals, first by heading on to Divers to score the first, then, with the score at 1–1, "after 25 minutes of the second half, the Celtic forwards came away in most determined style and McMahon, putting on a determined effort, fairly ran the ball through, Wilson being powerless to save". Then finally with time running out, McMahon passed to Blessington to win the game for Celtic. Celtic thus finished 1893 well on top of the League with 23 points from 13 games (this meant that only another five League games were left) while Hearts only had 18 points from the same games played, and Rangers who had played only 11 games had 15 points.

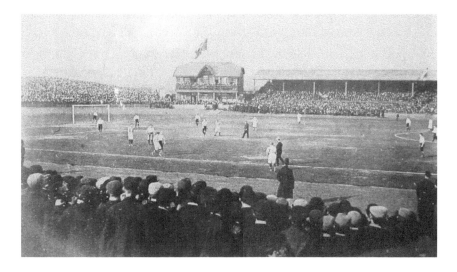

A fine picture of Celtic Park taken from where the Main Stand is now

1894, however, started badly with a couple of defeats in friendlies from Rangers and Everton before the Scottish Cup game against St Bernard's in which the Edinburgh side were torn apart with Sandy McMahon scoring four goals. In doing this, McMahon earned the praise of *The Glasgow Herald,* which said "Brilliant throughout, McMahon was the hero of the game and he quite excelled himself near the close". This was the game in which the Edinburgh side complained about the "lighting accoutrements" (their protest was thrown out) but the following week in the League at Logie Green in Edinburgh, Celtic beat them again, this time in the Scottish League, to strengthen their position at the top.

At the end of January, on the 27th, McMahon earned another International cap, this time against the Irish League on their first ever visit to Scotland. The game was played at Celtic Park before a poorish crowd of 4,000 spectators. The opposition was not great, it has to be said, but Scotland won very comfortably 6–0 with McMahon scoring twice and playing well throughout. It was a performance that he hoped would stand him in good stead for when the Scotland team would be selected to play against England.

February was a bittersweet month for Celtic. McMahon scored a first half hat-trick as Third Lanark were defeated 5–3 at Cathkin in the Scottish Cup semi-final, and then he scored another two against St Mirren as Celtic moved to within two points of the League flag. Celtic were now due to meet Rangers on two successive Saturdays. One was the Scottish Cup Final at Hampden on 17 February, and the other was the following week at Parkhead where a draw would probably be enough to give Celtic the Scottish League and a win certainly would do so.

The Scottish Cup Final, like last year's, was a bitter disappointment for Celtic, but as far as the game actually went, it seems that Celtic, quite simply, have to hold up their hands and admit that Rangers were, on the day, the better side. Maley was ill on the Friday, and played on the Saturday when perhaps he shouldn't have. He was given some "dope", as he himself put it, by the doctor, but that wore off in the second half when Rangers scored their three goals. Ironically it was Maley himself who scored Celtic's consolation goal, but it was too late for a fight back. McMahon is described as having given the Rangers defence some bother, but it was not one of his better games.

The game was played after a week of heavy Glasgow rain, and there was a case for the game not being played or yet again like, at least three previous Scottish Cup Finals, being played but then classed as a "friendly". Perhaps fearing (with good reason) some disorder among the 17,000 crowd in that eventuality, the SFA decreed that this would not happen and, the game being at Hampden, Queen's Park used hayseed (imported from Celtic Park) to give the players a foothold. *The Glasgow Observer* talks about the huge crowd, which congregated before the game, and was impressed by all the various forms of transport including "a growler with six or seven occupants" and "a flash hansom, which contained the scion of a commercial family". A "growler" was the technical term for a cab for four people, and was normally only deployed for funerals, but clearly such was the enthusiasm for this game that any form of transport came in handy.

It was generally agreed that Johnny Campbell had a very poor game – perhaps because of the wet conditions, or perhaps he too was suffering from the same unspecified illness that Maley was suffering from, but McMahon was affected by the poor performance of his left wing partner. They were a duo, and when one of them was off, the other was affected as well. In any case, Rangers took a hold of the game from the start, and were well worth their 3–1 win.

Students of the Celtic paranoia complex whereby Celtic feel that everything is against them, will have cause for concern in the way that some newspapers report the game. *The Glasgow Herald* for example, says "the result, which needless to say, was greeted with unbounded enthusiasm…" a comment, which perhaps means that the writer himself had a little "unbounded enthusiasm". And why should it be "needless to say"? On the other hand, even Maley himself in his curious account of this game, does say that Rangers had a large support. Indeed in some ways this day, the first time Rangers actually won the Scottish Cup after over 20 years of trying, was perhaps the birth of Rangers as a major force in Scottish football. *The Glasgow Observer* sighs with disappointment but nevertheless admits that "the better team won". The teams were:

Rangers: Haddow; Smith and Drummond; Marshall, A. McCreadie and Mitchell; Steel, H. McCreadie, Gray, McPherson and Barker.

Celtic: Cullen; Reynolds and Doyle; Curran, Kelly and Maley; Blessington, Madden, Cassidy, McMahon and Campbell.

Referee: J Marshall, Third Lanark

But for Celtic, there was a major compensation when the Scottish League was won the following week. The weather was once again miserable, with intermittent snow showers, but "upwards of 10,000 persons" were at Parkhead to see Celtic beat Rangers 3–2 and thus win the League Championship for the second time in a row. It was a victory that was all the more sweet for Celtic, who had lost three times previously to Rangers that season. Maley and Campbell were both out, but replacements Charlie McIlheney (sometimes called McEleney) and John Divers played admirably and after McMahon scored the first goal, Celtic looked comfortable, playing with a steely determination to get some kind of revenge for last week's reverse. The other Celtic goals were scored by Blessington and Madden, although some say that it was Joe Cassidy who scored the last one.

The Scottish League, as we have said, although gaining in prestige was not yet considered to be quite so important as the slightly more spectacular Scottish Cup in these days, but it was still a considerable achievement to have won it for two years in a row. McMahon was delighted by this, but he still also had two big dates to come as well. The first big date for McMahon was also a big date in the history of Celtic FC and more particularly the new ground, which was now looking "trim and well appointed" as well as being "spacious and commodious". In fact it ticked enough boxes to ensure that it was given the job of hosting the Scotland v England International on 7

April 1894 – the object of the exercise when the huge stadium was conceived and planned.

But it was not achieved without a great deal of work from a great deal of people with even players like McMahon not afraid to dirty their hands from time to time. The ground was indeed the best in the kingdom with particular attention being paid to the Press facilities. The new craze of the moment was telegraph and telephone links. No effort was spared to ensure that each national English newspaper would be supplied with a line for the evening editions of 7 April. And of course already a great deal of effort had been spent on the normal journalistic things like desks, inkwells, (copiously supplied with ink) and paper. Refreshments would also be provided in the Press box and a corps of boys with bicycles (another new craze of the age) ready to take copy to the offices of the Glasgow newspapers.

Then in late February, Celtic's hosting of the game was put in some doubt by a storm, which blew off some bits of the roof from the Main Stand (where the North Stand is nowadays) into the Jewish area of the cemetery on the other side of Janefield Street. Queen's Park and Rangers both immediately offered their grounds for the International, but Celtic's army of volunteers rallied and repaired the damage within a matter of days.

All this was watched with amazement by the rest of Glasgow and Scotland, for it was now apparent that, with the growth of Celtic, enthusiasm for this game of football knew no bounds. But for McMahon, the important thing was to be selected for the game. He was painfully aware that he had played the last two games for Scotland against England and had been on the losing side. He was anxious not to appear a kind of a Jonah, particularly as the game was to be played on his own home ground. He played well at the trials held at the beginning of March, was not too concerned to miss the Wales or the Ireland games – for he felt that his fine performance against the Irish League at the end of January had proved his form

– and was delighted when the side was announced for the England game and along with Dan Doyle and Jimmy Blessington, there was the name of Alexander McMahon.

It was a sign of McMahon's versatility that he was listed as centre-forward. He had played at inside-left for Celtic that season, and of course along with his friend Johnny Campbell, they were by far superior to most left wings of the day. But he had of course played at centre-forward in the past, and the Scottish selectors in their wisdom thought that this was the best place for him in the context. There was the usual amount of mumping and moaning about the team selection in the press and elsewhere, but McMahon was simply delighted to be given a third chance to play for Scotland against England, knowing full well how much this game meant to everyone.

45,107, by some distance a Scottish record crowd and one which astounded Glasgow, appeared at Celtic Park that bright and breezy day. A comparatively new feature was the amount of spectators from outwith Glasgow with the railway companies offering trips from Dundee, Edinburgh and even Aberdeen. From places like Motherwell and Hamilton, dogcarts were deployed to ferry passengers, as well as horse-drawn trams.

Rain had been threatening in the morning, but after about 12.00 the conditions settled as the crowd began to make its way eastwards from the centre of the city in time for the 3.30 pm kick-off. Celtic FC are praised by *The Glasgow Herald* for their prescience in building an extra embankment on both ends to house the crowd. At several points however, the pressure was just too much and the crowd encroached. One was a particularly serious looking "trespassing" in front of the Press Box on the London Road side of the ground, but the intruders were pushed back "with good humour" by Captain Boyd and his 170 policemen before Dan Doyle led Scotland out. The teams were;

Scotland: Haddow; Sillars and Doyle; Begbie, McCreadie and Mitchell; Gulliland, Blessington, McMahon, McPherson and Lambie.

England: Gay; Clare and Pelly; Reynolds, Holt and Needham; Bassett, Goodall, Smith, Chadwick and Spikesley.

Referee: Mr J Reid, Ireland.

If Sandy was not disconcerted by the huge crowd, he must have been the only one. "After seven minutes play a scene that cannot well be described announced that Scotland had scored the first goal of the game. They came away in a body in splendid style, fairly brushing everything before them, and McMahon sent in a fine shot, which Lambie sent through. Hats, sticks and handkerchiefs were thrown into the air and the scene baffles description," says *The Glasgow Herald* capturing the scene in a fine piece of writing. England however scored before half-time, and half-time was spent with no one listening to the pipe band, but engrossed in discussing with each other Scotland's chances of victory!

In the 75th minute, McMahon, who had alternated between the centre-forward and inside-left position, put Scotland ahead. *The Glasgow Herald*, by error, gives the goal to McPherson, but other sources say it was McMahon who "banged the ball through" following some fine work from Lambie and McPherson. Celtic Park was in a state of "fervent turbulence, like the Cape of Good Hope in a storm," after the goal was scored, and McMahon must have thought that he was about to become the hero of the country, but then with time fast running out, England equalized with a long drive from Reynolds which caught goalkeeper David Haddow of Rangers unsighted.

Still, 2–2 was a respectable result, and it was good enough to give Scotland the international Championship. McMahon felt that he had expunged the memories of 1892 and 1893, and the result was celebrated as if it had been a victory. McMahon felt that he had played well, and it was nice to have his hand shaken by supporters of Queen's Park and Rangers, as well as those of Celtic. Those who selected the Scottish League side to play the English League agreed that Sandy had had a good game for he was invited to play for the Scottish League at Goodison Park in Liverpool two weeks later.

It was a lovely day on 21 April 1894 before 25,000 spectators and a fine game ended 1–1. Oswald of St Bernard's scored Scotland's equalizing goal late in the game, and McMahon is frequently mentioned as playing well throughout the game, although on one occasion he conceded a free-kick when, "he put Holt of Everton higher up in the air than the referee thought proper". Clearly, McMahon, although more frequently the victim of fouls, was quite capable of occasion of dishing it out as well.

The season which had seen a fair amount of friendlies played by Celtic against English teams now fizzled out as far as McMahon was concerned. He played in the Glasgow Charity Cup semi-final and its replay in early May against Third Lanark, but in the 20th minute had to retire because of an injury. The injury is not specified, but Maley says that the reason McMahon missed the Final was because he was ill, rather than because he was injured. In either case, for the second year in a row, Sandy McMahon missed out on a Glasgow Charity Cup medal with Jimmy Blessington scoring both goals as Celtic beat Queen's Park 2–1.

1893–94 was thus another good season for Celtic and McMahon. He was now clearly established as Scotland's leading goalscorer, and the future looked bright. The legalisation of professionalism now meant that he could earn money from playing football without the constant fear that one day the law might ask questions about where his money was coming from. He would be earning considerably more than the average labourer or navvy in 1894, although he would still consider himself to be of the same class as they were. There was not yet the grotesque difference in the earning of professional footballer players' vis-à-vis the rest of society that there would be 100 years later.

The difference lay in the fact that McMahon and indeed most professional football players enjoyed what they were doing. They were not necessarily, of course, all full-time professionals, but even if they were just part-timers, they were earning money for doing a job that they loved. There were disadvantages, of course, in the ever constant danger of injury from the brutal tackles that were all too prominent, and there was very little in the way of security of contract, but it was still a good life, infinitely better than down a mine, in the shipyards or in a sweated labour factory.

Summer 1894 was a good time for McMahon and Celtic. For all sorts of reasons, 1894-95 was to be a lot less happy.

5.

1894–95

Celtic's seventh season was their worst to date. Yet it was not a total disaster either. The good points were the victories in the Glasgow Cup and the Glasgow Charity Cup with hegemony over Rangers and Queen's Park clearly established, but in the national competitions, teams from Edinburgh came to the fore. Celtic finished a poor second to Hearts in the Scottish League, and the Scottish Cup was won by the now defunct St Bernard's who beat Renton 2–1 in the Final. Celtic, admittedly without McMahon, had gone out at the quarter-final stage to Dundee at their new ground at Carolina Port. It was a mark of how fast Celtic were spreading that this season, in which they had established themselves as the best team in Glasgow, nevertheless they thought of themselves as a failure because they were not the best team in Scotland.

It was, as we have said, a good season for Edinburgh. For Glasgow, Celtic had a poor season, Rangers after winning the Scottish Cup in 1894 failed to replicate their form and Queen's Park were still going through the trauma of having to realise that no-one listened to them anymore and that everyone had gone their own sweet way of profes-sionalism. Hearts were going through a good phase of their history – they would win the Scottish Cup the following year in 1896 and the League again in 1897, and an additional warmer of the cockles of the hearts of Edinburgh football supporters was that Sandy's old favourites Hibs, the team still supported by many members of his family were also having a revival.

A Second Division of the Scottish League had been formed for the 1893–94 season and Hibs won it. This did not guarantee them promotion to the First Division for there would be no automatic promotion and relegation for some time, but when they won the Second Division again in 1894–95, they were duly admitted to the First Division for 1895–96. Edinburgh's star was thus in the ascendancy. One could indeed argue that 1895 was the zenith of Edinburgh football, for since then successes have been few and far between. St Bernard's of course are no longer with us, failing to re-emerge after World War II, and Hearts and Hibs, although they have both had their moments of spectacular triumph and both have produced a fair amount of brilliant players who have served Scotland well, have failed to sustain any lasting success on the Scottish scene.

From these events, the Scottish football historian is glad to observe that the game of football was spreading throughout the country, but the Celtic team's performances brought little but misery to their fans. There were other factors, which caused distress as well, namely on-going and ill-concealed discord among fans and officials. Such things are never conducive to success on the field – whether we are talking about the 19th century or the present day – and there can be little doubt that the seeds of the monumental disaster that was to come the way of the club in 1897 were sown in season 1894–95. A great deal of the trouble on the field stemmed from the brilliant but unstable Dan Doyle, but there was also murmurings in the background, which had started as early as the previous summer, about certain unresolved irregularities and allegations of ballot rigging in the voting procedure of the election of the committee.

McMahon himself was out of action in season 1894–95 on three occasions. His fitness problems over the summer meant that he was not able to begin until 8 September, then he sustained two really bad injuries, both times in games against Rangers – whether by accident or deliberate crocking we are not sure – and lost his International place as a result. He did play in the League International, but that was a very embarrassing 1–4 defeat. On the other hand, there was the occasional moment of brilliance, and the end of the season was a glorious triumph for him.

Sandy's first game of the season was also the first game ever played at Love Street, Paisley. A crowd of over 8,000 with many visitors from Glasgow came to see the impressive new facilities, although many of the Celtic persuasion were mainly there to see the return from injury of their hero Sandy McMahon. They were well rewarded with a good goal in the first half and another one at the start of the second when he seized on an opportunity presented to him by hesitation among the St Mirren defenders. Joe Cassidy scored the other goal in Celtic's 3–0 victory.

A couple of weeks later in a rough but exciting League game, Celtic beat Rangers 5–3 at Parkhead before a crowd of 20,000 spectators which may have risen to 30,000 by half-time as more men found their way from the pubs! McMahon didn't score but played his part in the game, exerting a calming influence when things showed signs of getting out of hand. The Glasgow Observer claims that a few insults like "Fenian!" "Irish!" and "Papist" were hurled by some of the Rangers players (not supporters!) at the Celtic men, who no doubt were fully capable of replying in kind. Several times the referee, the much-respected Mr Baillie of St Bernard's was compelled to bring a few players together and to tell them to "calm down".

October 1894 was a good month for Celtic and McMahon. There were four wins for the club and three goals for Sandy, but the first match in November was the one that indicated that winning the League for the third year in a row was going to be a big ask for Celtic. Once again 20,000, including a "fair speckling of capitalist trippers" (as Hearts supporters were quaintly described) came to Celtic Park to see this undefeated Hearts team who had been very impressive that season. Indeed they proved their worth when they scored early on.

There are reports of McMahon being badly treated (he was obviously marked out as the danger man). On one occasion he, "picked up the ball and in his best style wormed his way through several opponents," only to pass to Johnny Campbell who shot past the post. At another time, according to *The Glasgow Herald*, "several men lay heaped in the net, but the ball was not sent in with them," as Celtic pressed desperately for an equalizer, but as often happens in these circumstances, it was Hearts who ran up the field and added a second.

The following week Celtic went to St Bernard's, to Logie Green, where they attracted a crowd of 8,000 which included a "large Glasgow contingent" and won 2–0, McMahon scoring one of the goals and setting up Joe Cassidy for the other, and therefore they began to approach the Glasgow Cup Final with a degree of confidence. The opponents were to be Rangers who seemed to be "full of goals" for they had beaten Partick Thistle 5–3 in their semi-final.

17 November 1894 saw this momentous and fateful Glasgow Cup Final. It would prove to be a bittersweet occasion for Celtic and for McMahon. 20,000 crammed into Cathkin to see the game in "unfavourable weather", and at one point there was a crowd break-in. This was a regular curse of late Victorian football, it seems, due to the increasing popularity of the game and the inadequacy of some of the stadia. This one occurred at one of the corners because of over-crowding but the police "persuaded them not to come on to the pitch". McMahon, now the captain of the side, would look back on this game with mixed memories. On the one hand, he won a Glasgow Cup medal (his second), but on the other he sustained a knee injury following a few hefty challenges, and disappeared soon after half-time. Maley too was injured, but after being off for a spell, was able to resume.

It was one of Celtic's best performances in their first decade. Dan Doyle and John Divers had scored in the first half, and Sandy McMahon had come close on several occasions until he came into contact with the brutal Nicol Smith. History is not kind to the fair-haired

Nick Smith. Ten years later in the Glasgow Charity Cup Final of 1904, he would inflict bitter revenge on Jimmy Quinn for Jimmy's famous Scottish Cup hat-trick, and here, he seems to have been deliberately deployed to maim Celtic's best player Sandy McMahon. Sandy was injured on many occasions in tackles that would not be tolerated by modern day referees, but things were a lot tougher in the 1890s. It would also be grossly unfair to imply that Celtic were shrinking violets or injured innocents in this game, for Rangers' other Smith, the very talented Alec Smith also had to retire from the fray after one or two encounters with Celtic's full-backs Tom Dunbar and Dan Doyle.

Sandy limped through the last few minutes of the first half, then reappeared but briefly in the second half, before having to retire, his knee having given way entirely. Celtic, down to nine men until Maley reappeared, fought well and by sensible play kept Rangers from scoring. The man who earns the most plaudits was right half Charlie McEleny, a hard man whose war cry that day and others was "Up sleeves and at-em, Celtic!"

Celtic ran out 2–0 winners. McMahon watching from the sidelines and barely able to walk, was nevertheless unable to suppress a smile that the brutal tactics of Rangers had not won the day. "There was a scene of great enthusiasm at the end, several of the players being carried to the pavilion," says *The Glasgow Herald*. *The Daily Record and Mail* describes the game as a, "hard trying ordeal in which stamina was very much required and given by all". It then adds incongruously in the context that the game was "free from fouls", an absolutely astonishing comment and totally at odds with other accounts of the game! The teams were:

Celtic: McArthur; Dunbar and Doyle; McEleny, Kelly and Maley; Campbell, Madden, Cassidy, McMahon and Divers.

Rangers: Haddow; N. Smith and Drummond; Marshall, Pray and Gibson; Cowan, McCreadie, Gray, McPherson, A. Smith.

Referee: T Lamb, St Bernard's.

The Glasgow Observer spends more time and space discussing the funeral of Tsar Alexander III of Russia, but "A Celt" is jubilant with this triumph which he sums up as "two goals, nine men, a cripple, Rangers beaten and John Glass takes the Cup". His account however is churlishly ungracious as he also tells us at length how, "the Glasgow establishment as represented on the pavilion steps" were "pitiful to witness as depicted in their demeanour as the Celtic triumph became more and more apparent" and that even at the traditional after-match banquet a certain "coldness" was in evidence. The Celtic paranoia, whether justified or otherwise, is clearly on view here from an early stage of their history!

Celtic with the Glasgow Cup.
McMahon is second from the left in the middle row

It was a significant, but quite clearly a Pyrrhic victory. Maley and McMahon were now both despatched to Manchester for treatment from a Mr Allison, and in McMahon's case, he was now out until the middle of February 1895. During this time, he missed a fairly "interesting" time in Celtic's history with a certain amount of evidence of gross disharmony on and off the field. Dan Doyle, that stormy petrel of Victorian football, and a few others caused a great deal of trouble, and it is hard not to believe that McMahon's calming influence might not have helped. As it was, when McMahon returned in the middle of February, the team were already out of the Scottish Cup (a 0–1 defeat at Dundee's new stadium called Carolina Port), behind in the League, and without any kind of a win since 2January.

Even before the defeat at Carolina Port, there had been a clear indication of how much McMahon was being missed when Hibs (then, of course, still in the Second Division) actually beat Celtic at Easter Road on 15 December in a Scottish Cup tie. Fortunately, Celtic were able to find grounds for protest and won the replayed game, but the whole business was unsatisfactory, raised serious questions about how good Celtic actually were without McMahon, and did very little for the often strained relationships between Scotland's two "Irish" sides. It was often said that the real haters of the Irish were the Irish themselves!

It would have indeed been interesting to know McMahon's feelings about all this, given his still very strong feelings for Hibs. The protest for the first game seemed to centre on the fact that two Hibs players had played for other teams in the past and were not properly registered. Hibs sources describe this as petty and vindictive, if technically correct, and claim that Celtic, being one of the strongest teams in Scotland at the moment, were able to bully the other teams into voting in their favour. In any case, it did Celtic little good, for by the time that the saviour McMahon came back, Celtic's season was more or less over – at least as far as Scottish honours were concerned.

McMahon's first game back was against the strong going Hearts at Tynecastle on 16 February 1895. It was a game that Celtic really had to win to have any kind of hope of winning the Scottish League. It turned out to be one of the worst games in Celtic's seven-season history as the team went down 0–4 to a strong Hearts team. The game was played on a slippery pitch with the snow having recently melted, and several puddles could be seen. Doyle wasn't playing but appeared to act as linesman! Madden, McEleny and Maley were all absent with no adequate reason given, and Kelly failed to appear in the second half, presumably injured. McMahon, still not all that fit, hardly got a kick of the ball, and the only Celtic player to emerge with any credit was goalkeeper Dan McArthur who was praised for keeping the score down to four. Rangers lost to Third Lanark that day, and Hearts were now in effect League Champions. It was their first League triumph, and the first time that the League had not been won by a team from the west of Scotland.

The season now fizzled out depressingly for both McMahon and Celtic. The team did gradually get back to winning ways, but too late to have any impact on the League. McMahon had been out for so long that he could not realistically have expected a "cap" for Scotland against England. It was perhaps as well that he did not play that day, for Scotland went down 0–3 to England at Goodison Park, Liverpool. His colleague Dan Doyle did play – but only after he had mysteriously disappeared the night before and turned up again only a very short time before the start of the game! Amazingly, Doyle was allowed to play, but a lot less amazingly in the context of the circumstances, he played badly and Scotland lost.

Sandy's only representative appearance that season was an embarrassing one. It was for the Scottish League v English League on 13 April. The game was played at Celtic Park, and possibly for that reason, six Celtic players were chosen – McMahon, McArthur, Doyle, Kelly, Madden and Divers. It was a fine spring day, and a goodly crowd of 30,000 turned up. McMahon scored in the early stages, but Scotland were not much in the game until the later stages when a desperate effort was launched. McMahon had one chance, which might have brought Scotland back into it, but fired high over the bar, and the game finished 4–1 in favour of the Englishmen.

McMahon continued playing the odd friendly match that Celtic arranged as their season fizzled out. He wasn't playing against St Mirren on 20 April – possibly he and some other players had gone to Ibrox to watch the Scottish Cup Final between St Bernard's and Renton, or even further afield to see the English Cup Final at the Crystal Palace in London where Aston Villa beat West Brom 1–0 with a goal scored in 20 seconds. He was certainly interested in English football, as indeed English football remained interested in him.

Spring 1895 was dominated by scandal, rather than football. As in later years, (1963 for example where everyone talked about John Profumo and Christine Keeler), this one was about sex, in this case Oscar Wilde who caused more than a little stir in the Celtic community. Wilde was an Irishman, but his trail involved "the love that dares not speak its name" – namely homosexuality, an activity, which however widely practised in certain upper class circles, was anathema to polite Victorian society and to the Catholic Church in particular.

But as would often be the case in future years, as far as Celtic were concerned, the dreadful season of 1894–95 ended with a sting in the tail, and Celtic supporters had at least something to be happy about in the Glasgow Charity Cup. For McMahon, this became a sort of redemption, and his performance in the Final was something that would be talked about for a long time.

New players had been signed in the shape of Peter Meechan from Sunderland for the right-back position, and Tommy Morrison a right-winger from Glentoran. Morrison had two nicknames in "Ching" and (bizarrely) "Sandy Row", and he was an immediate success. In addition, McMahon who had been again out for another spell near the end of the season, came back in time for the Glasgow Charity Cup, and Charlie McEleny, a man "with a tremendous thirst for hard work" but who had been sadly inconsistent hitherto, suddenly found form. There was in addition a certain determination that the Glasgow Charity Cup, which the team had won in 1892, 1893 and 1894 should remain at Celtic Park, even in spite of the many disappointments that the team had suffered this season.

A 1-0 win over Clyde on 14 May saw Celtic into the Final at Cathkin on 25 May. Their opponents were to be Rangers, a team who had, like Celtic, suffered from a very poor season, and who had, of course, lost to Celtic in the Glasgow Cup Final in November and were thirsting for revenge. It so happened, however, that this was one of those days when everything that Celtic tried, worked successfully. The 4–0 score line could easily have been doubled.

The crowd was 15,000 and the primitive Cathkin Park struggled once again to contain the crowd. The admission charge was one shilling – rather too much, some felt – and there were reports of spectators climbing over the fence, and (turnstiles not yet being in place at Cathkin) "taking advantage of their vast numbers to charge the pay boxes". In addition, outside the ground there was an eminence at the top of Preston Street, which, although some distance away from the ground, allowed well over a hundred people to watch the game for free.

McMahon had been made captain (in a move perhaps to quieten the rebels, on the terracing and in the dressing room, who made their opposition to the incumbent James Kelly quite clear – a clear harbinger of things to come over the next 100 years for the Kelly dynasty!) and the players responded to his positive leadership. He was well supported by Charlie McEleny whose clarion call that day was once again the "up sleeves and at 'em, Celts", which had made its debut, as it were, in the Glasgow Cup Final in November. There was also a new player called Willie Ferguson who had taken over from Johnny Campbell (currently being wooed by Aston Villa) on the left-wing.

Half way through the first half McMahon had put Celtic ahead. Just before half-time, James Kelly, playing the attacking centre-half role, silenced his critics to make it 2–0 for Celtic. In the second half the dispirited Rangers could make no impact on the well-organised Celtic defence, and Celtic remained very much in charge. The "tactics of the Rangers defence were exceedingly shady" in the opinion of several newspapers. Peter O'Rourke, enjoying his brief moment of glory at right-half, took long throw-ins and caused all sorts of panic in the Rangers defence. McMahon scored again with a run, even though he was being constantly fouled, and a well-judged shot, and just as time was running out, he scored with a great header from a corner kick, rising, "with a Rangers hanging to each leg" (in the graphic but unlikely words of *The Glasgow Observer*) to score one of his best ever goals. The teams were:

Celtic: McArthur; Meechan and Doyle; O'Rourke, Kelly and McEleny; Morrison, Madden, McMahon, Divers and Ferguson.

Rangers: Haddow; N Smith and Drummond; N Gibson, W Gibson and Mitchell; Cowan, H McCreadie, McPherson, King and A Smith.

Referee: Mr W McLeod, Cambuslang.

*A rare action picture of the Glasgow Charity
Cup final of 1895 at Cathkin*

Celtic had now won the Glasgow Charity Cup for the fourth year in a row, in spectacular style this time, McMahon was clearly back to full fitness, and the future began to look a little brighter. The season had been disappointing, but there had been a few good points as well, and if this season taught Celtic anything, it was just how much they depended on the skills of Sandy McMahon, both on and off the field.

6.

1895–96 – MCMAHON ON SONG

Season 1895–96 was as good as the previous (and the next) season was bad. McMahon stayed comparatively free of injury and possibly as a result, the team had arguably the best season of its short life. There was one disappointment, and it was a big one – in the Scottish Cup against Queen's Park in January – but the club was well rewarded with success in the other three competitions, in the case of the Scottish League this was achieved a few weeks before the New Year (it was the habit in those days to try to get the Scottish League finished early to leave space for the Scottish Cup and International games). This season thus emulated 1892 in the winning of three trophies out of four. McMahon excelled throughout, but was disappointed not to regain International recognition

There were a few changes in personnel. One that particularly affected McMahon was the transfer of Johnny Campbell to Aston Villa. The left wing partnership of McMahon and Campbell was of course famous throughout the length and breadth of the British Isles, and it was no great surprise when Aston Villa were attracted by Campbell. They apparently offered the fairly astronomical wage of £4 per week. But according to Willie Maley, it was, "the stupid action of a very prominent committee man," which precipitated Campbell's departure, for Campbell was a true Celt, from Saracen Street, and was always quoted as saying that the first football result he looked for in his Saturday evening paper was that of Celtic. He would not be the first nor the last Celt to leave the club, and then come back!

As to who the committee man was and what his stupid action was we cannot say, but it was Celtic's loss. Yet the good form of season 1895–96 made sure that the loss was not obvious. It became clear however during the following season of 1896–97 that Celtic had made a very big mistake indeed.

Celtic in season 1895–96.
McMahon is sitting in the middle of the front row

There may have been an attempt by the Aston Villa club (winners of the English Cup in 1895 and generally regarded as the best in England) to dislodge McMahon as well, but if there was, nothing happened. Sandy, possibly remembering his ill-thought-out and somewhat immature flirtation with Nottingham Forest in 1892, was delighted to remain and play for the team with whom he now had a symbiotic relationship. His popularity among the support was proved week after week when he got his own special cheer the first time that he touched the ball – "if not adulation, certainly apprecia-tion", as a contemporary Press report has it.

At centre-forward this year, Celtic had acquired another man from Hibs, He was not the first nor the last to move westwards from one Irish team to another, but Allan Martin played for Celtic for only one season and returned to Hibs at the end of it. He had a tremendous season for Celtic, scoring prolifically and freely, and fitted in perfectly with other forwards like Jimmy Blessington and Sandy McMahon to regain the Scottish League Championship and restore the faith of the supporters, which had been put sorely to the test in the travails of the 1894–95 season.

As often with good Celtic seasons, it didn't necessarily start all that well. There was a very bad tour of England in early September which saw defeats to Manchester City, Liverpool and Newcastle United – something that did little for the club's credibility, for, "friendly" or not, losing to an English side was a painful experience. And the Newcastle game let to a salutary lesson for Sandy McMahon. He had picked up a knock against Liverpool so had not played at the new St James' Park. He was then persuaded foolishly by Dan Doyle to stay on in Newcastle for a night out. The night out lasted into a couple of nights, a few crucial trains were missed, and the four players who had stayed on were too late home for the game against Rangers on the Saturday.

McMahon may not have been playing in any case against Rangers because of his injury, but he was technically suspended along with Doyle, McManus and Cullen. Reserves had to be drafted in and the club was put in the embarrassing position of having to cancel the reserve fixture against Motherwell. Ironically, the team beat Rangers 4–2 without McMahon and Doyle, but after that things took a bit of a dive with heavy defeats by Hearts and St Bernard's as an Edinburgh complex seemed to develop.

These were all well attended games, and they were all hammerings, which made it hard to imagine the success that was to come this season. On 24 August, at Easter Road after Hibs unfurled the Second Division flag (which they had won last season) Celtic scored first, but then Hibs equalized and in a flurry of goals in the last 10 minutes, ran out 4–2 winners before a nasty Hibs crowd who still felt sore that Celtic had stolen their players in the early 1890s. McMahon, being one of those who was seen to have jumped ship, was singled out for barracking – something that must have hurt Sandy.

The Edinburgh Holiday Weekend of 14–16 September saw Celtic lose eight goals to Edinburgh teams and score none. Hearts came to Celtic Park on the Saturday and won 5–0 before 15,000 disappointed and bewildered fans. Hearts were of course Scottish League Champions in 1895 and there was no disgrace to be beaten by that fine side. A 0–5 thumping however was not easy to swallow. There was a reason and an excuse as well. McMahon missed that one, not yet having recovered from the injury sustained at Liverpool. But he was in the team that went to St Bernard's for the Edinburgh Holiday fixture and lost 0–3.

Had this happened in the modern era, there would have been an outcry and the sacking of a manager to appease the mob, but this was 1895 and there wasn't even a manager to sack! But although supporters moaned and said that "there is something wrong" while adding dark allusions to associations with bookmakers and other things, it was in fact just a run of bad luck. Calm appraisals of the situation followed, and slowly, with their star man McMahon back, completely recovered from injury, the form of the team began to turn. By the time that September was out, the team had notched an excellent win at Dumbarton with Divers, Blessington and McMahon all finding the net, and the defence warding off a late Dumbarton rally.

The training regime was also improved. The trainer was now a man called Tom Maguire who organised things like distance walks to Broomhouse, and swimming at the new baths recently opened in Parkhead, one of the many laudable attempts of Victorian society to do something about what politicians called "the great unwashed". Sandy clearly revelled in such activities. He realised that there is no excuse for a professional footballer not being fit. He said quite categorically that a professional player is cheating the public if he does not strive for fitness.

It was October that the team really hit top form. First of all, Hibs came to Parkhead, and on a wet and slippery pitch, revenge was taken for the defeat at Easter Road with a fine 3–1 win. McMahon set the ball rolling with a good goal, and then Doyle and Martin scored the other two. Alan Lugton's excellent *The Making of Hibernian* quotes a poem on this game, which brilliantly catches the mood. The poem is obviously written from a pessimistic Hibs perspective, but it does well to set the scene, with a touch of Homer's Iliad not far away.

> *Hibernian! Hibernian! Beware of the day*
> *When the Celtic shall meet thee in battle array!*
> *My spirit foresees the result of the fight*
> *And the dreaded green jerseys are scattered in flight.*
>
> *Alas for your pledges to victory vowed*
> *For Breslin the dauntless and Murphy the proud.*
> *Your halves are outwitted, your backs in broil,*
> *And bould Murray is sat on by Battles and Doyle.*
>
> *Fierce rages the conflict. Hark, hear ye that roar?*
> *The Duke and the Rooter have opened the score*
> *Uprouse ye, Auld Reekie, press on to the front!*
> *Now hurry up Hibs and still lead the League hunt.*
>
> *Oh, Martin! Oh, Martin! How can you have heart*
> *Against your old comrades to play such a part?*
> *Wirrasthru! Drop the curtain, the battle is done,*
> *The Celts are the victors by three goals to one!*

Clyde were then put to the sword with a 5–1 score. Next Celtic travelled down to Sheffield to beat Sheffield United 1–0 at Bramall Lane, with Sandy McMahon, now universally referred to as "The Duke", even in England, scoring the winner with a terrific shot. Then progress was made in the Glasgow Cup as Celtic beat Cambuslang 6–1, and finally at the end of the month came the record League score of Celtic 11 Dundee 0.

There were extenuating circumstances, as far as Dundee were concerned. There had been heavy snow overnight, but as it was still October, it melted fairly rapidly. The pitch however had been left very wet and slippery. Dundee, struggling in the throes of their own domestic difficulties and infighting, were a very poor side and by half-time, they had not only lost six goals but they had only nine fit men. Centre-half Longair was concussed, left-half Ferrier had a dislocated ankle and although inside-left McDonald was still on the pitch, he had injured his ribs and was virtually useless on the left wing.

Celtic took full advantage of all this, 11 goals were scored, but it is not possible to say with any degree of accuracy who scored them all, as reports vary and indeed the newspaper reporters themselves do not seem to have any clear idea. Martin seems to have scored about five, McMahon possibly three and Battles, Blessington and Ferguson may have scored as well. Once again we must remember that newspaper reporting of football matches in the 1890s was far from an exact science, particularly, as in this case, when things became hectic and complicated, and in the absence of numbered jerseys it was not always possible to identify clearly each player.

There was a little criticism in certain quarters about Celtic in this game for their merciless approach, but it must be stressed that everything was within the rules. Celtic were already well on top before anyone was injured. The injuries to the Dundee players were not caused by foul play. They were genuine accidents, even though

Barney Battles (ironically called "gentle Barney") was at one point spoken to by the referee Mr Baillie of St Bernard's, (Barney himself had to retire injured a little later) and praise should be given for the way that Celtic entertained their 11,000 crowd with some fine goal scoring. The Daily Record and Mail talks highly about Celtic's team work, but Maley in The History of the Celtic seems actually to be of the opinion that Celtic were "holding back" and that the game was "farcical". The Glasgow Herald, who clearly had not sent a reporter to this match, virtually eschews any detailed comment about this game, and prefers to deal with another high-scoring game – Third Lanark 6 Clyde 2.

Another point in doubt about this game, incidentally, is what colour of strip Celtic used, for Mr Baillie thought that Celtic's green and white vertical strip clashed with Dundee's blue and white, and in those days, it was the home team that had to change, (on the grounds presumably that they had their change strips available) but there is no evidence about what colour they changed into. Whether Celtic wore their green jerseys or their white ones is not clear.

The high scoring continued into November. Celtic had now caught up the arrears in the League race, and reached the Glasgow Cup final with a 5–1 drubbing of Partick Thistle. The following week in the Scottish League, Martin scored five as Third Lanark were on the wrong end of a 7–0 doing with McMahon, playing slightly further back and spraying passes to Martin in particular, earning the loud cheers of the Celtic Park crowd. They were in high spirits as they left the ground that dreich November afternoon to await the horse-drawn trams (or simply walk) to get back to the centre of the city or to their own towns and to talk excitedly about next week's game, which was the Glasgow Cup Final at Ibrox against Queen's Park.

The Daily Record and Mail quotes Alex (sic) McMahon as captian (sic) talking about the defeat of Third Lanark. He says that, "It was another big win" and that, "Celtic are too strong for Cathkin this year," but that he hoped, "to be on the winning side next Saturday". The same newspaper says that, "Martin is the finest centre that the club has produced".

Celtic were, of course, the holders of the Glasgow Cup, and in spite of dreadful weather on 16 November 1895 a crowd of 25,000 turned up at Ibrox to see the game. We are told the details that there were 50 policemen on duty, four of them mounted. This was a sensible precaution in view of the excitement and large crowds generated by football matches in the 1890s. Queen's Park seemed to have more supporters than Celtic had, but Celtic were by no means under-represented, even though their supporters had to stand in the heavy rain on an exposed mound.

There was a strange piece of class distinction at this game in that Queen's Park were given the dressing room facilities of the covered stand where the Govan Stand now is, but Celtic had to make do with the more primitive accommodation in the old pavilion on the south east side of the ground. It was difficult not to detect an element of social snobbery in all this, and those of the Celtic support who look for such things had much to go on, as Rangers now seemed to be collaborating with the Gentlemen of Scotland to keep them away from the vulgar professionals of the East End! It could of course be paralleled in cricket, a sport with an appalling apartheid-type ethos, which had Gentlemen (amateurs) and Players (professionals) coming out on to the field through separate gates! In Scottish football however, this particular piece of discrimination caused a tremendous resentment among the Celtic faithful.

The continuous rain over the previous 24 hours meant that the pitch now resembled "a quagmire, a sea of mud mixed with sawdust", the sawdust a testament to the heroic attempts of the Rangers committee and groundsman to keep the game on. It meant though that the pitch would be very heavy, and that the team with the greater stamina would win the day. In this respect, it was felt that Celtic, professional and well trained, would have a distinct advantage over the clerks, bankers, students, teachers and lawyers who made up the Queen's Park team.

Queen's Park won the toss and opted to play with the strong west wind (the rain had now eased slightly) but it was Celtic who were first on the attack with inside men Blessington and McMahon taking advantage of the iron grip that the half-back line of Maley, Kelly and Battles had taken of the game. They forced a series of corners, and from one of them Willie Ferguson ("the star of the front rank, and the coolest man of the 25,000 present" according to *The Glasgow Observer*) sent over an inch-perfect cross for Allan Martin to put Celtic one up and to delight the Celtic section of the crowd, who may have been outnumbered (three-quarters of the crowd were Queen's Park supporters, according to one account), but were far from outshouted.

Queen's Park equalized through R.S. McColl (the famous "Toffee Bob" whose name can still be seen on newsagents and confectionary shops on Scottish high streets) half way through the first half, and then as battle raged from end to end, McMahon had the bad luck to see a shot hit the post and another shot saved by the goalkeeper. But then the game and the destination of the Glasgow Cup seemed to hinge on a bad injury to Barney Battles who had to limp off, and while he was off, Queen's Park scored twice, as the outnumbered Celtic defence tried desperately to re-organise. Mr Baillie's half-time whistle came "with the Queen's Park star in the ascendant" and winning 3–1.

Maley's account of the game, laced as it is with paranoia and persecution complex, says that the crowd, "was delirious with joy at the prospect of a Celtic defeat, not knowing what the second half was to bring", but he also tells us that, "many invaded the pitch at the beginning of the second portion, but in an orderly enough manner, and the police were not long in returning them to the terracing". This is odd, but the invasion at the Copeland Road end of the ground and in front of the North Stand seems to have been nothing more than an attempt to get away from the worst of the crushing. 26,000 (Maley says 24,000) was an astonishing crowd for a domestic match in the mid-1890s, and possibly too much for the still primitive Ibrox.

The Glasgow Herald agrees with Maley that the break-in (such as it was) was "orderly" but then indulges itself in one of its periodic paeans of praise for the Queen's Park side that it clearly loved. It waxed eloquent, heroic and bordered on the poetic with phrases like, "Celtic…never looked like a winning team, the amateurs fairly taking it out of them and playing them at every turn", "the Queen's never played in a pluckier or more determined fashion…and fairly pulverised them, at all events during the first ten minutes". "The Queens were cheered to the echo and well did they deserve it, for never did a team respond more nobly to the demands made upon them…The Celtic forwards were blocked, baffled and beaten back in all directions, while the Queens' forwards fairly played McMahon and Doyle, meeting them in fearless style and playing them to perfection".

This is odd stuff, given the eventual result, although Maley does agree about, "the cheers which greeted every kick of Celtic's opponents", but then the chronicler of *The Glasgow Herald* (and over a century later we can still almost sense the tears in his eyes) is compelled to reluctantly record that Ferguson made in 2–3 after twenty minutes of the second half and that, ten minutes, later McMahon equalised.

The floodgates were now opened, and at this point professional training clearly made itself felt. Ferguson scored with twelve minutes remaining (Queen's Park and *The Glasgow Herald* were convinced that it was offside, but the days when Queen's Park could cow and intimidate referees had long gone, and Mr Baillie was no fool), and then as Celtic, with McMahon outstanding, simply took command

and ran the show so well that a further two goals were added near the end, (one by Ferguson and one by McMahon himself) and Celtic ran out 6–3 winners to retain the Glasgow Cup and to cheer up their fans, and to leave all Queen's Park supporters and neutrals awestruck on that grim November day.

Words like "stamina" and "pluck" were frequently used with James Kelly singled out for praise as a "man of metal" but captain McMahon said that he had always been confident even when the team were behind, and a conversation between himself and Waddell of Queen's Park is quoted. It was along the lines of what Waddell said to McMahon at half-time and what McMahon said to him at full-time. It apparently went along the lines of, "We are now in charge," from Waddell and "I always felt we could do it," from McMahon, but McMahon was gracious enough to praise Queen's Park as well. Such magnanimity was rare in late Victorian football writing.

It is odd that McMahon is described as "captain". Normally for this season the captain is given as James Kelly. It is possible that the *Daily Record* makes an error here, for there is no indication of Kelly having been removed from the job. McMahon was probably the vice-captain and may simply have been the man on the spot to talk to the reporter. Kelly and McMahon would have made a fine leadership team on the field, for although McMahon possessed the tact and diplomacy to do the job, – and certainly the playing ability and technical nous – he possibly lacked the "gravitas" and "dignitas" which the revered Kelly had in abundance, even though Kelly's popularity with the Celtic fans was clearly declining.

McMahon was quoted as saying that he, "had no doubt of the result even when Queen's Park were leading. Celtic's defence did not handle the two opposing wings in the first portion in their usual style but made ample amends in the second when they played a different game. Celtic were good value for the Cup – and well trained, even though ground conditions did not favour close combination".

Celtic had now won the Glasgow Cup four times as distinct from Queen's Park and Rangers with their twice each. Once more there were street parties with music and dancing, and once more McMahon, who now had three Glasgow Cup medals, felt humbled at the acclamation that he and his fellow players received, as they returned in triumph to the east end. The writer of *The Evening Times* who writes from a Celtic point of view lapses into doggerel verse;

> *Hurrah! At last the whistle sounds the call.*
> *Alas! Alas! Q.P. the jig is up!*
> *Six goals to three. You must feel rather small,*
> *Brave, Bold Celts. You've nobly won the Cup!*

The teams on that memorable day of 16 November 1895, "that lit a beacon in the Celtic heartlands to pierce the November gloom," were;

Celtic: McArthur: Meehan and Doyle; Maley, Kelly and Battles; Madden, Blessington, Martin, McMahon and Ferguson.

Queen's Park: Anderson; Gillespie and Smith; Allison, McFarlane and Stewart; Crookston, Waddell, McColl, Cameron and Leslie.

Referee: Mr J Baillie, St Bernard's.

This was good, but there was more to come yet. With Celtic still on a high following their Glasgow Cup success, the team now had to go to Tynecastle for a fixture that had the appearance of being virtually a League decider. In a 10 team League, each team played 18 games, and Celtic, Hearts and Hibs all played 12, points 18 (two points for a win). It did not take a genius to work out that whoever lost the game at Tynecastle would be severely and possibly irreparably damaged in the League race. Hibs were due at Ibrox that day to play Rangers, a team whose early lapses had made them only an outside contender for the Championship.

An astonishing amount of Celtic supporters made the trip to Edinburgh on the 11.00 train to help swell the 15,000 crowd on a windy but dry day of 23 November. It was a day on which the Celtic team of McArthur; Meechan and Doyle; Maley, Kelly and Battles; Madden, Blessington, Martin, McMahon and Ferguson, playing with the confidence and composure of a team with recent success, simply took Hearts apart. Some say that Martin scored a hat-trick (others give the third goal to McMahon) and Blessington scored the fourth as Celtic won 4-1 with Hearts goal being a late consolation.

McMahon was quoted as saying that Celtic had "deliberateness of method" and "earnestness of purpose". "It was our day easily. We got fairly knocked, but we got four goals without the knocking" – a statement that sounds odd, but means presumably that Celtic were on the wrong end of rough treatment, but did not retaliate and scored four times nonetheless – "We played an open game and Martin's play pleased me immensely".

But not for the first or last time, Celtic found the natives at Tynecastle a little inhospitable. "Blood ran free and feeling high" was a quote in *The Glasgow Observer* – the "blood" reference, one hopes to the internal feelings of supporters rather than blood being spilt in the environs of the ground! *The Glasgow Herald* is disgusted by the behaviour of Hearts' Scotland internationalist Isaac Begbie, but also says something that runs contrary to the perceived wisdom of the sporting demeanour of Sandy McMahon. "Kicking had become very common in the first half but McMillan and McMahon now stood in the centre of the field letting out (sic) at each other's shins until the referee brought them to order".

But Celtic left the field 4–1 winners, and within minutes of the full time whistle a telegram arrived at Tynecastle with the news that Rangers had beaten Hibs 4–0. This meant that Celtic were now clear at the top of the League. Celtic's loyal knot of supporters took it upon themselves to escort their favourites to Haymarket Station lest they be "assailed" by "disgruntled Edinburgh men", but the team could hardly believe what they saw when they arrived at Glasgow Central Station little more than an hour later. News having travelled quickly on the modern telegraphic system, the Station was packed with well-wishers, and a flute band had been hired at short notice to play Irish songs like *God Save Ireland, A Nation Once Again,* and *The Wearing O' The Green* mingled with a few current music hall favourites. The players were "chaired" off the train to their waiting horse-drawn brake. Not for the first time, McMahon was astounded at just exactly how much this team Celtic meant to its community.

Indeed the frenetic communal singing of *God Save Ireland* with its explicit and powerful words followed by its passionate chorus, sung by wild looking and yet triumphant Irishmen must have discomfited and possibly even terrified the douce Glasgow populace.

High upon the gallows tree
Swing the noble hearted free
Whom vindictive tyrants cut down in their bloom
But we met them face to face
With the courage of our race
And now we march undaunted to our doom!

God Save Ireland, cry the heroes
God Save Ireland, cry they all
Whether on the scaffold high
Or the battlefield they die
What matters when
For Ireland dear they fall?

Further progress towards the League Championship was made on 30 November when Celtic went to Love Street and in a rough game (as St Mirren v Celtic games tended to be) came back from 0–1 down to win 3–1 with two goals from Jimmy Blessington and one from Willie Ferguson, McMahon having a hand in all three. "McMahon and Ferguson were steady throughout but brilliant at the finish," says *The Daily Record and Mail*. Hearts lost to Third Lanark that day in a thriller and Hibs to St Bernard's, giving Celtic a distinct advantage.

But the same Stockbridge side, which had done so well against Hibs, put up a brave fight at Celtic Park the next week. The pitch was hard and snow lay on the surrounds, but Celtic adapted better to those difficult conditions in the first stages with McMahon scoring with an angular shot, then feeding Martin from the wing for the second goal after the Edinburgh Saints had equalized. With darkness falling fast, the teams did not even leave the field at half-time, but a man was seen to run on to the field to tell everyone that Hearts were being heavily defeated at Ibrox. Indeed they were – collapsing to a 7–2 defeat while Celtic held on grimly to their 2–1 lead in the semi-darkness with the only light coming from the pavilion. "It was a very poor game" according to *The Daily Record and Mail*.

The correspondent of *The Glasgow Observer* was even less impressed. Under the heading "Shooting Gallery Bottled Up" he is extremely disappointed at this "semi-failure" against the "Eastern Saints", as he describes St Bernard's, as distinct from the "Western Saints" (St Mirren). There is even a criticism of Sandy McMahon whose, "messing roused the ire of the stand and the once idolised Duke was laughed at and even hissed for his fatuous attempts at useless trickery". If Celtic played like that against Rangers, he said, they would have a "forlorn hope" of victory. Full time, however, meant that if Celtic could beat Rangers at Parkhead next week (December 14), the League flag would be theirs.

The reporting of this game and the comments of the curmudgeonly correspondent of *The Glasgow Observer* are interesting, but in the context of Celtic supporters throughout the ages, not really surprising. Celtic's fan base, obviously huge, does contain, it has to be said, more than a few who do not really support the team at all but appear to enjoy criticising and carping. It has been no uncommon sight in living memory to hear men like Jimmy Johnstone, Kenny Dalglish and Paul McStay barracked mercilessly, so we should not be entirely surprised at this vituperation of the team – even when in December 1895 they were on the actual cusp of a great victory!

Rarely had Glasgow been so excited about a football match. The interest was "like a Scotland v England game". It was of course McMahon's job to calm everyone down and to keep them focussed on the task in hand. This was one of his good points of course in that, as well as being the personality goalscorer, he was also every-one's favourite uncle, always ready for a chat with players, and never ignoring the approaches of supporters, however importunate and annoying, if they met him in the street or the environs of the ground. It was Jock Stein who said that football is nothing without fans…but other people like McMahon realised that a long time before.

Even in bad weather 24,000 came to Celtic Park that dull and rainy December afternoon through the 24 entrances, eight of which were now the modern "turnstiles", as distinct from the more primitive pay boxes which of course could be easily "rushed" by those wanting free admission! Another modern touch was the employment of six operators for telegraphic messages for the newspapers, something that happened with "commendable celerity". In view of the fact that it was December with little daylight, the game that was to kick off at 2.00 – rather too early a time, it was felt, for it might prevent, "some of the artisans from being present", and the ground would open at 12.15. Celtic, we are told, received several "Good luck" telegrams from ex-players like Johnny Campbell, "friend Jerry" (Reynolds) and Jimmy "Tooty" Davidson.

The showery weather was not conducive to good football, but the rain was intermittent and all Celtic's goals were scored when the rain was off, according to *The Daily Record and Mail*. Martin opened the scoring, Rangers equalized but then, "a smart header from McMahon saw the ball strike the inside of the upright and go down. McLeod and Smith got the ball away but referee Dickson who was in position, promptly gave the goal to the joy of the Celtic following". Mr Dickson had already had to call all the players together to tell them to behave themselves, but in the second half, play was so one-sided that the Rangers players visibly gave up and their supporters disappeared, leaving Celtic Park to the cries of joy from the Celtic faithful. "A big crowd, a great match, a terrible afternoon and an unexpectedly large majority" is how *The Daily Record and Mail* sums it all up.

"Nothing but disaster followed the Rangers in the second half," as Blessington, Martin, Battles and McMahon ran through a panic stricken defence with ease, and full-time in the crepuscular light came to Rangers like the battle in Homer's Iliad where "Night brought blessed relief to the hard pressed Greeks". But for McMahon and Celtic, joy was unconfined when the referee blew to signal a 6–2 victory. The Scottish League had been in existence for six years, and Celtic had won it three times. *The Daily Record and Mail* is in little doubt about who the star man was, "Parkhead's only Duke was the hardest working forward on the field". It went on to say that "Courageous and plucky throughout, Sandy's heading was a treat". In his dribbling, it is said that he "wriggled with eel-like grace".

The Glasgow Observer uses the Irish battle cry "Faugh-a-Ballagh" (meaning "Clear The Way" and much used by Irish Brigades in the American Civil War and elsewhere) to describe the Celtic performance, which was as good as last week's display against St Bernard's was bad. Clearly hot on Irish military history, the writer says that McMahon and the rest of the Celtic forward line, "went through their foemen as the Irish Brigade pierced the serried Saxon foes at Fontenoy" (a battle in the war of the Austrian Succession in 1745).

The writer also praises the crowd "a vast crowd which never winced" under the relentless rain, although some members of the Rangers brake clubs saw, "some benefit in an early departure". The Celtic fans however left the ground talking animatedly about "drenching rain, semi darkness, rapid scoring and rough play". He also singles out McMahon, Martin and Ferguson who "in that order, did giant service" for Celtic.

An analogous situation in more modern times would be the winning of the Scottish League Cup final in a 2–1 win over Rangers at Hampden Park on 4 December 1982 in meteorological circumstances which would compel the non-footballing population to question the sanity of football fans. Most of us that grim December day at Hampden in 1982 were reconciled to serious health problems like pneumonia the following week, but who cared? Similarly who bothered about getting wet in December 1895 when you have won the Scottish League Cup?

On that night of December 14 1895 the East End of Glasgow was one huge party with songs, music and laughter in spite of the dreadful December weather of "Biblical rain". The team had bounced back from their poor season in 1895 to win, before the same year of 1895 was out, the Glasgow Cup and now the Scottish League. All their team were heroes, but none more so than the great Sandy McMahon who may have been "hissed" in the St Bernard's game, but was now once again the hero of the hour. Christmas was, of course, no great festival in Victorian Scotland, –it was not even a public holiday until 1958 – but this occasion was as if "the New Year had come early, and there was another New Year party – the real one – to come". Once again, Celtic supporters could go to their work on a Monday with a smile on their faces!

The club proved generous for this success, awarding all players a £10 bonus, an astonishing amount for the time. Celtic and their increasing number of followers spent a good Christmas and New Year, relishing the triumphs of late 1895 and looking forward to competing in and possibly even winning their second Scottish Cup in the New Year where they were paired against Queen's Park at Parkhead. "No other tie matters," said some papers and the game on 11 January 1896 was much looked forward to. There was talk (which skipper McMahon had to try to quell or at least cool down) of Celtic sweeping the boards that season and winning every trophy. Fate and frost however were to play a part.

Celtic, League Champions.
McMahon is in the front row with the ball at his feet.

Celtic, Champions of Scotland, had gone on a triumphant tour of England over Christmas, and came back to play a friendly on New Year's Day against Rangers at Parkhead. It was an interesting and hard-fought draw but Barney Battles was sent off for retaliation. It was silly and in fact a fairly brutal charge on Barker who had admittedly kicked him once or twice, and although the game was just a friendly, the game was still under the jurisdiction of the SFA and the referee Mr Robertson of Queen's Park, reported Battles. Barney was then summoned to attend a disciplinary hearing on January 14, three days after the scheduled Queen's Park Scottish Cup-tie, which seemed to be the number one topic of conversation in Glasgow.

McMahon had been injured, but his "wound had now healed up" and "shooting in practice was a notable feature on of his preparation". Queen's Park on the other hand were under-strength, and it was widely expected that Celtic would win on 11 January, but fate took a hand when a frost came down and ruled the game off. Celtic tried hard to get the game on, and possibly the decision was taken just too early, for a rapid thaw set in and allowed, for example, Third Lanark to play little over a mile away at Cathkin.

It was a fateful decision. The game was rescheduled for 18 January. This meant that Barney's hearing was now held BEFORE the game, rather than AFTER. Barney was duly suspended for a month following Mr Robertson's report, even though Barney bravely and honestly defended himself. He claimed that it was "unfair", it was a friendly in any case, he apologised and would willingly pay a fine or accept an admonishment.

He had a case. In the first place the referee Mr Robertson was ill and could not attend, but sent in his report in which he agreed that Battles had apologised for his action. This cut no ice, and although Mr Kirkwood of Dykehead put up a vigorous case for Battles to be admonished – the game was after all, a friendly – the meeting was an ugly one with tempers lost, the suspension stood. Given the time in which it all happened, and the fact that Queen's Park and the SFA were still seen as being "in cahoots" and possible even the same establishment, Celtic supporters were not slow to see a certain element of bias in all this.

Be that as it may, Celtic now had to line up to face Queen's Park on 18 January without the influential Barney Battles. He was replaced at left-half by John King, a useful player but no more than that, and Celtic suffered as a result. Newspapers are all unanimous that Queen's Park simply "played better" than Celtic on the day, even though Celtic, playing towards the pavilion end and the breeze, through a penalty converted by Dan Doyle and a fine strike by Sandy McMahon, led 2–1 at half-time. Scotland international Willie Lambie scored an equalizer for Queen's Park from the penalty spot, and then two late goals for the Queen's, one coming from a very rare error on the part of goalkeeper Dan McArthur, won the day for them, and silenced the Celtic majority of the huge 28,000 crowd.

It was a massive disappointment, and effectively meant that there was little left for Celtic to play for that season until the Glasgow Charity Cup in May. There was a Glasgow League formed that season, but it was a competition that lacked credibility and did not last long, even though Celtic did get a little revenge for their Scottish Cup exit with a 2–1 win over Queen's Park the following week. Friendlies were the order of the day for the team who were the Scottish League and Glasgow Cup winners and McMahon kept scoring the goals and playing well. The game against Third Lanark on Leap Year's Day of 29 February saw a fine goal from McMahon and a quixotic description of how there, "was not much dancing or mud-larking" (we are glad to hear it!) between himself and Ferguson. But there was no getting away from the fact that he and Celtic had missed out in the main tournament of the day, the Scottish Cup, won that year by Hearts in an all-Edinburgh Scottish Cup Final played against Hibs at a place called Logie Green, home of St Bernard's.

McMahon did win another Scottish League cap against the Irish League on 15 February. He was one of five Celtic players, all chosen, presumably, because the game was at Parkhead and Rangers players were unavailable, as they were playing in a Cup tie. The Scottish

League won 3–2 – a rather disappointing result for them – and McMahon was not considered for the other League or full Internationals that spring, even though he was described as "passing with marvellous accuracy". He would have been vexed to have missed the big International against England, played at Celtic Park and won by Scotland 2–1 before a crowd which was well in excess of 50,000 and which was greeted with huge acclaim throughout the land. Jimmy Blessington was Celtic's only representative on that epic occasion.

Sandy may have been a victim of the circumstances of 1896. This was the first game that "Anglo-Scots" (Scots men who played for English teams) were allowed. It was a contentious decision. It meant that Tommy Hyslop of Stoke City and Jack Bell of Everton found themselves in the forward line, and it is possible that Sandy McMahon might have earned a place otherwise. In the event, it proved the wisdom of the Celtic Committee in building their new huge ground. Indeed they might have built a bigger one yet, for the ground strained to hold the crowd with even troops from the Maryhill Barracks standing by in readiness in case of disturbances or to help out with casualties caused by overcrowding.

The meaningless Glasgow League and Friendlies against English teams continued – one of them dubbed the World Club Championship against Aston Villa on Monday 20 April. It was so called because both teams had won their respective Leagues and it gave McMahon a chance to play against his old friend Johnny Campbell. Sadly only 9,000 were attracted to Celtic Park to see Celtic win 3–2. It was a fine night and the pitch was in good condition, and those who did turn up saw a great game. Celtic's right-half that night was one John Gillespie of Queen's Park who had a month previously captained Scotland against Wales in their 4–0 win at Carolina Port, Dundee. One presumes that Aston Villa agreed to this move, and it would be interesting to know if Gillespie, the nominal amateur, was paid for his Celtic appearance!

Johnny Campbell, still much loved by the Celtic faithful, was given a great cheer as he appeared and even a polite round of applause when he scored the first goal in five minutes! But Celtic fought back and for a long time the score was a very even 2–2, but then, "as darkness began to fall, just on the call of time, McMahon scored a third goal for the Celtic". Campbell was seen to congratulate Sandy at full-time, and it was clear that he had enjoyed playing once again at Celtic Park. He did of course return to Celtic in the future, but at the moment he was still enjoying a great career with Villa.

Even fewer (only 2,000) turned up to see Everton a couple of days later revealing a certain amount of "ennui" and "turnstile fatigue" with friendlies. It also betokened as well perhaps the demand of fans for competitive games, something that they had now accepted as the norm. "Prestige" did not mean quite so much as a piece of silver. But the Aston Villa game did allow Celtic to call themselves the Champions of the World, even though that title meant absolutely nothing in 1896!

It was almost a relief when the Glasgow Charity Cup started in May. There was more than a little interest in this, for Celtic had won this trophy in 1892, 1893, 1894 and 1895, and to win it five years in a row would be rather special. Three trophies would make up for the crushing and gnawing disappointment that still hung over Celtic Park since January after the defeat by Queen's Park in the Scottish Cup. Celtic were boosted by the return of their prodigal son Charlie McEleny who had spent the season with Burnley. He was a fine player, a skilful wing-half, but like Tommy McInally in the 1920s, did not work nearly hard enough at his game, and his prodigious talent was never exploited to the full. Like Tommy McInally, however, he did have a few moments of glory in his short career, and the Glasgow Charity Cup of 1896 was one of them.

McEleny took over from Willie Maley at right-half. Maley at 28 was hardly too old but he had suffered from a few injuries of late.

In addition he was increasingly showing signs of being interested in other sports, notably cycling and athletics, as well as the internal politics and administration of the club, something at which he excelled. But it was also becoming clear that Maley was becoming more and more frustrated with the way that the club was being run.

As if Celtic had been waiting for this competition, someone seems to have pressed a button, and the team hit top form. On a fine sunny but breezy day on 9 May 1896, 20,000 turned up at Hampden to see the semi-final. Celtic beat Rangers 6–1 with *The Daily Record and Mail* in ecstasy about Celtic's performance, "McMahon's fine accurate passing perhaps giving him pride of place". Opening with the sun behind them but against the breeze, Celtic were three up at half-time. For the first goal the "Duke" and the "Wee 'Un" (Willie Ferguson) teamed up brilliantly on the left-wing for Ferguson to score, then Madden scored a second and just before the turnover, McMahon "plonked the ball in the net for the third time".

In the second half the "McMahon orchestra" ran past the panic-stricken Rangers defence at will to the massive approval of the Celtic crowd while the Rangers support were divided, with some staying to applaud and others disappearing to get at least some solace in the fine May weather. The wonder was that Celtic did not score at least double figures, but they stopped at six with Martin, Battles and Martin scoring before Yuille got a consolation goal for Rangers near the end. In the tradition of such things, the triumphant Celtic supporters, given the absence of most Rangers fans, cheered that goal as well!

This set-up a Cup Final between Celtic and Queen's Park at Ibrox on 16 May. The sun was baking hot at 4.00 pm for the slightly disappointing 12,000 crowd, and no favours were done to anyone when the teams finished 1–1 at 90 minutes and 30 minutes extra time had to be played. *The Glasgow Herald* is distinctly upset at the result, saying twice that Celtic were lucky to win the trophy, and that the thing that everyone would remember was the Queen's Park equalizing goal of Willie Lambie. This seems to be nothing other than sheer prejudice, for other sources agree that Celtic and Queen's Park both deserved a great deal of credit, although *The Daily Record and Mail* says that, "McMahon and Ferguson alone played to reputation," and that there was a tremendous amount of "wilful kicking out," meaning, presumably, long clearances rather than kicking lumps out of each other!

McMahon had scored the first goal with, "a wonderful effort, which defeated Anderson with a shot that he could not possibly reach," and it was McMahon who scored the winner in extra-time. *The Glasgow Herald* declines to give any details about how the winning goal was actually scored other than that it was McMahon who finished the move, and the newspaper finally reveals its preferences by finishing off waspishly by saying… "and they (Celtic) were certainly lucky in winning." Jealousy is clearly a terrible thing for a Victorian journalist, but lucky or not, Celtic had now won three trophies out of four that year and the Glasgow Charity Cup for five years in a row. McMahon, now the proud possessor of three Glasgow Charity Cup medals, (he had been injured in 1893 and 1894) was rightly feted as the hero of the hour both as the inspired playmaker and as the goalscorer. The teams on that hot day at Ibrox were;

Celtic: McArthur; Meehan and Doyle; McEleny, Kelly and Battles; Madden, Blessington, Martin, McMahon and Ferguson.

Queen's Park: Anderson; Gillespie and Smith; Allison, McFarlane and Stewart; Crookston, Waddell, McColl, Cameron and Lambie.

Referee: Mr J McPherson, Cowlairs.

Sandy's happiness was crowned by his marriage that month (12 May before the Glasgow Charity Cup Final) to Annie Devine whom he had been courting for some time. It was a sign of the honour and esteem in which he was held at Celtic Park that he was voted a wedding present of £20, an astonishing amount for 1896. His best man was his friend Johnny Campbell, who had recently won an English League medal with Aston Villa. There will not have been many other weddings in which the groom had recently won a Scottish League medal, and the best man an English one!

Returning from honeymoon he then finished the season by winning the Charity Cup and then going with Celtic on a tour of the Highlands, taking advantage of the improvements in travel, particularly the railways. They played and defeated Aberdeen Victoria and then Inverness Caledonian. They were much feted in both venues, for the name "Celtic" now meant a great deal in Scottish circles. And so did the name "The Duke". There were many dukes in the Royal Family all waiting impatiently for some advance up the pecking order when "old Queen Vic" would eventually die, (she was now nearly 80) but to all Scotland, the Duke was none other than Sandy McMahon.

7.

1896–97 – THE HORROR STORY

Season 1896–97 was a momentous and turbulent one in the history of Celtic FC. Sooner or later, there had to be a bad season, for the success since 1888 had been consistent and sustained. Even 1894–95, their worst season to date, was by no means bereft of silverware. But the 1896–97 season came as a shock to all the many supporters of the club, and was harder to bear because it was all self-inflicted. It was characterised by a shocker of a Cup defeat, major internal dissension and trouble, and no honours won.

It was hardly a coincidence that most of the season was played without Sandy McMahon, the Duke, the Prince of Dribblers, the hero of the Celtic support, and if there was ever the slightest doubt about the contribution of McMahon to the cause since he joined Celtic in 1890, then his absence in this season proved it. Without McMahon, Celtic more or less fell apart. There were other factors as well, but it is hard to resist the conclusion that the calming influence of the Duke might not have made a huge difference. He was missed on two fronts – one was his sheer playing and goal scoring ability, particularly with his head, and the other was his dignity and authority in the dressing room.

Another popular Celtic poster of the 1890s

The season had opened with a 1–3 defeat at Hibs, but after that, form had settled down, and good results were being produced. McMahon scored a particularly good goal at Carolina Port, Dundee on 3 October in a 2–2 draw, which has the scribe of *The Daily Record and Mail* going into raptures. "If ever a shot was unsaveable, it was that one of McMahon. McMahon immortalised (sic) himself to the match by the brilliant manner in which he scored the Celt's (sic) second goal, and unquestionably it was an effort all too rarely seen nowadays on the football field". All this in front of a record crowd for the ground of 13,000, which raised the phenomenal amount of £355. There was a piece of drama before the game as well in the shape of a fire on the train bringing supporters to Dundee between Bridge of Allan and Dunblane! Fortunately no one was killed and they all arrived safely in Dundee to see Sandy at his best.

By the end of October, the team were very much in contention for the Scottish League, and, very importantly in late Victorian Celtic circles, the team were still in contention for the Glasgow Cup. In fact they had reached the Final by beating Queen's Park 4–2 on Hallowe'en. *The Daily Record and Mail* states that, "McMahon and his colleagues exhibited a perfection in combination, a freedom of grace and action that has never been surpassed by a Celtic team in any previous context against such renowned opponents."

This semi-final game was played at Hampden before a crowd of 14,000 which would have been a lot more, if greed had not persuaded the teams to double the gate from sixpence, the normal gate for games like the Glasgow Cup, to one shilling, something that would have made a huge dent in the pocket of Celtic fans. The absent missed a great game, with McMahon described as "in brilliant form" as Celtic won 4–2. *The Glasgow Herald* in a lengthy diatribe or rant about the virtues of amateurism as against professionalism is compelled, nevertheless, to admit that Celtic were far superior to Queen's Park. One of the reasons given being that the amateurs are compelled to cram all their preparation into "a panic form of training" on a Friday night as distinct from six days which Celtic had at their disposal.

So amateurism had lost the argument. Celtic now found themselves in the Glasgow Cup Final against Rangers. But there was a "previous" here. On 10 October at Celtic Park in the Scottish League match between the two sides, a contentiously disallowed headed goal by Divers had led to scenes of disorder in which the referee Mr Duncan Campbell of Bridge of Weir escaped to the dressing room at the end only through the strenuous efforts of Willie Maley and a few of the Celtic committee men. Some Rangers players escaped the "flailing fists" of some of the crowd only with a great deal of difficulty, and the policemen on duty had been compelled to use their batons, their "cudgels of office", to control the spectators.

It had been a shame that this happened, for the 1–1 draw had been a great game of football, described with a touch of hyperbole perhaps, as "the greatest club struggle of modern times". The game was played in heavy rain on a very wet pitch but had still attracted a crowd of 24,000. McMahon scored in the early stages against the wind for Celtic, then Rangers had equalized almost immediately and the game had been an absolute thriller with no real indication of dirty play, although *The Glasgow Herald* says that "fouls against the Celtic were frequent".

The Celtic crowd clearly felt that Mr Campbell was being too harsh on their players, but Rangers were not able to exploit the free-kicks. It was against the rules in 1896 to score direct from a free-kick – all free-kicks were indirect – and the well-drilled Celtic defence was able to mop up any trouble. Celtic for their part were not able to pierce the Rangers defence until late in the game when, "Divers headed through what seemed a legitimate goal," in the opinion of both *The Glasgow Herald* and *The Daily Record and Mail*. The decision of offside was, "anything but well received," by the Celtic crowd. *The Glasgow Herald*, neutral whenever Queen's Park were not playing, hedges its bets, saying that it looked a good goal and that everyone else seemed to think so, but that the referee was in the best position.

A 1–1 draw it remained, and that was how it finished, although both sides made Herculean efforts to win the game. "McMahon's brilliant bursts, accurate placing and back heeling were unsurpassed". Full-time brought the distasteful incidents already described and it seemed like Celtic would have to answer to the complaints of Rangers and the referee. As it turned out, neither the referee, clearly a forgiving man, nor Rangers – there was still a tolerably good relationship between the officials of both clubs – made any official complaint, and officially the matter rested…but strong feelings had been aroused. Dan Doyle, now the captain, and Sandy McMahon were both quoted as saying that the goal scored by John Divers would have won the game if it had been allowed to stand.

Cathkin Park on 14 November 1896 was the venue for the Glasgow Cup Final between the two big professional sides of the era, Celtic and Rangers. The crowd of 13,000 was disappointing, but supporters could hardly be blamed for not turning up on such an awful day with wind and rain. It was in fact an archetypal Glasgow November day, (one wonders why the penny never dropped to the Glasgow FA that having their Final a month earlier or several months later might produce a better day and therefore a bigger crowd!) and the amount of shelter at Cathkin was minimal. The game ended 1–1, both teams scoring when playing with the wind, (McMahon equalising for Celtic with a fine header) and Celtic not quite capable of forcing a winner, although McMahon had a reasonable chance at the end, with "fouls a frequent occurrence".

That Celtic were sore about this game is given a certain credence by the fact that they were, "conspicuous by their absence at the Bath Hotel," at the reception organised by the Glasgow FA. Celtic had a grievance about Turnbull's goal for Rangers – at least Willie Maley did, claiming years later that, "one of the forwards was actually sitting on McArthur's chest, what time (sic) a colleague was 'scoring' the equalizer."

Maley's memory is certainly faulty here, for Rangers scored first in that game, and the equalizer came for Celtic. He may be thinking of the replay the following Saturday, 21 November at the same venue. Weather conditions were only marginally better. Again the crowd was in the region of 13,000, "a good crowd considering the high cost of admission," and once again they saw a feisty encounter, which was a lot nastier then the previous game. Mr Robertson of Partick Thistle was the referee and he was to be a very busy man, the point not being missed in the national Press that the teams were playing each other too often.

The Press is of course hinting here at what was being increasingly perceived as a piece of fraud with replays between teams with large supports being a common occurrence. No one can prove or disprove this of course, but certainly there were two side effects. One was that, "the best laid schemes o'mice and man gang aft agley," and the attendances were often a little disappointing, and the other was that players began to know each other too well, and a few vendettas were carried over from game to game.

Be that as it may, Blessington scored first for Celtic, and then just after the turn around, Turnbull equalised for Rangers, but the moment that defined the game (and possibly Celtic's season) came in the 60th minute when Sandy McMahon was badly injured and had to limp off, "an injury to his leg being the cause," as *The Glasgow Herald* blandly puts it. In a game between two equally balanced teams, the loss of a star player reducing the team to 10 men makes a huge difference, and of course, there would be no substitutes allowed for another 70 years. Rangers scored soon afterwards through Alex "Cutty" Smith and remained on top until the end, finishing, without any argument, the better side. Indeed only "McArthur's really marvellous saving" kept the score down to 2–1.

This was a really bad day for Celtic, but one is struck and appalled by the blatant Rangers sympathies of *The Daily Record and Mail*. Usually true colours are raised in the modern world when Rangers win, and 1896 was just the same with detailed and gloating descriptions of people wandering round Glasgow "in triumph" and "saying Good Old Rangers" to each other. A woman had asked the Rangers taxi if her small child could touch the Glasgow Cup, and other details like that are lovingly included.

To be fair, it has to be said that Rangers, who had had a poor season in 1895–96 winning nothing, did not often achieve the success that their increasingly demanding support were expecting. Such triumphalism, however, on the part of a supposedly neutral newspaper did little to scotch the incipient Celtic paranoia complex, but even *The Daily Record and Mail* is compelled to admit that the injury to Sandy McMahon was a crucial factor in the game. The Press is coy about telling us how he sustained his injury, but the Celtic version is that it was a quite deliberate crocking of their star man.

For the second week in a row, neither John Glass the Chairman, nor John H. McLaughlin the Vice-Chairman attended the meal (implausible excuses about other commitments and illness having been given) at the Bath Street Hotel at which the Glasgow Cup was presented to Rangers, while several Celtic players either visited the toilet during the presentation or glowered their feelings of injustice. So, while Sandy McMahon nursed his injury, the comparatively young Willie Maley, still in 1896 only a Committee man, was compelled to grit his teeth and deliver the losers' speech on behalf of Celtic FC. He probably made the right noises, but inside his feelings, as evinced in his memoirs and book, were totally different! The teams were:

Celtic: McArthur; Meehan and Doyle; Russell, Kelly and Battles; Divers, Blessington, King, McMahon and Ferguson.

Rangers: Dickie; Hyslop and Drummond; Gibson, McCreadie and Mitchell; Low, Miller, Turnbull, McPherson and Smith.

Referee: Mr Robertson, Partick Thistle.

This game was this a huge disappointment to Celtic and their supporters. But it was the way that the game was reported that would have repercussions. *The Daily Record and Mail* says that, "Meehan and Battles of Celtic and McPherson of Rangers were unduly rough and left a bad taste in the mouth of some spectators," but that was mild compared with what other papers said. *The Glasgow Herald* does not apportion blame but mentions several times in its report that the game kept being stopped for fouls.

What happened next was of great significance to Sandy and Celtic, but he was in no way able to involve himself or have any influence on the dreadful events that were to unfold for the remainder of this season. Sandy's knee had been giving him problems for some time, and wiser counsel might have been to take a rest from competitive football for a spell, even giving the Glasgow Cup Final replay a miss. But he had insisted on playing in this game, and a nasty series of tackles from some Rangers players, in the manner of a boxer going for the cut eye of his opponent, in the Glasgow Cup Final replay meant that McMahon was now out for some considerable time.

So important was McMahon to the club's revival that Celtic, on the advice of Professor Knox of Glasgow University, were prepared to send him, after some medical treatment, to Matlock in Derbyshire, near Manchester ("Cottonopolis", as the Press dubs it) a hydrotherapy institution like Crieff Hydro or Seamill Hydro in Scotland, where his knee would get the best possible attention. Apart from a comment on the value of McMahon to the side, it is also interesting to note that Celtic had the money and were prepared to pay for this. Such enlightenment was rare in football clubs, and even rarer in Victorian employers! The real cure was rest, enforced rest, and it is a fair bet that Sandy hated every minute of this. And while he was recuperating, what a distressing catalogue of events the Celtic historian is compelled to record in the winter of 1896/97!

Being in Matlock, McMahon was thus powerless to stop the players' strike of the following week, when John Divers, Peter Meehan and Barney Battles all refused to play against Hibs at Parkhead because of the presence in the Press Box of a reporter from *The*

Glasgow Evening News and its sister journal *The Scottish Referee*. This man's reporting of the Glasgow Cup Final replay had been seen as being biased and he had said that, "Celtic were always the aggressors," in the fouling department when no mention had been made of the tackle or tackles which had crippled McMahon. The matter came to a head on the Saturday, but there was an indication in the middle of the week that all was not well, for *The Daily Record and Mail* has a cryptic comment that, "One or two Celtic players had an interview with the club's committee. Result? The maintenance of discipline among rank and file." Maybe, but only for a day or two.

Celtic, of course, however much they may have sympathised with the players, could not remove the journalist concerned, for "the freedom of the Press" was a much cherished concept in Victorian Britain. In addition, it would have involved being seen to give in to blackmail. John Glass would later say, "We would rather lose twenty Cups and Leagues than tarnish our reputation."

Possibly there were other issues at stake here and the demands for the removal of the journalist were possibly just the "casus belli", the symptom of the malaise rather than the real problem. After all criticism of a team in the Press had happened before – it has certainly happened since and continues to do so – and players really should be a little more pachydermatous (thick-skinned) and should remember the old truism that the way to shut them up and to hurt them is by what one does on the park the following week.

For a spell, it seemed that the whole Celtic team were to refuse to play, but eight of them cracked under the pressure put on them by the Celtic committee, leaving only the three ringleaders. The players concerned were immediately sent home to be dealt with later. Celtic were forced to start this game after a delay of about 20 minutes with only ten men, one of them being Willie Maley who thought he had retired, while another player, Tommy Dunbar, was summoned from the reserve game at Hampden to make up the 11. The game against

Hibs ended 1–1, when Celtic really needed to win to strengthen their position in the Championship race. Indeed, once again, Dan McArthur came to the rescue, saving "shot after shot" and "could not be passed".

It is not hard to believe that the presence of McMahon, reasonable and moderate, would have mollified matters, or at least prevented it getting to the silly and self-destructive level that it reached. The players probably did have a grievance, and may also have had a point in believing that their committee had not really done enough to protest at the treatment the players received from those journalists. The sensible thing for the players to have done, of course, would have been to play the game under protest and then seek redress after the game, having in the meantime perhaps even won the game and thus strengthened their position. McMahon, wise in counsel and as conciliatory as a cooing dove, might have been the man to suggest just that – but he was far away. In the circumstances, the team did well to draw, but the real winners that day were Hearts who benefitted from the "points divide" as the Press would call a draw.

Indeed the three strikers must be held culpable in the eyes of history for this very issue. A win would not necessarily have won the League but would have put them in a far better position to do so. As it happened, the support, totally unaware of what was going on until they read the newspapers on the Monday, were disorientated and arguing among themselves, some of them believing that Barney Battles could do no wrong, others saying that while the club themselves were to blame for allowing this situation to develop, players who refused to play for Celtic were guilty of some kind of mortal sin!

The Press themselves now all ganged up against the Celtic rebels. *The Daily Record and Mail* is sneering and patronising, sarcastically comparing the three men with the three who defended the bridge (Horatius and two others) in Ancient Rome – a hit perhaps at Celtic whose supporters sang *A Nation Once Again,* which contained the lines;

> *When boyhood's fire was in my blood*
> *I read of ancient freemen*
> *For Greece and Rome who bravely stood*
> *Three hundred men and three men!*

But then it states that, "We greatly fear that certain gentlemen have been afflicted with swelled head, and the best cure for swelled head is attenuation of the pocket." The Celtic Committee, whatever their private feelings might have been, were compelled to agree, and the three men were suspended, the wages that they had lost being given to charity. In the long term, Meehan never played again for Celtic, and Battles and Divers were away for a long time before being brought back. This action of course seriously weakened the team and led directly to the defeat by Rangers in the Scottish League on 19 December.

Worse was to follow in the New Year. James Blessington and Joseph Cullen were fined three guineas for a "disturbance" in Dunlop Street on New Year's Day 1897. What it was about we cannot tell, but it was symptomatic of much more trouble at Celtic Park. Although we are told that the Celtic Committee and players "did the pantomime" at a Glasgow theatre on New Year's Night in an apparent show of harmony and unity, the team had lost that day to Hibs in a friendly, and would lose again to Rangers in a Glasgow League game the following day.

In spite of all that, they were loudly cheered by Celtic fans who were "sighing for the reappearance of the Duke", even though "Darling Willie" Groves had returned from Hibs to take Sandy's place. "Darling Willie", a great star of the early 1890s, had been with Aston Villa and West Brom where he had failed to distinguish himself, before returning unsuccessfully to Hibs and now to Celtic. It was later discovered what the cause was. He had not yet totally recovered from a bout of tuberculosis, that scourge of Victorian society, and his return was a dismal failure.

Sandy McMahon. How Celtic missed him this season!

The crisis came in the game against Arthurlie in the Scottish Cup on 9 January 1897. Arthurlie were a small non-League team, which played at Dunterlie Park, Barrhead, and even in Celtic's current travails, seemed to present few problem to last years' Scottish League winners. On the morning of the game, there was no inkling of what was to happen. *The Daily Record and Mail* concedes that they were, "ill prepared for heavy cup engagements but the League club (Celtic) is fortunate in being drawn against a second class opponent and should qualify easily for the next round". Then, in an ironic Cassandra-type prophecy, it goes on to say that, "Celtic furnish a few surprises occasionally. They may give us another today." They did indeed, but not in the way that was expected.

The three suspended players were obviously still out, McMahon, Madden, Dunbar and McEleny were injured, centre-half Davie Russell missed a train and Dan Doyle and Pat Gilhooly simply failed to turn up (Doyle presumably on a "bender" or having found an accommodating lady!) and Celtic kicked off with seven men, although a few reserves arrived later. There is a certain doubt as to who actually played, and it is not impossible that Celtic offered a game to some young lad who happened to be there! *The Scottish Sport* for example claims that one of Celtic's goals was scored by a man called McIlvany, although Celtic had no such player!

Arthurlie's 4–2 victory was a dark, dark day in Celtic's history and McMahon, who had been in Glasgow over the New Year but was now back in Matlock to resume his treatment, must have been devastated when he heard the news. Certainly Chairman John Glass was similarly upset, for he was seen to leave the game early. *The Glasgow Observer* while making a brave attempt to pretend that it never happened, or that it was "just a football match", says that the big problem was the absence of Sandy McMahon. "It was a paralysing blow because Sandy could almost win matches single-handed".

Various other excuses were made such as the slope of the pitch at Dunterlie Park, Barrhead where Arthurlie played. It was indeed called "the dump" or "the hump" and the slope was as pronounced as that at Carlton Cricket Club in Edinburgh, although the claim that looking down from the top of a slope to the bottom was, "like looking out of a tenement window at the street below," seems a trifle exaggerated. It was also narrower than what Celtic were accustomed to, thus inhibiting Celtic's passing to each other and the speed of the wingers.

Other unconvincing excuses included the weather, the referee and the partisan, unwelcoming crowd, but the truth was that Celtic had no one to blame but themselves. It was a classic piece of amateurish self-destruction, and right up until the 1960s when the last supporter who was alive in 1897 eventually died, the name "Arthurlie" sent a shiver down every Celtic spine. It was a Scottish Cup tie, and once you are out of that competition, you remain out for another year. No Celtic team took the field in a Scottish Cup tie for decades after that without being aware that there had been a game at Barrhead in January 1897.

Those of us who can recall Inverness Caledonian Thistle in 2000 will have some sort of idea of what Arthurlie did to the club in 1897. Indeed the parallels are striking – incompetent management, bloody-minded players who did not realise what the wearing of a Celtic jersey actually means, the absence through unavoidable reasons of injury of key, even star players, (Sandy McMahon in 1897 and Henrik Larsson in 2000) who might have saved the day. In the long term in both cases the club learned a lesson and appointed a good manager, but that would be in the future.

Monday's newspapers of 11 January 1897 shed crocodile tears for Celtic, singling out James Kelly as a man who always gave his best for the club, and what would he be feeling now? Apart from the long term injuries, James "Duster" Orr was genuinely injured and watched the game, John Divers was "ill" (in fact, he was still suspended) and Sandy McMahon was still "recruiting" (sic, a Victorian use of the word, meaning "recuperating") near Manchester but of the rest, only Kelly, Crossan, Blessington and King had appeared at training, we are told by *The Daily Record and Mail,* scarcely able to conceal its glee at the demise of the great Celtic side.

In early 1897 with the kiss of death now firmly on Celtic, and with McMahon not even an impotent onlooker, as he received letters and the occasional telegram in the treatment room of his clinic near Manchester, the team proceeded to blow what little chance they had in the Scottish League by losing to Dundee at Carolina Port and then St Mirren in Paisley. Hearts with a late run would win the League that year, but for Celtic, the season fizzled out with the team in crisis.

Any little chance they may have had of an honour came when they lost 1–4 to Rangers in the Glasgow Charity Cup, thereby failing to win the trophy for the sixth successive year. For the first time since season 1889–90 Celtic failed to win any of the four major honours that they competed for. Even at this early stage of Celtic's history, such things sat ill with their vast support.

There was even the possibility that Celtic might now implode and disappear altogether. This happened to many teams in the Victorian era – Renton, Abercorn, Cowlairs, for example – and even though Celtic had come so far in such a short time with their magnificent stadium and many talented players, they were by no means immune from this possibility. No one before 2012 could have predicted what happened to Rangers; Celtic might have suffered the same fate in 1897.

But Celtic were made of sterner stuff. The club meant so much to so many people that this was not allowed to happen. In addition Celtic were blessed, in the main, by good leaders who appreci-ated what the club symbolised to their followers. The club altered appreciably after this, as it had to, and perhaps there had to be an "Arthurlie" to tell everyone that changes were necessary and indeed inevitable, if the club were to survive. In addition, there had never been a major financial problem. The club clearly lost money after the Arthurlie disaster, but the finances remained sound enough.

The bad long-term effect of these shenanigans was that they "let in" Rangers. Rangers would win the Scottish Cup in 1897 and again in 1898 as they built the team, which would win four League Cham-pionships in a row between 1899 and 1902. A serious challenge by Celtic rather than the feeble collapse of 1897 might have meant that Rangers history would have been somewhat different. Rangers, a team with hitherto only moderate success, would very soon attain equal status in the land to Celtic, and would now replace Queen's Park as the challenge to Celtic.

The devastation of the Celtic fan base was total. They kept attending in ever smaller numbers such games as there were, but without stars like McMahon, there was little to enthuse about. Some fans now began vicariously to follow the fortunes of Aston Villa where Johnny Campbell now was. Indeed the thought must occasionally have crossed the mind of Sandy McMahon in his Manchester clinic that possibly he might not want, on his recovery, to play for Celtic in the shambles they were in. Campbell, in his visits to see him, made it very clear that he (McMahon) would be very welcome at the currently very successful Aston Villa. But McMahon was a Celt. Indeed he was very grateful to them for his treatment.

As far as Celtic were concerned though, the one good thing about all this was that the club's structure changed and that Willie Maley changed from being "match secretary" to "secretary/manager" and he was paid for this job. This major regime change determined the future course of Celtic, for Maley was a determined, visionary character. Maley of course would not have allowed the Arthurlie fiasco to happen if he had had more executive power. Maley said that it, "was nothing less than astonishing in its utter feebleness". Other players would have been sought at an earlier stage, and Doyle by not turning up would have signed his own death warrant, as far as Maley was concerned. As it is, the damage done in 1896–97 was severe and deep, but at least for the start of the new season, Maley knew that he could count on the services of his friend and colleague, Sandy McMahon. And there was more good news yet.

It may be that the now recuperated McMahon was part of a Celtic delegation that visited the Crystal Palace in London on 10 April 1897 to see the English Cup Final. The attraction was of course Johnny Campbell who scored the first goal in Villa's 3–2 defeat of Everton to win the Cup for the third time. It was, of course, a great day for Villa, for the misfortunes of Sheffield United and Derby County meant that they also won the English League on the same day! In the midst of all the justifiable Villa celebrations, however, it is also possible – indeed it is likely – that McMahon and Tom Maley had an unofficial chat with Johnny about the possibility of a return home to Celtic. Both Tom Maley and McMahon would have realised that Campbell would not have needed a great deal of persuasion. The phrase "pining for home" is applied to the return of Tommy McInally in 1925. It could also have been applied to Saracen Street's Johnny Campbell.

In the meantime Dan Doyle had reconciled himself to the International scene. He was in the Scotland team that beat England 2–1 at the Crystal Palace on 3 April, and behaved impeccably. It might have been felt that given what happened two years ago in Liverpool that he should never have worn a Scottish jersey again, but he was simply too good a player to leave out.

It took a great deal of time, but McMahon's knee healed up. Before the end of the season he was back doing light training, but was not risked even in any of the friendlies that Celtic played at the end of the season. But he returned with a great deal of optimism for the future, both himself and Willie Maley hoping that the nightmarish winter of 1896–97 had passed and that better times lay ahead.

8.

1897–98 – RECOVERY

No easy task faced Celtic in their attempt to rehabilitate themselves after the shocking and dreadful events of 1897. There were many changes of personnel. The three troublemakers of last year – Battles, Meehan and Divers, good players all of them, had now gone, as had Johnny Madden, but new arrivals included George Allan from Liverpool and Jim Welford from Aston Villa. Sandy McMahon was still taking a long time to recover from his injury, and although he played a few practice matches, it was well into September before he made his competitive debut that season. Even then care was taken and Maley was determined that McMahon was not to be rushed back. He was simply too valuable a commodity.

But the greatest "recruit" of them all was Johnny Campbell. "Recruit" is of course the wrong word, for he had been away for two years to Aston Villa, with whom he had won the League in 1896 and the League and Cup double in 1897 and thus emulated "proud Preston" who had done likewise in 1889. A good sixty years and more would pass in England before anyone would do this again, and Maley was aware that no-one had achieved a similar feat of a League and Cup double in Scotland. One would have thought that Campbell would have been very happy to stay with Aston Villa but he possibly felt that he had done all he intended to do with Villa. He was, in any case, a Glasgow man, Celtic through and through and the thought of a return home was irresistible. No doubt Celtic offered as much money as Villa did, but that was irrelevant. He was going home.

For Sandy, this was excellent news. Not only was Campbell a close personal friend of his, having even been best man at his wedding, but the left wing pairing of "McMahon and Campbell" was already a legend in the as yet brief annals of the club, and a return to the glory days of yore seemed to beckon. But it was not as simple as that either, for McMahon, a proven goalscorer, could play in the centre as well as inside-left. It would all depend on the team that Maley chose.

Celtic in season 1897–98, McMahon is seated second from right

As to what extent Maley decided such things as team selection, we cannot be sure. But he was certainly the conduit between the players and the "Limited Company" as it called itself, and such was the strength of his personality, his vast footballing knowledge and his basic ability to get on with both the Directors and his players that it is hard to believe that he did not, in practice, exercise control over quite a few things at Celtic Park. The Press certainly seemed to think so, for "Maley" and "Celtic" were virtually interchangeable concepts, and he was frequently referred to as Willie Maley, Celtic FC, even when taking part in some other sport like cycling and athletics, as he loved doing.

And of course it was Maley's natural affability and geniality that made sure that Celtic were seldom out of the newspapers and the public limelight. Like Stein, some sixty years later, Maley appreciated the value of a "good Press". To his players he may have on occasion

seemed unapproachable, distant and even boorish and unpleasant
– this was certainly true of his later years – but to the Press and public, he was quite the opposite and would never miss an opportunity
to show everyone just exactly what Celtic meant to him. Curiously
enough, there is again a parallel with Jock Stein who was not always
loved by some of his players.

Maley also cultivated other teams, never neglecting the smaller
teams in Scotland, for he thus built up a network of contacts
throughout the land, all of whom were willing to do some unofficial
scouting or spying for him. He had his enemies as well, of course,
but his constant willingness to take his team to play friendlies all
over the British Isles ensured that a great deal of good will was built
up towards Celtic. He often said that his greatest friend in football
was no less a person that William Wilton, the manager of Rangers.

A man by no means impervious to the Celtic paranoia complex,
as some of his writings will prove, Maley nevertheless had the good
sense to set all the luggage to one side as he set out to build a fine
Celtic team. He probably realised that it would take a few years to
build up a team of "invincibles", that it would be a gradual process
and that the backbone of such a team would be a nucleus of young
players. In the meantime however it was important to keep Celtic
winning honours. The team must always have a winning mentality.

James Kelly having now retired from the playing side of the
game, a new captain was a necessity. McMahon might have seemed
to be the perfect character. Indeed he had been the captain before
his injury in 1896 but the job was in fact given to Dan Doyle. There
were possibly several reasons for this. One was the obvious one that
a captain did (and arguably still does) tend to be a defender rather
than a forward. This may be for the rather naïve and vacuous reason
that the defender is looking forward all the time and can therefore
see more of the game than a forward who must of necessity be looking back some of the time!

But perhaps the Directors felt that Dan Doyle, commonly known as "Ned" (after Ned Kelly the famous Australian outlaw of Irish descent, perhaps, and identified in popular culture with the character in the popular song sung by supporters – *The Wild Colonial Boy*?) and in recent years called the "Wild Rover" by Marie Rowan in her excellent biography of Dan, was a better candidate for the captaincy in that he was more "in your face" aggressive than the more retiring McMahon.

Yet another reason might have been the very fact that Doyle was indeed a wild boy. He had on more than one occasion disgraced himself e.g. with the Scotland team in 1895 in Liverpool when he had disappeared the night before the game for reasons as yet unexplained but widely guessed at, and there was still a major question to be asked about what he had been doing when the team were at Arthurlie in January. Perhaps the Directors and Maley felt that if they gave him more responsibility, he might yet turn up trumps for the club. There was little doubt about his playing ability. His character would now be tested.

In addition there was the inescapable fact that there was still a doubt over McMahon's short and long-term fitness. But for whatever reason he was chosen, Doyle could hardly have found a more reliable and trustworthy lieutenant than Sandy McMahon. There were no tantrums, no feelings of rejection nor refusal to work with Doyle. McMahon, already a close friend of Maley to whom he was more temperamentally similar, now worked well with Doyle and substituted for him as captain on the odd occasion that Doyle was unavailable or injured.

Indeed the fact that they were totally different characters worked to Celtic's advantage. Each had a few qualities that the other lacked. Doyle was impetuous, unstable and wild on the one hand, but immensely talented and even brilliant on the other. He was charismatic, handsome and had the look of the handsome hero in the myriads of soppy romantic fiction that characterised the late Victorian age feeding the demands of the now increasingly better educated young women. McMahon was schoolmasterly in looks, tall, angular and with a very respectable look about him. He was reliable, hard-working, diligent and with the ability to get on with everyone. What was never in doubt was that both men were totally committed, and loved the Celtic.

1897–98 was to be a difficult season for many reasons, not least because at last there were signs from Ibrox that William Wilton was now getting together a good Rangers team. Celtic would in fact lose to them in both Glasgow competitions, and would lose to another Glasgow team, Third Lanark, in the Scottish Cup, but the Scottish League would be wrested back after a campaign, which featured some brilliant high-scoring performances in the midwinter months.

That McMahon was back was shown in two wonderful games over the Glasgow Autumn Holiday weekend. First Clyde were put to the sword to the score of 6–1 with McMahon scoring two goals in the first half and then Celtic "doing much as they pleased" in the second half according to *The Glasgow Herald*. Johnny Campbell had now returned, of course, but was now playing at inside-right with Sandy at inside-left and in the centre, George Allan.

Even better was to come on the Holiday Monday when Celtic beat Rangers 4–0 at Ibrox. The wisdom of playing such a high profile fixture on a Holiday Monday was questioned however when 31,000 crushed into Ibrox with a certain amount of minor injuries through over-crowding. There was an overspill onto the ground just as the teams came out at the start of the second half. Fortunately no one was seriously hurt, and everything went well for Celtic in the glorious weather. McMahon once again scored the first goal, and was the orchestrator of the fine play throughout. His friend Johnny Campbell said, "I am as proud today as when I helped Aston Villa win the

Cup". (He is referring to that day in April at the Crystal Palace when Villa beat Everton 3–2.)

Various press reports enthuse over Celtic that day, "the finest football seen in Scotland this season"…"Celtic forwards really magnificent"…"Celtic back to their predictable best after the travails of last season", yet there were a few bad days as well. A depressing goalless draw with St Mirren and a narrow 1–0 win over Third Lanark were disappointing, but then there was a fine 3–2 win over last year's Champions Hearts on 23 October with Johnny Campbell scoring a late winner in a game that was described as "terribly fast and certainly worthy of the reputation of the teams engaged".

But the Glasgow Cup was a setback. Three attempts were necessary in order to split Celtic and Rangers – people were already beginning to ask questions about this – and it was only in extratime in the third game that Rangers got the better of Celtic. Rangers were two up at half-time in the first game at Parkhead before a huge crowd of 36,000, and with Willie Orr off injured and Sandy McMahon hobbling, thanks to one or two rather severe tackles from the ever notorious Nick Smith, things did not look good for Celtic. Yet the injured McMahon still had enough skill left in him to play his part in fashioning the two goals required to keep Celtic in the Cup. But they left it late in the gathering Glasgow gloom of 30 October, before Pat Gilhooly pulled one back in the 83rd minutes and then amidst, "scenes of excitement seldom seen at a football ground," Davie Russell scored the equalizer with a long fast shot, "as the Celtic supporters shouted themselves hoarse".

Because of his injury in the first game, McMahon missed the intervening League game, a 2–1 win at Carolina Port, Dundee, but he was back for the replay of the Glasgow Cup semi-final at Ibrox. This time, before 30,000 spectators, the game finished 1–1 with Gilhooly of Celtic and Turnbull of Rangers both having an opportunity to finish the tie, but both firing over the bar. Before that, according to Maley in *The Story Of The Celtic*, Celtic three times hit the upright. Ibrox won the ballot for the third tie the following Saturday, 20 November 1897, and this time, extra-time was decreed in the event of it being necessary, the kick-off being brought forward to 2.00 pm to cover for this possibility.

The precautions were justified, for the third game finished 1–1, before Rangers showed that they had a little more stamina than Celtic and scored twice in the extra-time period through Bob Hamilton. This caused *The Glasgow Herald* to fire a broadside and to reflect that Celtic were not as well trained as they might have been. This seems a fairly harsh verdict, because it was in extra-time after three gruelling ties, but the fact was that Rangers won through. In truth there was little between the sides.

Celtic and McMahon were upset by this, naturally, but had reason to be proud of the part they played in the three games that had Glasgow talking for so long. The month of December saw Celtic make amends to their supporters for the disappointment of the Glasgow Cup with four straight wins over Third Lanark, Partick Thistle, St Bernard's and Clyde. A total of 24 goals were scored and McMahon was heavily involved in the scoring or the making of them all. Christmas Day saw a 9–1 win over Clyde with George Allan scoring five goals. With Campbell now established at inside-right, McMahon's partner on the left wing was now a young man called Peter Somers, a man with a very bright future ahead of him, and who would learn a great deal from watching the play and deportment of Sandy McMahon.

A feature of McMahon's play was that he was always a very good winter player. When the conditions were muddy, McMahon, who was never the fastest of players (Maley would say of him years later "of speed he had little"), was not unduly slowed down, whereas other players, particularly defenders, were. On a frosty day (there would not be undersoil heating, of course, for virtually a hundred years after McMahon's time), he had a remarkable ability, for a tall man, to keep his feet. And of course, although most writers agree with Maley that speed was not Sandy's strongest asset, nevertheless he did have a "turn of speed" i.e. the ability to move short distances quickly, something that is almost as important as speed itself. He was deceptive in that regard.

New Year's Day 1898 saw astonishing, albeit predictable, scenes at Celtic Park with the referee Mr T. Quairns of Clyde compelled to abandon the Celtic v Rangers after 70 minutes because of repeated crowd encroachments caused by gross overcrowding. *The Glasgow Herald* is glad to report that there was no disorder or fighting (there might have been, given the day that it was and the two clubs involved) but feels that the crowd was inadequately policed, and that Celtic FC had quite simply underestimated the amount of people who would turn up and pay their sixpence to get in. Laudably, Celtic, with the interests of their fans at heart, had refused to put up the prices to nine pence or perhaps even a shilling, but the result was utter chaos with a crowd of about 50,000 there in a ground which could theoretically hold that amount…but only if adequate preparations had been made, and if the club realised just how many people wanted to turn up.

£1,479 was taken at the gate, but quite a few supporters had managed to climb the gate or rush the inadequate turnstiles or pay boxes. Celtic came in for a certain amount of criticism for not closing the gates earlier but their defence was that they feared disturbances in the environs of the ground. They also claimed that their ground could and indeed had (at the International match of 1896, for example) held bigger crowds, but that the problem here was that the crowd on this occasions was badly distributed.

It certainly does seem that overcrowding was a significant problem for Scottish football in the 1890s. To an extent this reflects the growth of interest in the game, a growth that was perhaps just a little too fast for the game's own good. Football was now undeniably the biggest working class occupation in Scotland, and although the game had undeniably started in England, the centre of the world game was now, without a great deal of doubt, Scotland, and Glasgow in particular. Popular heroes like Sandy McMahon contributed to this.

James Handley in *The Celtic Story* would describe Glasgow and football in these terms, "…the fact is that Glasgow takes its soccer very, very seriously. It is the most football conscious city in the world. It supports six senior clubs…besides scores of junior, juvenile and amateur teams. Its playing pitches dotted over the city are crowded with all sorts and sizes of footballers on free days and in the summer evenings. Any piece of waste ground is a magnet that draws the smaller fry to try their skill with a rubber, or even a paper ball; and the younger men at the dinner break in the works bolt their food in the canteen and scramble out to while the rest of the hour away in kicking a ball. A sports writer in a mild parody declared 'All the town's a park and all the men and women football players', while another added 'Glasgow has a Barnum and Bailey biggest-show-on-earth complex on football with the biggest grounds, the biggest crowds, the biggest bottle assaults, and our newspapers devote bigger space to the sport than the papers of any other town in Britain. Everything is on a gargantuan, exaggerated scale.'"

In these circumstances, a certain amount of blame must be attached to the clubs themselves for failing to provide adequate accommodation for the vast crowds that now attended football games. There would of course be a spectacular disaster in 1902 involving fatalities at Ibrox, but there were several other occasions when disasters were only narrowly avoided. The warnings were not heeded. Celtic, for all their self-righteousness about, "the interests of spectators being paramount," were very lucky on this and other occasions not to have similar things happening at their ground.

The phenomenon of the cult hero had now appeared. Prior to

the rise of football, heroes had been the unlikely ones of the Royal Family, the Duke of Wellington, or some music hall artiste or possibly even the cricketer W.G. Grace. But now with football having reached the mass market, people like Sandy McMahon suddenly found themselves the topic of conversation in the shipyards, the factories, the schools and the pubs. This insignificant-looking and naturally shy man (being so tall, he found it hard to hide among the undernourished of London Road and the Gallowgate) was flattered and occasionally overwhelmed at the amount of attention he received, and at the massive size of the crowds who flocked to see him, even when on this occasion, there were unfortunate and even dangerous consequences.

The football that had been seen in that ill-fated match on New Year's Day 1898 was, "of the highest order," but there were times when the touchline simply disappeared as the fans took over. The referee was patient and waited for the crowd to clear several times but eventually had to signal for the end of play with the score at 1–1. Both goals had come early, and if anything Rangers were looking more likely to score a winner when the game was abandoned, leaving Celtic at the top of the table with 26 points from 14 games and Rangers with 23 from 13. (Two points for a win in 1898.)

While arguments raged about whether the result should stand or whether a replay should be ordered behind closed doors if necessary (it was eventually replayed on 11 April by which time Celtic Park had an iron fence, "making it look like a menagerie or a prison"), Celtic had another important game in the Scottish Cup the following Saturday. As luck would have it, Celtic had been drawn to play at Arthurlie again on 8 January, exactly a year after last year's catastrophe, and much was the speculation throughout Glasgow that lightning would strike twice, while Celtic supporters talked about the "curse of Arthurlie".

They need not have concerned themselves. The circumstances

were different. Willie Maley was now in charge, Doyle turned up (remarkably, he had been forgiven for last year's misdemeanours and was, as we have seen, the captain) and Sandy McMahon was not injured this year. McMahon scored first, then fed Adam Henderson for the third before scoring again – all within the first 20 minutes. From then on, the game was simply no contest and with Celtic having no great vindictive desire to reach double figures, they contented themselves with 7–0, as indeed it should have been last year as well. Nevertheless, a huge sigh of relief was heard from everyone at Parkhead at the partial exorcising of a ghost that would, nevertheless, live long in the memory of Celtic demonology.

But the value of McMahon to the Celtic cause was proved in the next round against Third Lanark on 22 January, and once again it was in the negative sense of how much Celtic missed him. Having presumably picked up an injury in a League game against Dundee (and it is not impossible that it was a "collision" with his direct opponent, the disgraced Barney Battles who was now appearing for Dundee!), McMahon was out for the Scottish Cup tie at Cathkin Park against Third Lanark. He did not, "feel equal to the strain of a hard Cup tie," according to *The Glasgow Herald*. Left-winger Adam Henderson was also out, and Celtic thus had a makeshift left wing combination of Alec King and George Allan, which was uncharitably described as "non-existent" in *The Glasgow Observer*.

McMahon as a player was clearly missed as Thirds won 3–2, but he was also missed as a positive influence. The full-back combination of James Welford and Dan Doyle argued furiously with each other after the loss of an early goal, and there was no-one to settle things down between them as McMahon was forced to watch impotently from the stand. 14,000 disappointed Celtic fans expressed their feelings about the players at the end, for a complex about the Scottish Cup was beginning to build up. Celtic had not won the trophy since their only success in 1892 and had not been in the Final since 1894.

Willie Maley himself expressed concern about this, for the team could apparently do well in both Glasgow Cup competitions and in the Scottish League (which they had won three times out of seven seasons) but the Scottish Cup eluded them. The Scottish Cup, of course, reckoned to be the most prestigious of them all, did not allow for any second chances. As *The Glasgow Observer* rather weakly, unoriginally, but still grimly effectively put it, "in the Cup, there are no byes, simply goodbyes".

But there was still in 1898 the Scottish League, and the following week, with McMahon fully restored to fitness and form, and with the worthy Adam Henderson also back, Celtic took a decisive step in the direction of lifting that trophy and flag with a 3–1 defeat of Partick Thistle before a somewhat diminished crowd of 5,000 at Celtic Park.

The performance of the team had been much enhanced by the club having taken their players to Rothesay (to stay in non-licensed accommodation, of course!) in midweek for some training but also some relaxation as well. Maley appreciated the value of such occasions, for it gave his senior and more reliable players like Sandy McMahon the opportunity to talk to some of the wilder elements like Doyle and Gilhooly, to play cards or dominoes or table tennis with them, to tell them their value to the team…and then enquire ever so gently what the problem was? They were great players, and the club needed them to be at the top of their form.

Maley was an able psychologist and McMahon was his trusted lieutenant. Doyle was of course the captain on the field, and an inspiring one at that, but Maley and McMahon were the motivators. In addition, there was organisation and thought going into the running of the club. The contrast between the energetic and methodical arrangements of Maley this year and the shambles of the previous one could hardly have been greater.

Where McMahon was given the opportunity to show his prowess was in the soirees held in the evening. It was the custom when

Celtic were away on a training session for the players to entertain each other and the other guests (often elderly but wealthy old ladies charmed by the affability and geniality of Maley) by providing a concert of songs, piano recitals and recitations. McMahon with his encyclopaedic knowledge of Burns, Shakespeare, Dickens and other literary greats, excelled in this.

The Scottish League was duly won on 12 February. There were eerie parallels to an event some 88 years later as Celtic beat St Mirren quite comfortably, but the League victory was confirmed by Dundee beating their nearest challengers, through the agency of a man who was undeniably a Celtic lover through and through. In 1986 it was Albert Kidd who scored twice against Hearts at Dens Park; in 1898 it was Barney Battles against Rangers at Carolina Port! On both occasions Celtic were playing and winning handsomely against St Mirren, although the parallel breaks down with the venue. 1986 was at Love Street; 1898 was at Celtic Park.

Barney, of course, had left Parkhead after his "subversive trade union activities" in November 1896, and had ended up at Dundee via Liverpool. Like many a Celt, Johnny Campbell for example, he made little attempt to hide the fact that he was "pining for home", and his success in scoring the equalizer for Dundee against Rangers that day and then the winner in a scrimmage following a penalty kick was something that he was particularly delighted about. He possibly, indeed probably, hoped this achievement would be a strong pointer in persuading Maley and the Directors to offer him the olive branch. *The Glasgow Observer* could hardly be more obvious in its opinions "St Bernard Battles, Patron of Parkhead…surely after today the Celts will forgive and forget the dressing room revolt?"

Celtic of course were immense in their own game against St Mirren at Parkhead. The attendance was described as meagre in the wind and the rain (once more a few parallels with Love Street in 1896 where the attendance was considerably less than one would have expected, for the weather was indeed awful) but Sandy McMahon was in tremendous form. This day, he won his fourth League flag for the team. He didn't score but "orchestrated and organised" the forward line. The sometimes erratic Pat Gilhooly scored twice, and Davie Russell got the other in the comfortable 3–0 victory, St Mirren's cause not being helped when their centre-forward Mullen picked an argument with the referee and was sent off.

Celtic before a game played against Sheffield United in March 1898.
McMahon is sixth from the left.

It mattered little, for Celtic were the Champions in any case. They came off the park that day to meet a sympathetic newspaper reporter who was able to tell them that Dundee had beaten Rangers, and that Celtic were the League champions for the fourth time. And worthy champions they were! They had not lost a single League game, and *The Glasgow Observer* avers that, "never in the club's history has it been served by such a steady set of fellows". It also tells us that they were given a £10 bonus for winning the League for the fourth time by their grateful Directors.

The game against Rangers, which had been abandoned on New

Year's Day was replayed on Monday 11 April and ended up goalless before a small crowd of 11,000 who had been somewhat sated
with pointless games this season. The Glasgow League, for example,
was a good idea but suffered from the fact that it was often played
with depleted teams whose players were on International duty or
who were simply being "rested", and the simple fact that the Glasgow
teams were playing each other too often. This particular Glasgow
League did not last too long.

Sandy would have been disappointed to miss the Scotland versus England International that season which ended in a 3–1 win for
England at Celtic Park. Two of England's goals were scored by the
famous Steve Bloomer of Derby County, and it would have been nice
to see how McMahon would have done. England's best goalscorer
on the same field as his Scottish equivalent would have been good
to see, but then again the Scottish team selection was a haphazard,
unpredictable and amateurish business in those days (and would
remain so for a long time!).

More interest was engendered by a couple of games that Celtic
played against Sheffield United that spring, especially the one on 16
April by which time both were champions of their respective coun-
tries. The game ended in a 1–1 draw and McMahon with, "a swift
oblique shot low down," scored Celtic's goal. What was more upset-
ting for Celtic however and a clear indication of how well Rangers
were beginning to play came when the Ibrox side won the Scottish
Cup beating Dumbarton 5–1 in the Final. Rangers then won the
low key Glasgow League, and finally put Celtic out of the Glasgow
Charity Cup by beating them 2–0 in the semi-final at Cathkin before
20,000 spectators on 7 May. *The Glasgow Herald* exonerates McMahon and the other Celtic forwards for the defeat and places all the
blame on the inexperienced half-back line of Goldie, Hynds and
Orr, and says that Rangers were worthy winners.

Season 1897–98 was thus a mixture of good and bad for

McMahon. He had little to reproach himself with and might even have considered himself unlucky not to earn more International recognition. It was a shame that injury prevented him from playing in the game that saw Celtic's exit from the Scottish Cup. The Scottish League had been won, but there were now disturbing signs from their Scottish Cup victory that the team from the west of the city sometimes calling itself "proud Scotia's darling club" – in a conscious and deliberate attempt to emphasise their Scottishness, as distinct from the Irishmen in the east of the city, and perhaps the precursor to the religious bigotry and hatred that were to foul their reputation in the 20th century – were now beginning to rise to wrest hegemony away from Celtic.

9.

1898–99 – ALEXANDER THE GREAT

This was a strange season for Celtic. In the first place, it is one of those seasons, at least as far as the Scottish League is concerned in which Celtic historians must hold up their hands and say that Rangers were the better team. Indeed the facts are inarguable. Rangers played 18 League games and won them all, (including two comfortable wins over Celtic) a 100% record and thoroughly deserved their first outright League Championship. It is the only time in history that has happened – even Maley's great Celtic sides of 1907, 1908, 1916 and 1917 and the great Rangers teams of the 1920s or 1940s lost or drew the occasional game, as indeed did Jock Stein's talented players of the 1960s. Full credit must therefore be paid to William Wilton for his efforts in building a strong team to challenge Celtic, Hearts and Queen's Park.

On the other hand, Celtic after a September that was not so much indifferent as sheer terrible, made the brave decision to bring back Barney Battles. They had to swallow a certain amount of pride to do so but were then able to recover, and by the end of the season, they had won three trophies (if one counts the little valued Glasgow League) including the one that was considered to be the most valuable of the lot – the Scottish Cup, something that they had not done for seven years. Never again until 1961 would seven years pass (if we discount the war years) without Celtic winning the Scottish Cup at least once in that period – something that hurt quite a few older supporters (and some young ones as well) on that awful night of 26 April 1961 when the Cup was lost to Jock Stein's Dunfermline. It would be 1965 before that was rectified, and that would make it 11 years since 1954!

The decision to bring back the colourful but controversial Barney Battles, was one which would have been approved of by Sandy McMahon. It was not impossible that the shrewd Maley even consulted Sandy on this matter, knowing that Sandy would be able to judge how the players would react to this. Barney being the character that he was, could certainly cause trouble, but he was committed to the Celtic. In addition, he was contrite and apologetic, he would appear to have learned his lesson, and was indeed, like Tommy McInally of 25 years later "pining for home". There was certainly little doubt about how the fans would react, as a popular jingle of the time would indicate;

> *Back to the Celtic again!*
> *Back to the Celtic again!*
> *Get out your rattles,*
> *For brave Barney Battles*
> *Is back to the Celtic again!*

And there was even the one that bordered upon blasphemy when Barney seemed to replace St Patrick;

> *Hail Glorious Barney Battles*
> *Great prince of Parkhead.*
> *You're back with your darlings*
> *And peace has been made!*
> *With McMahon and Battles*
> *And dear captain Ned,*
> *Now Erin's green valleys*
> *Look down on Parkhead!*

McMahon, one imagines, would not have been unsympathetic to the original claims and demands of the militant three in that infamous game in 1896. The reporting of the previous game (in which McMahon had been badly injured) had been biased and unfair, but of course McMahon, being injured and out of the side and even out of the city of Glasgow in any case, had no voice in any decision. He was certainly aware that the team had missed the thrusting hard work of Barney Battles in particular, and Barney had always remained popular with the support, never more so than when he did his "Albert Kidd" act of winning the League Championship for Celtic while playing for Dundee at Carolina Port last February.

In fact the decision had been forced upon Maley and the Board of Directors. Two defeats at the hands of Hibs in September, a feckless draw with Hearts and then an embarrassing 0–4 thumping from Rangers compelled some sort of action. Even McMahon himself was affected by the dismal performances of the rest of the team and his form suffered, as the crowds began to "catcall, hiss and boo" or more significantly, failed to turn up. The 0–4 defeat by Rangers had been particularly hard to take, for it was Rangers' first ever League win at Celtic Park, and it had occurred before a huge crowd of almost 45,000. Rangers had gone ahead with an early penalty, but then there occurred a second half collapse of monumental proportions, not helped by injuries to Welford, Storrier and King.

It became common in the 20th century for Celtic fans to walk out on their team when they were being annihilated. One recalls the spectacular and almost eerie event of 15 May 1963 when 50,000 turned their backs on Celtic in mute protest at a feckless 0–3 defeat to Rangers in the Scottish Cup Final, but this day in September 1898 is the first time that it is recorded as having happened en masse. "The crowd departed prematurely" is the way that it is described. Some of them would take a long time before they returned as well.

The last straw came on 1 October when the team went down to another 0–4 defeat, this time to St Mirren. Admittedly Welford and Storrier, the full-backs, were both still out injured, but *The Glasgow*

Herald pulls no punches when it says that, "the Celts were out-played in every department". There was also a little crowd trouble at this game (no uncommon occurrence at games between St Mirren and Celtic, it has to be said) but Maley realised that this could not go on. He acted quickly. By the following Monday, with the tacit, possibly reluctant support of the Directors, he had gone to Liverpool to bring back the errant but now repentant Barney Battles in his melancholy exile on Merseyside. Barney took little persuasion. John Divers would similarly be brought back in a few weeks' time.

Celtic won their first game with Barney back against St Bernard's, ("St. Bernard of Parkhead against St Bernard's of Edinburgh", it was dubbed!) a 1–0 win which attracted a larger crowd (12,000) than might have been expected. The standard of play was not much improved, if truth be told, but there was greater animation in the crowd, and this was borne out in the Glasgow Cup semi-final at Ibrox; when with a bit of luck they might have won rather than drawn against Rangers. The wind played a dominant part, but Celtic thoroughly deserved their late equalizer, which came from a long drive from Davie Storrier. Indeed the consensus of neutral opinion was that Celtic were by some distance, the better side.

For the replay a week later, most people similarly thought that Celtic were desperately unlucky not to get at least a draw. On the heavy ground at Parkhead, Celtic twice missed a penalty kick, twice hitting the bar, and, inspired by McMahon, pressed all the time in the last 20 minutes, but could not get round the very professional Rangers defence which contained Scotland Internationals like Neil Gibson. Rangers ran out 2–1 winners, but it was a moral victory for Celtic. McMahon would blame himself for not insisting on taking the penalty kick, but although the Celtic community were disappointed, they were aware that things were gradually getting better.

From then on, Celtic turned on the style and, with one exception, played the football that their fans loved. The exception however was a bad one – another defeat by Rangers, 1–4 at Ibrox this time with McMahon scoring Celtic's consolation goal. Rangers were already League Champions by this time and had built up an air of invincibility about them. Sadly, as would happen so often in the 1940s and the early 1960s, Celtic seemed happy to believe in the theory of the inevitability of a Rangers victory. This distressed McMahon, but he and Maley would now work on the psychological aspect of all this. Some 65 years later, Jock Stein would similarly identify the "Rangers complex" as one of his major problems to deal with.

Training now became a priority with players frequently taken away to hotels for a few days break before a big game, and on occasion, players were taken on horse-drawn coaches to places like Eaglesham, Hamilton and Kirkintilloch and invited to run all the way back to Parkhead. This sounds gruelling stuff, and one wonders how the wilder elements of the squad coped with it all, but for McMahon, it was a great challenge and gave him much enjoyment. He was painfully aware that he was now closer to his 29th birthday that he would have liked to be, but wanted to stay in the squad as long as he possibly could.

On the days away, McMahon's talents came to the fore. Not only was there the importance of enjoying themselves and building up an esprit de corps, but Maley was always, as we have seen, very keen that the Celtic squad, on their days away, should take it upon themselves to entertain the other guests at the hotel. This was as much part of the "missionary" part of Celtic as his desire to play good football. It was important, apart from anything else, to allow the good people of Scotland to see the acceptable side of Irishness. In the ongoing battle for Irish Home Rule, it was vital that "Ireland" should not be solely identified with the violence of the Fenians. Charm was more essential.

The pay-off for all this bonding came in the fine form shown in the early months of 1899, which included a run on the Scottish Cup leading to their first Final appearance since 1894. McMahon scored in every round against the Sixth Galloway Royal Volunteers, St Bernard's, Queen's Park and Port Glasgow Athletic. The Queen's Park tie at Hampden was actually abandoned when "Bad light stopped play", as they would say in cricketing circles – something very familiar to the full-backs James Welford and Davie Storrier, both great cricketers, Welford having been a professional with Warwickshire and Storrier in the less exalted circles of Arbroath and Forfarshire.

The abandonment was all brought about when a combination of darkness and fog prevented play. The game did not kick off until 3.30 pm, a tad too late for a dull afternoon in mid-February. Celtic were winning 4–2 half way through the second half (McMahon having scored twice) when the referee Mr McPherson took the players off. This did not go down at all well with the Celtic players or indeed some of the crowd who had been charged one shilling (double the normal) for admission, and the Glasgow police had to be called upon to enforce law and order, but most observers agreed that the fog and the darkness made it impossible for the referee and indeed the spectators to follow the game.

Celtic were all for playing out the remaining 23 minutes the next week, but the SFA and Queen's Park were adamant that there should be a full replay. Illogically however, they decided that the replay should be at Celtic Park (normally venues were changed only after a drawn game). Any lingering feeling of being hard-done by was however dispelled when 35,000 turned up (paying only the normal sixpence for admission) and Celtic won 2–1 with the on-form McMahon scoring twice, soon after half-time. One was a rebound off the post, which McMahon was on hand to score, and the other was a "grand, high shot" which gave goalkeeper Waller no chance.

Before this happened, McMahon's fine form had earned him another International appearance when he was invited to play for the Scottish League against the Irish League at Solitude, the home of

Cliftonville in Belfast on 11 February. He duly scored for Scotland "with a high shot", according to *The Glasgow Herald,* but *The Belfast News Letter* describes it somewhat differently when it says that McMahon "displaying any amount of speed" sent in a "long shot" which deceived the goalkeeper. But whether McMahon's shot was high or long, it mattered little. The result of the game was a somewhat embarrassing 3–1 defeat for the Scotsmen who had fielded a weakened team, with no Rangers players, as there were Scottish Cup ties on that day. Doyle and Battles also played but "failed to impress". The young Peter Somers was also given a game, and it was felt that he was due "another chance", although he was a "palpable delinquent" when it came to offside. Sadly for Sandy, there were no other International appearances that year.

The report of the game in *The Belfast News Letter* is worth reading in itself as an excellent piece of Victorian journalism. Scotland is described eccentrically as "the Land of Cakes". The "elements were in a tearful mood" is a lovely way of describing the rain. Some Scottish supporters were there wearing "dadges" (apparently a flat bonnet with a Scottish thistle sticking out of it) and expressing themselves with "rugged emphasis". A man called McMaster of Glentoran was covered in mud and looked "blacker than the Ethiopian" (a phrase than no journalist would dare to use today!) and he returned to the pavilion at one point and emerged with "a clean face and pair of knickers". The paper also perhaps hints at one of the reasons for the Scottish League's poor performance when it states that they had been in Ireland since Friday morning and had had plenty of opportunity to "recover from such fatigue as the journey may have given them". A certain amount of Irish hospitality, possibly too much, one feels, may well have been dispensed to the players on the Friday night.

There is a reported embarrassing incident at the meal after this game. The Scottish League's President John H. McLaughlin of Celtic did not turn up with an excuse of "indisposition", a lovely word, which can cover anything from illness to "can't be bothered" or drunk or whatever. Indeed there is a pattern of John H. McLaughlin not being happy with formality when things have not gone his way! He was notorious for suddenly taking ill between the end of a game, which Celtic had lost and the beginning of the meal.

The Scottish players, particularly the wilder elements like Doyle and Battles and a few of the Hearts players, had been nursing a grudge against the referee Mr Hugh McCormick, President of the Irish Referees Association. He had been perceived to be incompetent, and even biased, in particular expressing some delight in the Irish victory. The meal over and drink beginning to flow, the speeches began. Everyone listened politely until it came to the time for the customary toast to the referee. A few of the Scottish players got up and walked out!

The Scottish League cap won by McMahon in
this game against the Irish League

But the thing that dominated Sandy and Celtic's thinking in spring 1899 was the Scottish Cup Final. Having defeated the surprise semi-finalists in Port Glasgow Athletic, they discovered that the opponents were the apparently all-conquering Rangers. Rangers' semi-final against St Mirren took place only the week before and was a narrow 2–1 win for the Ibrox men, who radiated confidence, and not without cause, for, "they and defeat were strangers to each other," in the words of *The Glasgow Herald*.

This was a vital game for Celtic for many reasons. A Scottish Cup complex was beginning to develop for Celtic, and Rangers were the winners for the last two years. Moreover Rangers were the runaway Scottish League winners with a 100% record, and were certainly the favourites, having defeated Celtic on three occasions, once luckily in the Glasgow Cup, but twice conclusively in the Scottish League. Victory in the Scottish Cup would mean that Rangers would emulate the feat of Queen's Park and Vale of Leven who had both won the Scottish Cup three years in a row in the early years. Moreover no team had, as yet, in Scotland won a League and Cup double and Celtic were all that stood between Rangers and this feat.

Celtic, therefore, needed to win this game; otherwise the inferiority complex would intensify and harden. Maley had already issued a few statements moaning about the attitude of some of his players – this would be a recurring theme of his whenever the team began to disappoint – and it was clear that Rangers success this year was having a bad effect on him.

Both teams took their players off for training. Celtic went to Loch Katrine for a few days but returned to Glasgow the day before the game to give the players a chance to socialise with their wives and families before the big day, whereas Rangers went to the Clyde coast. During all this time, the entertaining skills of McMahon were much called upon. Some of the younger players would have been nervous, and some of the wilder boys would have needed to be held in check. Maley could hardly have found a more willing colleague than Sandy McMahon. Dan Doyle had now disappeared out of the picture and Davie Storrier, the amiable Arbroath man and cricketer for Forfarshire, was now the captain. He too had the ability to bring out the best in his players.

Eager enthusiasm seized the support and indeed all of Glasgow in that month of April. The Scotland versus England International that year was played at Villa Park. It was a disappointing 1–2 defeat, and possibly for the first time, it began to appear that the Scottish Cup Final was more talked about than the Scottish International team. Given the good form of Rangers, it was only natural that their supporters brimmed with enthusiasm and confidence, but Celtic fans began to hope that with McMahon on form, and the team having had a great boost from the return "home" of Barney Battles, perhaps it was time to revenge these awful defeats that Rangers had inflicted on them earlier in the season. The cynics however, both in the Press and outwith, predicted with a certain degree of confidence that the first game would be a draw!

The Glasgow Observer with "Man In The Know" talking from "Celtic Inner Circles" (something that gave credence to the rumours that "Man In The Know" at this time, was no less a person than Tom Maley, the brother of Willie) tries to rally the troops, but one gets the impression that he is not always totally convinced himself. "Will the Celtic Win?" he asks, then states, "After weeks of weary waiting, (since their semi-final win on 11 March) the Celts are once more to face their Glasgow rivals. A better couple could not contest the Final, and the meeting is sure to be the event of a rather poor season…Like the good sportsmen they are, the Celts admire the Rangers' prowess, but they feel that just now they can turn out a team a bit in front (sic) of anything the Ibrox people can show. The forward line can play effective as well as pretty football. Campbell is back in his best form, Divers is doing splendidly at centre while

McMahon, the old reliable, has apparently forgotten how to play a poor game".

He then goes on to state that Celtic are in splendid condition, the players have trained "systematically" and have been offered a £20 bonus each (a phenomenal amount in 1899) for a victory. Celtic had looked particularly fit in a friendly game they played recently against Liverpool, whereas Rangers had had a tough season, had struggled against St Mirren in the semi-final and were just back from an exhausting tour of England.

Most unusually for a Scottish Cup Final in these days, the weather on 22 April was fine and the pitch at Hampden was excellent. Cathcart Road presented an extraordinary scene that day with the gates opened some two and a half hours before the kick-off at 4.00 pm. "Every kind of vehicular transport was pressed into service," including one or two motorised vehicles which baffled and terrified the late Victorian population. A favourite method of transport was a dogcart, but there were also bicycles, hansom cabs, trams, growlers and carts used to bring the 25,000 crowd to Hampden. In a primitive form of the supporters' bus, some groups would join together and hire a horse-drawn charabanc to take them to the game. These became known as "brake clubs".

At 3.30 pm a good half hour before the kick-off, the authorities, mindful, no doubt, of previous occasions and fearful of the possibility of disorder, took the decision to close the gates, leaving thousands outside to follow the progress of the game from the roars of those inside. It was a lesson that would soon be learned by Queen's Park. They were aware that Celtic Park could hold a lot more, and therefore earn more money than the current Hampden could, and that perhaps it might be an idea to invest in a new stadium. *The Daily Record and Mail* notes with approval that ex-Celt Paddy Gallagher albeit, "looking like a shadow of his old self," turned up from his nursing home at Bridge of Allan to cheer on his old team. Paddy, a veteran of 1892, sadly died a few weeks later, but he enjoyed this game.

The admission charge was one shilling, possibly still a bit much for the pocket of some supporters but this was a Scottish Cup Final and a huge cheer from the 25,000 crowd greeted the following teams as they took the field.

Celtic: McArthur; Welford and Storrier; Battles, Marshall and King; Hodge, Campbell, Divers, McMahon and Bell.

Rangers: Dickie; N. Smith and Crawford; Gibson, Neill and Mitchell; Campbell, McPherson, Hamilton, Miller and A. Smith.

Referee: T. Robertson, Queen's Park.

Both teams started brightly and both goalkeepers were soon in action with Celtic possibly having the edge on pressure. McMahon headed narrowly past, and similarly a shot from the same man was lacking only slightly in accuracy, but then a moment later McMahon was required at the other end to head off his own line when McArthur was beaten.

The game had been very even in the first half as both sides took time to settle. Things took a nasty turn, however, when Celtic's left-winger Jack Bell was badly fouled by Rangers notorious Nick Smith. Bell wanted to come off, and in truth was of little use to his team-mates but Maley insisted that he stayed on the field to hobble about for nuisance value, if nothing else. But Celtic were now gradually taking the ascendancy and in the 67th minutes, halfway through the second half, won a corner on the right. Johnny Hodge took it, swung over a high hanging ball and up rose the Duke to head home a glorious header. It was in the tradition of the goal he had headed home in 1892 and it would become the prototype and template for future Scottish Cup Final headed goals – McGrory in 1925, McNeill in 1965 and 1969, McGarvey in 1985, McAvennie in 1988, Van Hooijdonk in 1995.

This event, "created bedlam among the Celtic supporters," as they, "patted each other on the back and hurled their green favours in the air". There was however more than a little tension and worry in the air over the next twenty minutes. Two things worried the support – one was whether the players would give in to commercial pressures from their Directors and concede a goal to allow a replay and another big gate. The other was whether Celtic might simply not believe that they could beat Rangers and would cave in, particularly as with the injury to Jack Bell, they were virtually a man short. Their fears on both accounts were groundless.

Now Celtic took a firm grip of the game with Battles in particular winning every ball that came his way and feeding the forwards with some superb passes. Jack Bell, although badly crippled, still played a vital part in the second goal when a ball spun off a Rangers defender and came to Bell who immediately kicked it across the field with his one serviceable foot towards Johnny Hodge. Hodge collected the ball and ran through a static Rangers defence who appealed half-heartedly for some infringement to score Celtic's second and decisive goal. The game finished amidst intense cheering and singing with the words of *A Nation Once Again* being converted into *The Scottish Cup Once Again* even though the words did not quite fit the metre of the scansion! It was a great Celtic occasion, and McMahon was the hero of the hour.

The Glasgow Herald said, "the better team won definitely," and Celtic returned to their heartlands later that night with the Scottish Cup. The celebrations recalled those of seven years ago when the Cup was last won, but there was an element of relief in the celebrations too. The so called invincible Rangers had been beaten. The Cup had been presented once again in the Bath Street Hotel, and Celtic's Director John H. McLaughlin spoke magnanimously about Rangers and claimed (somewhat prematurely, one feels!) that, "sectarianism was a dead letter," in Scottish football, and that Celtic would take anyone, "from all quarters, regardless of sect".

Rangers, although disappointed at not having emulated the feat of Queen's Park and Vale of Leven in winning the Scottish Cup three years in a row, were in attendance and were "perfect sportsmen". It was a fine night for Celtic, however, and for Sandy McMahon. He now had two Scottish Cup medals, and he had scored in both, his headed goal in both cases being the talk of the fast growing Celtic support who raised their hero-worship of the Duke to ever higher and higher levels.

The Glasgow Observer the following week goes into overdrive, with "Man In The Know" stating that it was Celtic's fitness that won the Cup. Several players are singled out. James Welford, who had now the distinction of having won a Scottish Cup medal and an English one – the only Englishman to do so – was "superb" at right-back, and of the forwards, John Divers is quixotically described thus, "his arms move in windmill fashion and his elbows are always meeting with an opponent's ribs, accidentally of course," whereas McMahon and Campbell were, "quieter but no less effective".

McMahon apparently, after he scored the first goal, "dropped back between Divers and King, rendering the Celtic defence invulnerable". (This was a facet of Victorian football as well in that a centre-forward was also expected on occasion to be a centre-half, a positional manoeuvre that would be perfected ten years later when Jimmy Quinn and Willie Loney frequently changed position to the confusion of the opposition.)

"Man In The Know," then says that, "McMahon's display at Hampden is all the more creditable since he partly broke down while sprinting during the week". This rather disturbing sentence which does not specify what particular kind of "breaking down" occurred, perhaps indicates that McMahon, now older and less supple than he had once been, was becoming more and more prone to recurrences of old injury problems, but whatever it was, it did not last long on this occasion.

"Man In the Know," then finishes off by congratulating the Celtic Directors on their "glorious victory" which had been achieved after "grappling with misfortune" and "neither effort nor expense had been spared to bring the 'Blue Riband' back to Celtic Park". A happy summer would now be spent by the Celtic supporters, for the Scottish Cup was still considered by most in 1899 to be of far more value than the Scottish League. The Final, well publicised and well attended, certainly brought more glory.

But there was still more to come for Celtic and McMahon this year. Having now beaten Rangers in the Scottish Cup, they proceeded to beat them twice more. 4–1 was the score in the Glasgow League in a game, which attracted 18,700 to Parkhead (an astonishing crowd for the much despised Glasgow League) on the fine but cold day of 6 May, thereby winning that League in the process. McMahon opened the scoring, and from then on was cheered every time he touched the ball by his adoring followers.

Three weeks later the Glasgow Charity Cup was won for the sixth time this decade. On 20 May Sandy had been in superb form scoring a hat-trick against Queen's Park before 18,000 at Hampden in the semi-final, and then in the final on 27 May against Rangers at Ibrox before a somewhat larger crowd on a marvellous sunny day, Celtic won 2–0, the goals inevitably coming from McMahon (yet again) and the more and more impressive Peter Somers, a pert and confident young man with a great future ahead of him. Celtic and McMahon were so much in charge that *The Glasgow Herald* says that, "McArthur's post was almost a sinecure, and once again the peerless McMahon was cheered every time he touched the ball." The teams were:

Celtic: McArthur; Welford and Davidson; Battles, Russell and Orr; Hodge, Somers, Divers, McMahon and Gilhooly.

Rangers: Dickie; N Smith and Drummond; Gibson, Neil and Mitchell; Campbell, McPherson, Hamilton, Miller and A Smith.

Referee: Mr T. Robertson, Queen's Park.

Thus ended the 1899 season. It was arguably McMahon's best. He had stayed to a large extent clear of injury, had been talked about in terms of winning back his Scotland International cap (he perhaps should have been playing in Scotland's 1–2 defeat by England at Villa Park) and had finished the season in a blaze of glory. Celtic felt that their finish to the season meant that they were the superior team to Rangers. They had had the last laugh. Rangers had of course their 100% Scottish League record – something that has never since been equalled – and no-one of course would want to minimise that achievement, but Celtic felt they had more reason for optimism in the future, for now that Battles and Divers were back in the fold, the fight, determination and confidence were all back, as indeed was the upbeat nature of their support. And of course, they still had the Duke, the Prince of Dribblers and the hero of the age in Sandy McMahon. And in the Scottish Cup, they certainly had the last laugh.

An indication of how much the return of the Scottish Cup meant to the Celtic establishment came when they announced that the players had indeed been awarded a £20 bonus as promised, something that lifted McMahon and company into "superstar" status. This clearly caused a certain amount of envy among their supporters, – it would have been several months' wages for most of them! – and they were also amazed at the amount of times that Celtic seemed able to take their players away on "holidays" to places like Bute and Loch Katrine. Yet envy did not become jealousy, for as long as the players were able to produce the goods on the field, the supporters would remain happy. They now, far from being an illiterate, self-pitying, downtrodden sub-culture of Scottish society, had something to be cheerful about, something to boast about

Celtic at the end of their triumphant season of 1898–99. McMahon second from the right in the middle row

A subtle change had come over the Celtic support as well in the past few years. In the first place, there were more of them. Most of them of course still lived in Glasgow, in the East End and were Catholic and Irish, but increasingly it was becoming apparent, particularly in away games outside the immediate area of Glasgow, that lovers of Celtic were beginning to appear and they were not necessarily of the ethnic delineation that the bigots expected. Dundee and Aberdeen, for example, (Aberdeen were not yet in the Scottish League but Celtic's trips there to play friendlies were always well attended) now had active Celtic supporters who increasingly began to travel on the railway to watch them.

In addition Celtic fans who travelled on the "brake clubs" from shorter distances would find that the journey was often the best part of the day. Alcohol was naturally consumed, but there was also a great deal of noise and singing with bugles blowing and flags hanging from the side, as the brake would enter Hamilton or Port Glasgow or Paisley with the accompaniment of the raucous singing of *The Wearing O' The Green*. The horse was usually given a name like "Sandy" or "Barney" (sometimes "Parnell" or "Davitt") and was decorated in green colours. Even, occasionally, a few women were seen to join the merry band – something that shocked a few people in Victorian society.

But also within the Irish in Glasgow, the first topic of conversation was now not so much Irish Home Rule or how bad the English landlords had been to their grandfathers or how long it would be before there was a violent uprising (as was about to happen in South Africa, for instance) against British rule, it was more about how well the team were playing, and whether Sandy McMahon was to stay clear of injury or indeed how long he would continue to grace the green and white stripes. Football, in fact, the Scottish obsession for the next century and a bit, was now beginning to assume more importance than politics. Yes, the origins of the club were important, and no, the support would not forget their provenance, but, "the wearing of the green" was no longer a matter for which men and women might be hanged for, it was now more about who was going to line up alongside Sandy McMahon next Saturday!

Summer 1899 was a glorious one with the East End urchins showing again and again to each other how Sandy had jumped up to head home that first goal in the Scottish Cup Final. The arrival of the new season and the new century was eagerly anticipated. One leader column in a newspaper made an abstruse reference to "the Macedon Chief". This was of course, the famous Greek conqueror of the world, Alexander The Great!

10.

1899–1900 – THE NEW CENTURY

As the new century approached, Celtic began the new season fairly upbeat about what they were about to face. There seemed little doubt that the big two Glasgow teams were now Celtic and Rangers rather than Celtic and Queen's Park. Queen's Park still enjoyed the patronage of the middle classes and were much loved by *The Glasgow Herald* in particular, but their clear aversion to professionalism and to the Scottish League (they would eventually apply to join and would be accepted for the 1900–01 season) meant that they were no longer mixing with the big boys on a week by week basis. They still had their prestigious fixtures against London amateur teams like the Corinthians, but these games now seemed more and more irrelevant.

Increasingly, however, Queen's Park saw their role as the Scottish establishment team. They already had plans to build a huge new stadium to outdo both Celtic and Rangers in bidding for Scotland games and for Scottish Cup Finals. They also had their past glories to reflect on. Queen's Park had done so much to make football such a major and indeed unparalleled spectator attraction. There never had been such a popular mass attraction in Scotland as football, and that is, more than 100 years later, still the case. But in 1900 the influence of Queen's Park was a great deal stronger than their actual playing potential.

Rather than Queen's Park, it was Rangers under William Wilton and with a fine new stadium who were a real challenge to Celtic. Their geographical location as well meant that they were near to the shipyards of the Clyde, and when the shipyards stopped working at

12.00 on a Saturday, it was the most natural thing in the world for the workers to have their pint, then go to Ibrox to see what was in all conscience a very good team. The vile sectarian prejudice that befouled them so much after World War One now had its roots there – for no other reason than that Celtic were (wrongly) perceived as "the Catholic team" so therefore their strongest rivals would be "Protestants" – but religious prejudice was not yet the all-encompassing fiend that it was to become.

The fact that in 1898 Celtic won the Scottish League and Rangers the Scottish Cup whereas in 1899 it was the other way round meant that it was now clear who were the best two teams in Scotland. More and more supporters from beyond their natural catchment areas were attracted to each team, for everyone loves a winner. The two Edinburgh teams, on the other hand were more generally confined to their own city in terms of support, with Queen's Park's support, while still numerically strong, were now a lot less vocal and animated than the supports of Celtic and Rangers. They were middle class and subdued, although not necessarily any less committed, and their team, at least in the Scottish and Glasgow Cups, was still a force to be reckoned with.

Sandy McMahon got off to a bad start this season. The second League game was at Kilmarnock on 26 August 1899. It was a special occasion, for it was the official opening of Rugby Park, a magnificent new ground. The weather was fine and sunny, but McMahon was badly injured in the early part of the second half. Celtic were 2–0 up at the time, but then with only ten men, lost two goals to give Kilmarnock a draw and if it had not been for a magnificent performance by Dan McArthur in goal, Kilmarnock might have won.

McMahon's injury was unspecified but serious enough to cause him (somewhat embarrassingly) to miss his own Benefit match a couple of days later. It was a friendly against Rangers attended by 12,000 people (a huge crowd for a benefit fixture) and Sandy earned the princely sum of £400. A week later, *The Glasgow Observer* reported that Sandy was not only injured, but actually unwell and taking the air on the Kyles of Bute.

This caused no little alarm in the gossipy village that Glasgow can be. Sandy had of course been troubled with injury in the past and the team had suffered as a result, but in this case, he was out for all of September, during which time the team played reasonably well apart from a very bad 0–2 defeat by Hearts on the last day of that month. But the Duke was seen in the stand at that game, and it was clear that his return would not be long delayed. The lack of forward play in that game against Hearts was indeed worrying.

McMahon's return from injury or illness should have been the Rangers game at Ibrox in early October. In fact the game had to be played at Celtic Park because of building work still going on at Ibrox. Concern had been expressed about the wisdom of playing McMahon in such an important fixture, and there are a few comments about him not quite lasting the pace, but it was he who headed home Celtic's third goal which looked as if it might win the game until a mistake by goalkeeper Dan McArthur allowed Rangers to equalize. The splendid autumn weather had attracted 40,000 to see the game, kicked off eccentrically by Lord Emly of Limerick in a top hat.

The important thing however was that McMahon was back, and he had certainly contributed to the fine co-ordinated play of the Celtic forwards. But November saw Celtic continue their melancholy tradition of losing in the Glasgow Cup to Rangers after a draw. The plethora of drawn games in Cup-ties necessitating a replay and another large gate – a phenomenon that would of course become a major issue ten years later – was beginning to raise even more eyebrows than previously. Indeed, newspaper columnists on the morning of a game were beginning to predict a draw, hinting that they had some kind of inside information. On this occasion, however, the first game, played on a heavy pitch in wet conditions at Cathkin before

10,000 spectators was indeed a 1–1 draw. It had been a good game however. Celtic were probably the better team, playing their close passing game which impressed the correspondent of *The Glasgow Herald* who singles out McMahon for his co-ordination with Campbell and Bell.

Other things were beginning to dominate people's thoughts by this time, however, notably the conflict in South Africa, which was now openly being referred to as a "war" in the newspapers, and causing all sorts of arguments. Clichés like, "defending Britain's imperial interests," on the one hand were balanced with, "unnecessary slaughter," on the other, and a few letters were beginning to appear, asking the question why professional football players were allowed to play a game when they could be, "acting as bulwarks for the Empire". The fact that it was all about the super-power of the day seizing diamonds from a few Dutch farmers did not seem to come into the equation. Those opposed to the war, however, were not without support from some quarters. Large sections of the Liberal opposition, including future Prime Ministers Henry Campbell-Bannerman and David Lloyd George were distinctly un-enthusiastic about the whole venture.

But on Saturday 18 November, the day of the replayed Glasgow Cup Final, the topic of conversation was fog. Glasgow was very prone to fog, particularly in November, and before people realised the dangers of fog mixing with industrial pollution, "pea soupers" were common. The city that day was enveloped in a particularly dirty and dismal fog. Representatives of both teams were at Cathkin from an early stage, and agreed to play, something that would weaken Celtic's case later when they considered a protest. In the event, in spite of rumours sweeping the city that the game would be off, some 8,000 turned up at Cathkin to see what they could of the game.

Celtic were without Welford and Campbell, and Campbell in particular was badly missed, but the game was decided by two penalties both awarded within a minute of each other halfway through the second half. Celtic, unfortunately, missed theirs but Rangers were more successful and the one goal was enough to win the game, which finished in almost farcical conditions with some spectators leaving the ground in the belief that Celtic had scored a late equalizer at the far end! The referee Mr Baillie from Edinburgh refused to allow the players off the field at half-time, and the joke was that this was because they might not be able to find their way back again! The truth was that no one could see what was going on, and even Rangers themselves admitted at the post match banquet that the conditions were less than ideal. John Glass was now the President of the Glasgow FA and it was agreed that a donation of £100 from the profits should be given to the war fund for widows and orphans. The teams were

Celtic: McArthur: Turnbull and Storrier; Battles, Russell and Orr; Hodge, Gilhooly, Divers, McMahon and Bell.

Rangers: Dickie; N. Smith and Drummond; Gibson, Neil and Robertson; Graham, Wilkie, Hamilton, McPherson and A. Smith.

Referee: Mr J Baillie, St Bernard's.

The century then finished on a low note as far as Celtic were concerned with three miserable draws against teams that they should have beaten. The weather remained poor, Rangers had won the Scottish League for the second year in a row, and McMahon was injured yet again, missing two games, and the whole country was enveloped in depression with continuing reports of reverses and heavy casualties in South Africa.

Yet there was still a considerable amount of jingoism about as well. "Johnny Foreigner" had to be taught a lesson, it was felt, and shades of Palmerstonian "giving the Boers a bloody nose" were noticed, with campaigns for recruitment with the promise of regular pay and a trip to an exotic land a definite enticement for the urban poor of Glasgow and other cities.

It might have been thought that the Irish community in Glasgow might have experienced a certain "Schadenfraude" at the embarrassment of the British Empire, but apparently not so, with both John Glass and John H. McLaughlin speaking about the necessity to fight, hoping, one presumes, that Home Rule for Ireland was more likely to come about from a strong, triumphant and therefore grateful British Empire rather than a demoralised and weakened one. The same arguments would be used by people like John Redmond of the Irish Nationalist Party in 1914 to persuade Irishmen to join the Great War.

The Glasgow League was now called the Inter City League with the inclusion of Hearts and Hibs, but the change of name did little to raise its profile. A poor crowd was seen at Easter Road for the final game of the nineteenth century, and Celtic went down 0–1. The old century was thus going out with a whimper. What would the new century bring? Certainly things were going well for the team that had emerged as Celtic's biggest rivals, Rangers. They had won the Scottish League and the Glasgow Cup, and on the very cusp of the new century had officially opened their new stadium at Ibrox.

It might have been an idea to play the first game of the new century at Ibrox, particularly as the clubs had agreed to reverse venues for the game that was meant to be played at Ibrox in October, but for some reason that never happened. Whether this was because Ibrox was not quite ready to house such a huge crowd or whether quite simply Celtic turned awkward and uncooperative, is not really clear, but for whatever reason, the new century began at Celtic Park on Monday 1 January before a slightly disappointing crowd of 20,000.

It turned out to be Rangers first defeat in the Scottish League for nearly two seasons, as Celtic, in an entertaining game on a cold but dry day, won 3–2. McMahon had a splendid game leading his line as Celtic showed their fans how good they could be, and how, with a bit of luck, things could have been a great deal different this season. Jack Bell scored first, then John Divers added another two before half-time after Rangers had equalized. Divers then missed a penalty in the second half before Rangers pulled one back and strove hard for the equalizer, but Celtic held out and gave their fans some hope that they might yet come good in the Scottish Cup. They were after all, the holders.

The Glasgow Herald is interesting in its account of the game, or rather by its lack of account of the game. There is little more than a small paragraph. More attention in the sports pages is given to the Draughts Championship of Scotland which opened at the City Hall, and while there is a detailed account of how the New Year was celebrated in Glasgow and elsewhere including the interesting but debatable statement that, "money is more than usually plentiful with the working classes," the main focus is of course on THE WAR which merits a couple of pages in the centre, including a detailed account of the exploits of one Winston Churchill and his escape from the Boers.

Ominously, the Kaiser of Germany also had a great deal to say, some of it potentially alarming to British ears, in his New Year address to the German Army and Navy. But then again, in 1900 the Kaiser was looked upon by most people in Britain as an amiable, bombastic, occasionally tactless, fool with a withered arm. He was known as "l'enfant terrible" for his ability to rock the boat, but he was well connected to the British Royal Family and although he couldn't stand the Prince of Wales ("fat old Wales" he called him), the Kaiser was still very fond of his "Granny Vic".

For Celtic and McMahon, the early months of 1900 concerned little other than the Scottish Cup. Bo'ness were put to the sword with McMahon scoring four in the 7–1 victory, but then strange problems met them when they were drawn against Port Glasgow Athletic at Clune Park at the end of January. Not only were they made to feel not very welcome by some of the less intelligent natives who threw stones at the Celtic linesman, but in the 70th minute with Celtic well ahead, a hole appeared on the park and had to be filled with turf so that the game could continue. It turned out to be an old drain, and the grass had collapsed under the weight of the very heavy rain, which had at one point put the game in danger. But Celtic had played "football of the old sort" and ran out 5–1 winners with McMahon scoring the final goal.

A 4–0 defeat of Kilmarnock in mid-February then set up the semi-final that had all Glasgow and all Scotland talking. It was against Rangers at Ibrox. The cynics who had predicted a draw and therefore another big crowd at Celtic Park were to be proved right, but the first game at Ibrox (which attracted 33,000 admiring fans to see the new, revamped stadium) was a 2–2 thriller. Rangers had gone ahead early in the second half, but then Celtic drew level with a penalty. Then soon after that, Jack Bell scored what looked like a winner until a last desperate surge by Rangers saw them equalize after Celtic's goalkeeper Dan McArthur had twice saved, once diving courageously at the feet of the Rangers forwards and injuring his head. Celtic's close passing play had attracted a great deal of admiration in the Press, but ultimately the undignified "kick it up the park" earned Rangers their draw.

The replay was scheduled for a fortnight later on 10 March at Celtic Park (Scotland were playing Ireland on 3 March) and it was, quite frankly, one of Celtic's best ever performances against Rangers as they beat them 4–0 with McMahon scoring twice and Hodge and Bell once each. 32,000 (only marginally fewer than had been at Ibrox a couple of weeks previously) saw a very one-sided contest, described oddly by the curmudgeonly writer of *The Glasgow Herald* as, "none too brilliant". The Celtic crowd and the rest of Press seemed to disagree. McMahon was singled out for his "long, wide passing", (Celtic having apparently given up temporarily on their short passing game), and he was praised for his first goal, which was a well-angled shot from a corner kick.

"Bedouin" of *The Daily Record* was very impressed, possibly overdoing the word "beautifully". McMahon's first goal was, "beautifully shot across from an awkward angle," and his second was scored, "beautifully with a head off a free-kick," and he goes on to state that, "nothing finer was witnessed than Campbell and McMahon's inside work". At half time the boys' band from Slatefield School paraded the track, but the crowd did not appreciate fully their music because they were still "spell bound by the excellence" of some mighty play by McMahon and Campbell.

The Glasgow Observer, as effusive as *The Glasgow Herald* was grudging, states that, "Spectators were spellbound by the brilliance of Celtic's forward play," and McMahon himself made the esoteric quote that, "We have taken Kruger's advice and staggered humanity". It was a strange, undiplomatic, and possibly tactless remark, although maybe the erudite McMahon said it sarcastically. Paul Kruger, the leader of the Boers was seen as the Antichrist in the contemporary press and the full context of his statement was that if the Boers had to stay within the British Empire, it would be at a price that would "stagger humanity" – and of course in March 1900, the casualty lists, mounting steadily and inexorably, since October 1899 were doing just that.

McMahon's quote therefore that a victory over Rangers (however impressive), "staggered humanity" might have been seen as in bad taste, and possibly was considered offensive by certain people, but for the majority of the Celtic support, the victory had indeed been a staggering one, and of course Sandy McMahon, being Sandy McMahon, could be forgiven for the occasional remark that was less than what modern 21st century society might term "politically correct".

The fired up Celtic community now had a month to wait for the Scottish Cup Final against Queen's Park on 14 April. Celtic were of course the holders, and it would be Celtic's sixth Scottish Cup Final, for they had already beaten Queen's Park in 1892 and Rangers in 1899, but lost to the same opponents in 1893 and 1894 respectively, as well as their defeat to Third Lanark in 1889, the first year of their history. The game would be played at the new Ibrox Park. Queen's Park had been the kingpins of Scottish football in the 1870s and 1880s, but many people felt that their moment had now passed, particularly with their reluctance to join the Scottish League, which penalised them in the financial sense, but also in the footballing sense, for they were depriving their players of the opportunity to play against top class opposition.

But before the Scottish Cup Final, McMahon played another representative game for Scotland when he turned out for the Scottish League team against the English League on 31 March at the venerable Crystal Palace ground in a game delayed so that the crowd would have plenty of time to go the Oxford v Cambridge Boat Race first! McMahon enjoyed his trip to London and played well in the respectable 2–2 draw.

He would, however, have been disappointed not to be selected for the "Big" International the following week against England at Celtic Park – a game which is known to history as the "Rosebery International" because of the presence of Lord Rosebery, one time Prime Minister of Great Britain, to support Scotland, and which saw an emphatic 4–1 win for Scotland. Rosebery even donated Scotland his own strips in his racing colours, and had the Celtic Park pavilion bedecked in the same colours! In his speech after the game, Lord Rosebery after a conscious attempt to be Scottish with phrases like "michty me" and "och aye", uses strange imagery to describe the rivalry between the two nations when he hopes that, "no greater civil war will ever come between us," than football.

Celtic had two men in the Scotland team, Jack Bell and John Campbell. *The Glasgow Herald,* naturally and deservedly very upbeat about the exploits of Queen's Park's R.S. McColl upsets *The Glasgow Observer* by failing to give enough credit to John Campbell whose praises are sung by the rest of the Press, especially the English news-papers who, according to "Man In The Know", talked nostalgically about Campbell and his days with Aston Villa.

> *Oh, one more sigh*
> *Is the Birmingham cry*
> *For braw Johnnie Campbell!*

The immortal McMahon and Campbell

McMahon may have missed out on this occasion but he was, however, well involved in the Scottish Cup Final the following week. Special training for this game began on the Monday after the International. Celtic had been a fitter team than Rangers in last year's Cup Final, and it was as well that they were at the top of their game for this one as well. They already had, on the surface at least, a great advantage in that they were full time professionals as distinct from part time amateurs!

This Scottish Cup Final at the recently reconstructed Ibrox has gone down in history as the "hurricane Cup Final", but the strength of the wind must not be allowed to detract from the fine football played by Celtic and by McMahon in particular, both against and with the wind. When the wind was as strong as it seems to have been on 14 April 1900, and the game is played at a ground without too much cover especially from the west, it is sometimes as difficult to play with the wind as it is against it. *The Glasgow Herald* clearly miffed at the defeat of its favourites, accuses Celtic of time wasting and negative tactics particularly against the wind, "in a way that incensed the spectators" but is compelled to admit that McMahon and Bell "were in good form for Celtic".

The crowd was a disappointing 17,000 – the wind had caused rumours to spread about a postponement, (but it was a bright sunny day!) and in any case, the prices were raised again to a level which discriminated against Celtic (one shilling) with their poorer support but allowed the slightly better heeled lovers of Queen's Park to attend. For Celtic, right back Bob Davidson was injured, but there was a more than adequate substitute in ex-captain Davie Storrier to play alongside the mighty Barney Battles. The teams were;

Queen's Park: Gourlay; D. Stewart and Swan; Irons, Christie and Templeton; W. Stewart, Wilson, McColl, Kennedy and Hay.

Celtic: McArthur; Storrier and Battles; Russell, Marshall and Orr; Hodge, Campbell, Divers, McMahon and Bell.

Referee: J. Walker, Kilmarnock.

That was not the way they were listed in *The Glasgow Herald* of course. Queen's Park were given their Christian initial because they were amateur. Thus, for example, Queen's Park's goalkeeper was given as D. Gourlay, but Celtic's goalkeeper is simply McArthur! This piece of discrimination would sadly continue for some time.

Celtic's captain Henry Marshall won the toss and decided to take advantage of the wind first, but it was soon obvious that good football was going to be difficult, particularly as the ball used seemed to be lighter than usual and therefore particularly prone to be blown about by the wind.

Rather to everyone's surprise, Queen's Park scored first with a "snap" shot from Christie who took advantage of a temporary lull in the wind to shoot for goal when everyone expected a pass. But then McMahon took a grip on proceedings and Celtic went through a purple patch during which they scored three goals. "McMahon fairly distinguished himself by making the score equal, a lovely cross shot from the inside-left finding the desired haven", according to *The Evening Times*. That was in the 22nd minute, then a few minutes after that, he headed on a cross ball for Divers to score with another header, and finally after a prolonged period of total Celtic dominance, he fed Jack Ball just before interval to crash home a third off the post. He had also forced goalkeeper Gourlay to make a great save when he, "fisted past a beauty from McMahon".

Celtic's supporters, outnumbered but considerably more vocal, were delighted at half-time but very aware that the wind showed no sign of abating and wondered how their favourites would deal with the problems as Queen's attacked what is now the Copland Road end of the ground. But not only did Celtic start the second half well, they actually scored again, this time through Divers in the 55th minute. Playing sensibly against the wind, McMahon met a high ball, headed it down to Divers who ran on and scored.

4–1 and Celtic looked home and dry, but if anything the wind was intensifying and Sandy's defensive skills were now called upon as well as his attacking and creative ones. Queen's scored half way through the second half to make the score 4–2, but, "panic stations were not sounded," until well within the last ten minutes when Barney Battles rose to head clear and deflected the ball into his own goal. Queen's Park threw everything at Celtic, with R.S. McColl, Scotland's hero of last week's International against England, particularly dangerous, but Celtic's defence of McArthur, Storrier and Battles held firm. At times like this, a man with the dribbling skills and sheer all-round ability of Sandy McMahon is invaluable.

In Victorian football, there was not always as big a difference as one would expect between a defender and an attacker. A forward would be called upon in situations like this, –talented, but desperate attackers, a very strong wind and the feeling that the Scottish Cup is just minutes away. A "calm heid" is called for. McMahon was just that in the frenetic, stormy atmosphere of Ibrox that day.

He "took the dog for a walk" (as the saying went) to distant parts of the ground with the ball at his feet, to allow the defence a breather, riding tough tackles, shielding the ball from the opposition, but most importantly of all, holding on to the ball, as the minutes ticked away until, to the relief of all concerned in green and white vertical jerseys and the green-bedecked support who were singing "ditties and dirges which were lost in the wind", Mr Walker pointed to the pavilion. *The Glasgow Herald,* looking for crumbs of comfort says that Queen's finished "the fresher team".

"Man In The Know" in *The Glasgow Observer* the following week is in a surprisingly misanthropic, curmudgeonly, grumpy and paranoid mood after what was, after all, a great victory for the club and its supporters. "The International seemed to have taken all the interest out of this tie. The attendance was very poor and would have been poorer but for the large following of the Amateurs. The Celtic had very few friends and the behaviour of the crowd was little better than that howling mob which showed its hatred of the Celtic in the Anglo-Scots trial a few seasons back. But Celtic were not put off. As for McMahon and McArthur, it would take something stronger than an earthquake to put them off their game!"

Sandy McMahon thus, defying the elements and the constant barracking from the Queen's Park supporters, had his third Scottish Cup medal. He had scored in all three Cup Finals in which Celtic had won the Cup, and he and Johnny Campbell were the only Celtic players to have taken part in all their three Scottish Cup triumphs. Given the esteem in which the Scottish Cup was held then (and still is, thank heaven), there is little wonder that "the Duke" was still lauded to the skies.

It was of course the end of an era. It was a new century, and if Queen's Park had been under any illusions about whether profes-sionalism was here to stay or not, such ideas were clearly blown away in the winds of Ibrox that April day. Queen's Park may have still in 1900 have been the record winners of the Scottish Cup with 10 vic-tories, but they never again played in a Scottish Cup Final. Celtic had now won the trophy three times, as had Rangers and sooner or later, one of the clubs would overtake their number of victories. Celtic indeed did that in 1925.

Queen's Park might have changed this had they decided to turn professional, but laudably, they remain amateur to this day, living up to their Latin motto of "ludere causa ludendi" – to play for the sake of playing. Now looked upon as a quaint anachronism, they have at least stayed faithful to their ideals. One often asks the question of whether Celtic still continues to live up to their lofty ideals of providing soup kitchens for poor children! They probably do to a certain extent, but not nearly as much as most of their supporters would like.

But on 14 April 1900 for the very professional Sandy McMahon, there was the satisfaction of being acknowledged by Press and supporters as the best man on the field. Sadly there was no "Man of The Match" award in these days, but everyone knew how good McMahon had been. The reception was once again held at the Alexandra Hotel in Bath Street. John H. McLaughlin was now the President of the SFA, and he talked about the "good relationship" between Celtic and Queen's Park. For Celtic, John Glass graciously accepted the Scottish Cup, but there were a few sour notes when Mr Kirkwood the Vice-President of the SFA said that, "he could not say that they (Celtic) had played a great game that afternoon," (because of the weather, one presumes) and then Mr Lawrence of Dumbarton while proposing the health of the referee made the odd comment that he thought that referees had too much power!

Scottish Cup winners again! McMahon is in the
centre at the back of this picture

On the Monday after that, Celtic beat Rangers 2–1 in the Inter City League en route to winning, for what it was worth, the tournament, ("Man In The Know" is upset and embarrassed at the way that John Hodge "attacked" Matthew Dickie of Rangers), but Celtic were less successful in the Glasgow Charity Cup. The semi-final against Queen's Park at Cathkin on 8 May was bizarre when the referee, the well-respected Mr Murray of Stenhousemuir by error blew for time a full nine minutes early with Celtic beating Queen's Park 3–2. The crowd, feeling that they were being cheated, invaded the field, and even when the error was publicly acknowledged, refused to leave the playing area even when asked to do so, in order to facilitate the playing of the remaining nine minutes. There may have been a little more to it than that, for Celtic's goalkeeper Dan McArthur had been badly injured, and some of the fans possibly did not take kindly to the injuries inflicted on their popular goalkeeper.

It of course suited everyone (not least the Glasgow charities who would benefit) to have a replay, and this was exactly what happened on the following night. This time it was 6–1 for Celtic without McArthur ("if I'd been at Megarsfontein, (in South Africa) they'd have sent me home," he said in a comment about his many injuries) but with McMahon who did not himself score, but "supplied the ammunition" (as the South African War was still going strong, there was no lack of military metaphors in the newspapers) for the rest of the forwards to run riot.

The final on 12 May was a massive disappointment. It was a fine day with a pleasant breeze, but McMahon did not look fit, and with Orr and McArthur out, the 12,000 at Hampden saw Celtic outclassed by Rangers who won 5–1. *The Glasgow Herald* states categorically, "The game was but a short time in progress when it became manifest that the Celts were manifestly below form, mainly due to the numbers of cripples in their ranks," The teams were;

Celtic: Docherty; Storrier and Battles; Russell, Marshall and King; Hodge, Gilhooly, Campbell, McMahon and Bell.

Rangers: Dickie; N. Smith and Drummond; Gibson, Neil and Robertson; Campbell, McPherson, Hamilton, Miller and A. Smith

Referee: T. Robertson, Queen's Park.

It was a sad end to what had been an interesting season, which had at least landed the Scottish Cup. Celtic now three times winners had overtaken quite a few clubs, but Queen's Park's tally of ten seemed a long way away. McMahon, more and more plagued with injury, was still a class act and the adulation in which he was held seemed to know no bounds. Not many people possessed three Scottish Cup medals – but he and his friend Johnny Campbell did!

In some ways 1900 represented the zenith of Sandy McMahon. His career was far from over – indeed he had still some more International appearances to come – but from now on, there would be a slow and gradual decline. The team too seemed to have reached its peak. It would never again win the Scottish Cup or the Scottish League in McMahon's time, and it was gradually becoming clear to Maley that some wholesale changes would soon be required. The fact that Rangers had won the Scottish League Championship with such apparent ease for the last two years was a definite cause for concern. Maley was of course a close personal friend of William Wilton, his counterpart at Ibrox, but felt that Celtic should always be the top team. Some young blood was being looked for, and in particular stories kept reaching Maley's ears about a young lad called Quinn who played for Smithston Albion out Croy way.

11.

1900–1901 – DISAPPOINTMENTS

Season 1900–01 was generally reckoned to be one of Celtic's poorer seasons so far. Yet there were good things that happened as well. McMahon, although now past his 30th birthday, played consistently well all through the season, and round about the New Year there emerged the man who would, in time, become McMahon's successor in both the goalscoring and popularity stakes, Jimmy Quinn. And the team did play in the Scottish Cup Final, the one that was reckoned in 1901 to have been the best Scottish Cup Final ever. But Celtic lost it, and McMahon did not win his third successive Scottish Cup medal.

But to begin at the beginning, Celtic began with a draw with Partick Thistle followed by a run of victories, but once again, the initiative was lost to Rangers when they went out of the Glasgow Cup to them in the first round in September. Surprise! Surprise! The game needed a replay! The first match at Celtic Park on 15 September, played in heatwave conditions before 30,000 fans saw Celtic ahead at half-time through a great Sandy McMahon header. Then with only fifteen minutes to go, Davie Storrier scored again for Celtic and things looked good, until the Celtic defence went mad and conceded three goals, so that in the last minute Rangers looked as if they were going to win 3–2 until Johnny Hodge equalized with referee Tom Robertson of Queen's Park "pursing his lips" to blow the final whistle.

Naturally, the unusual circumstances of this draw led to the usual rumours, "which are hardly worth refuting," according to *The Glasgow Herald*. In truth this one was rather more suspicious than some others. The role of the Press is interesting in its reporting of all these drawn games. Clearly, without running serious risk of libel writs, a newspaper cannot say that a game has been fixed unless it has definite proof. But it cannot really ignore the speculation either, and the device that it uses is what the ancient Romans would call "praeteritio" i.e. pretending to say that one is NOT going to say something, but saying it so vigorously and so repetitively that the matter becomes a major issue and topic for discussion. So by denying the possibility that games can be fixed, it is effectively saying that they could be, and perhaps were! In Ancient Rome, Cicero would often say, "I am not going to say anything to the effect that my opponent is a coward…", but that very statement conjures up the possibility!

Having said that, "fixing" a football match is no easy matter, and the amount of people who would have to be involved immediately raises the possibility of someone squealing to the Press or even the police. Yet it has undeniably happened in places like Italy in recent years, and one would have to be incredibly naïve to say that it has never happened in Scotland. It remains an open question, and the clubs are at least guilty of a certain lack of tact in allowing it to happen as often as it did, particularly as there always seemed to be a pronounced reluctance of the authorities to allow extra-time.

Be that as it may, another 30,000 turned up at Ibrox to see the replay. They saw virtually a carbon copy of last week, except Rangers won 4–3 with McMahon at the death failing, "by a matter of inches," to get the equalizer which would have earned another replay and caused even more tongues to wag. The reality however was that for the third year in a row Rangers had put Celtic out of the Glasgow Cup, a competition last won by Celtic in season 1895–96. This was painful for McMahon.

Jim Scullion's magnificent collage of the early Celts.
Sandy McMahon in top left corner.

Things went better for a spell in the Scottish League. On a rainy day at Celtic Park in early October, with the attendance about one third what might have been expected on a better day, McMahon inspired Celtic to a narrow but deserved 2–1 win over Rangers, and then a week later against Queen's Park, who had now swallowed their pride and joined the Scottish League, he scored one of his marvellous goals with *The Glasgow Observer* telling everyone that, "the Duke wriggled and screwed through the Spiders' defence to score," the first goal in a 2–0 win. They would hardly be likely to use such imagery today.

McMahon's brilliance however is glossed over, however, in *The Glasgow Herald* which prefers to concentrate on the bad weather and how well the Conservatives were doing in the 1900 General Election, which became known to history as the "khaki" election because of the amount of soldiers voting while on leave from South Africa. (The 1918 and 1945 elections would have a similar nickname.) The

Conservatives, under Lord Salisbury, would win a ringing endorsement of the war policy with jingoism and war fever being the order of the day. This result hardly helped the cause of Irish Home Rule, but the Labour Party made a modest start by winning two seats.

Celtic, while generally playing well enough, had a few stumbles towards the end of the year. There was a defeat at Rugby Park, Kilmarnock and although a 1–1 draw at the new Dens Park, Dundee in mid-November was acceptable, losing to the same opponents at Celtic Park on 22 December was less so. Celtic paid the penalty, according to the Press, of persisting with a short-passing game on a heavy ground, and this defeat meant that the initiative in the Scottish League passed back to Rangers who could now more or less win the Championship if they beat Celtic at Ibrox on New Year's Day.

They did so, but Celtic were convinced that one of Rangers two goals was a handball. But there was some consolation for Celtic fans, for there was little doubt that Celtic's only goal was the best of the three, coming as it did from the old combination of McMahon and Campbell who one-two-ed the ball to each other before the Duke hammered home. It was late in the game by then, and hard as Celtic tried, they just could not get the equalizing goal, which would just have kept them in the Championship. As it was, Celtic needed to win their last game and hope that Rangers would lose all three of their games. That did not happen.

But other things did. A young man called Jimmy Quinn had joined the club as left-winger, and McMahon took him under his wing, for he saw quality there. Rab Finlay the existing left-winger had been poor and ineffective of late, and on a training trip to the Lorne Hotel, Rothesay, McMahon was seen helping the gauche and nervous young man, who had seldom in his life been out of the mining village of Croy, to adapt to what was expected from a Celtic forward. The trip to Rothesay was probably the first time that young Jimmy had ever seen the sea!

The trip to Rothesay was in preparation for what was to be called "the Cup tie of the Century" – a somewhat pompous title (but newspapers could be as silly in 1901 as they can be today) but bestowed on the meeting at Celtic Park in the Scottish Cup between Celtic and Rangers. Celtic took this game so seriously that they kept their players at Rothesay until the Saturday morning before travelling up to Glasgow.

Once again, the crowd on 12 January 1901 was in excess of 30,000 and a draw was confidently predicted. But if that was what was intended, Celtic did not co-operate and beat Rangers 1–0 in a game that was hard and tough on a hard pitch that was less than totally conducive to good football. Willie McOustra scored for Celtic in the first half, and Celtic remained on top until the 75th minute when goalkeeper Dan McArthur had to be carried off following an accidental kick in the head by a Rangers forward. John Divers had to be deployed in the goal and the last 15 minutes were likened, topically, to the siege of Mafeking as Rangers rained shots on the Celtic goal.

But captain Willie Russell had everyone well organised and McMahon proved his versatility by playing as a double centre-half with the young Willie Loney (another man in whom McMahon detected potential) and denying the eager Rangers forwards by compelling them to shoot from a distance. Nevertheless, full-time came as a blessed relief for Celtic, who had now for three years in a row removed Rangers from the Scottish Cup.

Young Jimmy Quinn was given his Scottish League debut in what was Celtic's last League game of the season against St Mirren the following Saturday. It was a tough game. Celtic had been involved in a few rough houses with St Mirren before, particularly in Paisley, but this time the trouble came from the fans rather than the players. It all started, ironically enough, with Sandy McMahon, the gentlest of men who was involved in an accidental collision with Brandon, St Mirren's right-back. The referee Mr McPherson of Cowlairs saw nothing untoward but some of the St Mirren supporters thought otherwise when Brandon was forced to retire. They invaded the field and someone landed a punch on John Glass, Celtic's President who was acting as linesman.

Further trouble came later in the second half, but that should not disguise the fact that Celtic won a good game 4–3, and the Celtic left wing combination of Sandy McMahon and Jimmy Quinn earned acclamation and applause for what they had done. It would be some time before the baton of Celtic's goal scoring hero was to be passed from Sandy to Jimmy, but it was already seen that the earnest young Quinn was learning from Sandy. The young maestro was earning his spurs by paying attention to the old one. It was almost like the apostolic succession.

This did not however quell or inhibit, in any way, Sandy's sense of humour. A story is told of how on one of their trips to Rothesay, a trick was played on young Jimmy by Sandy. They were sleeping four to a room, and early in the day, Jimmy had lost at cards and being a young player did not have enough loose change on him to pay the small debt that he owed. Sandy had said, "That's OK, Jimmy. Never mind about that," but then in bed that night, pretending to talk in his sleep, he kept saying, "That young Quinn, he wauldna pay for anything. He'll never put his hand in his pooch tae pay his gambling debts, so whit chance is there o' him ever buying a drink?" The other inhabitants of the room Willie McOustra and Johnny Campbell were of course in on the trick, and everyone burst out laughing when the shame faced Jimmy Quinn duly paid his debts in the morning, having borrowed money from others!

But the main talking point throughout the world at this point was the illness and eventual death of Queen Victoria on 22 January 1901. She had been Queen since 1837, but McMahon and others no doubt would have been baffled at the depth of the emotion on her death. Tributes to her, even from Celtic and Irish sources, were lavish and extravagant, and ignored the bad points like her self-imposed ten year sulk when her husband died, her general prickliness with Prime Ministers whom she did not like, and poignantly for Celtic fans, the apparent total indifference to the travails of Ireland. The Potato Famine had happened when she was Queen, and scarcely a finger had been lifted to alleviate the suffering. It was all the more surprising that Willie Maley joined in the general outpouring of grief, but then again his father had been a soldier in the British Army.

Quite a few people were unhappy when the SFA cancelled all football on 2 February. (One recalls how all football had to be postponed almost 100 years later in 1997 for the death of Diana, Princess of Wales – another decision bereft of any consultation with the fans, and frankly, out of touch with the prevailing mood, at least in Scotland.) Ironically and illogically in 1901, football had been allowed on the previous Saturday, 26 January, when the Queen was still lying in state, but the referee for Celtic versus Kilmarnock in the Scottish Cup failed to appear (he apparently misread Maley's telegram, thinking that it said "match off" rather than "match on") and a friendly had to be played. This was a shame, for McMahon headed a fine goal in that game.

The funeral obsequies over and the new King Edward VII now proclaimed King and on the throne, football resumed in February and McMahon had a good month. Kilmarnock were put to the sword 6–0 in the delayed Cup tie with McMahon again heading a goal from a free-kick. This set Celtic up with a very difficult away tie at Dens Park, Dundee on 16 February 1910. 16,000 attended (a huge crowd for Dundee, even for their fine new stadium, and swelled from early in the morning that Saturday with several trainloads from Glasgow to augment Celtic's already large local support).

Dundee had erected a temporary stand at the west end of the ground, (what was later called the Provost Road end of the ground) and after several fairly loud creaks, a massive crack was heard and the stand collapsed, fortunately without causing any serious injury. The matter was treated with a certain amount of levity and ridicule, but *The Glasgow Herald* intones portentously that "lessons should be learned", but sadly no one seemed to pay any attention, and a year later, a far more serious disaster occurred at Ibrox. Another one would occur at a cricket match in 1903 in Perth!

Celtic scored about the halfway point of the first half through Rab Finlay, but then Dundee laid siege to the Celtic goal where Dan McArthur's deputy, young Willie Donnelly played the game of his life. The young Irishman ignored distractions like the collapsing stand, encroachment on the pitch by spectators and general mayhem to deny the Dundee forwards time and time again. He was aided by sterling play from Barney Battles and young Willie Loney, but the toast of Glasgow and Dundee's large Irish communities that night was the previously unknown Willie Donnelly.

This was indeed young Donnelly's finest hour – indeed it was his brief moment of glory – and Celtic were now in the semi-final of the Scottish Cup, but for McMahon there was a pleasant surprise the following week when he was invited to play for Scotland against Ireland at Celtic Park. It was his fifth full International cap and his first since 1894. He made the most of it, scoring four goals but even then he could not be outdone for Bob Hamilton of Rangers scored five as the hapless Irishmen were thumped 11–0.

One might have thought that four goals would have been enough to earn him another game for Scotland that season, and maybe even a trip to the Crystal Palace to play in the "big" game against England, but that was not the way that things worked then. His friend Johnny Campbell was more fortunate however, playing well for Scotland in the 2–2 draw against Wales on March 30, and then again in the 1–1 draw at the Crystal Palace.

One of the stranger of Sandy's souvenirs is this teapot. Articles like this were often given after an International appearance.

The week before that however saw a very important win. This was the Scottish Cup semi-final game against St Mirren at Celtic Park. Memories of the rough game in Paisley a couple of months previously were high in Sandy's consciousness, and he noted that he again had young Quinn as a left wing partner. This partnership served Celtic well, and Celtic went through 1–0 to the delight of the 18,000 crowd. Johnny Campbell scored on the half hour mark and in spite of losing Bob Davidson for a spell with a nasty head knock (he recovered but had no recollection of what happened), Celtic stayed on top. By this time Dan McArthur had recovered from injury to play in the Celtic goal, and he too had a good game.

McArthur would be a lot less successful in the Scottish Cup Final on 6 April. The Scottish Cup Final of 1901 was hailed in the Press as being the best in the 28-year history of the trophy, and certainly from a neutral point of view, it seems to have been quite a spectacle, but a 4–3 score line is always a painful one for the losers. (90 years later the 1991 Scottish Cup Final ended a 4–3 win for Motherwell over Dundee United. It was similarly lauded as one of the best Cup Finals of them all – but not in Dundee!) In this case the finger of blame has to be pointed at a man who was previously looked upon as a great hero – the diminutive, courageous and agile goalkeeper Dan McArthur.

Celtic were aware that if they won this game, they would join Queen's Park and Vale of Leven in having won the Scottish Cup three years in a row – the same three years that Rangers had now won the Scottish League in successive seasons – and that a fourth Cup win in total would put them second only to Queen's Park in the list of winners. Hearts, their opponents, had won the Cup in 1891 and 1896 and felt that a victory in 1901 would make it a quinquennial event for them! (As it turned out they would win it again in 1906!) They had defeated Hibs in a replayed semi-final (the first drawn game looked upon with the same sort of suspicion by the Edinburgh cynics as the Glasgow draws were!) and had many fine players notably Charlie Thomson and the man who, arguably, would become the best individual player of the Edwardian era, Bobby Walker, although the lovers of Jimmy McMenemy would dispute that.

The game was at Ibrox. Once again the high admission charges deterred quite a few Celtic fans, and a disappointing crowd of 17,000 turned up to pay their shillings. Football special trains from Edinburgh meant that Hearts fans were there in great numbers, well dressed and looking considerably more prosperous than the Celtic fans who turned up at the gate, hoping perhaps for the opportunity to scale the fence, but if not, to listen to the shouts of the crowd and to gain admission for the last ten minutes when the exit gates were opened. In fact, the last ten minutes were very exciting, but heart breaking as well for Celtic supporters.

Hearts fans probably outnumbered the Celtic following as the teams ran out;

Celtic: McArthur; Davidson and Battles; Russell, Loney and Orr; McOustra, Divers, Campbell, McMahon and Quinn.

Hearts: Phillip; Allan and Baird; Key, Buick and Hogg; Porteous, Thomson, Walker, Houston and Bell.

Referee: Mr Jackson, Rangers.

Celtic are criticised in *The Glasgow Herald* for their "total disregard" of the necessity for long passes and concentrating instead on their short passing. This seems unfair, but the pitch was heavy after a great deal of recent rain and maybe a more direct approach might have produced better results. But one could hardly complain of the lack of entertainment. *The Daily Record and Mail* describes the pitch as "sloppy" (a misprint for "slippy", perhaps?) and well sanded, but is full of praise for Celtic's approach and sportsmanship.

Poor Dan McArthur! He had a hand, as it were, in all four Hearts goals. He could not stop Walker's shot for the first in spite of getting a hand to it. Then after McOustra had equalized with a header McArthur surprised his own right-back Bob Davidson with a throw out, which led to a shot from Hearts left-winger Bell. Dan should have clutched the ball but opted to punch it out. Bell banged the ball back in, he got a lucky deflection off Davidson (the goal is sometimes given as an own goal) and Celtic went in at half-time 1–2 down.

This was bad, but hardly disastrous. Celtic now had the benefit of the wind. The key goal for Hearts, however, came in the 60th minute, when Thomson scored for Hearts with a shot that McArthur could only parry and Thomson got a second chance. Celtic were now 1–3 down, and in Maley's words in *The Story of The Celtic*, chances were "the reverse of bright". But at this point McMahon stepped in. He realised that the close passing game was not working, so he began to use his wingers, McOustra and Quinn, feeding them long balls and allowing them to rampage down their wings. These tactics had an effect when Jimmy Quinn beat six or seven Hearts men and won a free kick. Barney Battles took the kick and Jimmy Quinn was there to put Celtic back in the game. Willie McOustra, according to some sources got a touch, but Jimmy is usually credited with the goal.

The Ibrox crowd now saw Celtic, inspired by McMahon, charge forward to save the game. Well inside the last ten minutes, Celtic won a corner on the left after another charge down the wing by Quinn. The youngster took the corner himself, found the head of McMahon, and Sandy continued his tradition of heading a goal in Scottish Cup Finals. The tie was now squared – or so it seemed.

The Celtic faction of the crowd now cheered Sandy to the echo thinking that he had saved the day. The exit gates now opened and the crowd began to leave, thinking that Celtic had deservedly earned a draw, with the cynics in loud voice telling everyone that, "I kent it wad be a draw!" "That's anither big gate next week". The crowd still inside the ground however had now changed character. Not only were the Celtic fans upbeat and singing their songs and talking about the old maestro Sandy McMahon, but they were now augmented in number by the dispossessed who had been waiting outside for the exit gates to open. In rushed the ragamuffins, the shoeless, the ill fed and the ill clad – but they now had something to cheer about! Their team had fought back; it appeared, to earn a draw and a replay!

One can only imagine the mortification of the Celtic community when, in the dying seconds of the game, Bobby Walker shot and Dan McArthur once again was unable to clutch the ball, and then Mark Bell, scarcely able to believe his luck, ran in and scored. Mr Jackson then immediately signalled for time, leaving a devastated Celtic team on the ground in various states of distress, none more so than the veteran Sandy McMahon. Nevertheless he went out of his way to congratulate the Hearts men, and more importantly to console those on his own side who were even more upset than he was, namely the

young Quinn and the distraught Dan McArthur. Dan had served
Celtic so well over the last several years, but he had now quite clearly
lost the Scottish Cup for Celtic.

Celtic put a brave face on things. They were magnanimous and
sporting in defeat, although John H. McLaughlin complained at the
Dinner after the game of the "paucity of attendance" and that the
price was possibly too much for the fans, even though it was a Cup
Final. But the Dinner did not last too long for Hearts had to catch
the 8.25 pm train back to Edinburgh where they received a great
reception. McMahon and the Celts on the other hand went home
quietly to lick their wounds. It was a sad, but dignified occasion for
the Celts.

The Glasgow Observer says there is no use, "crying over spilt
milk which only makes it more watery," and quixotically describes
the defeat as, "deserved yet undeserved". Two tactical mistakes very
made – one was the insistence on the short passing game, and the
other was for not settling for a draw after McMahon had equalized
late in the game. It laments the absence of the now retired Dan Doyle
"Dan would never have allowed the Hearts to get the leading (sic)
goal after McMahon had put his side level". The goal was left totally
unprotected by poor full-back play, it claims.

Apart from poor Dan McArthur, Willie Orr gets a pasting, and
we are given the extra piece of gossip that Davie Storrier (who didn't
play in the Final) has now been suspended and put on the open to
transfer list. He has been, "a lame duck for the Celts for a long time,"
and has been unable to keep himself fit. Nevertheless, Davie might
have made a difference if he had been able to play in the Scottish Cup
Final. Perhaps significantly, Sandy McMahon is not mentioned apart
from his goal – something that makes one, perhaps, think that the
1901 Scottish Cup Final was not his best game. Or perhaps, Sandy
having a good game was simply taken for granted!

Celtic's season now fizzled out. They might have won the

Inter-City League (as the old Glasgow League was now called with the inclusion of the Edinburgh teams) but had too many bad results. Then the Glasgow Charity Cup, played this year at the Exhibition Grounds (specially constructed for the Glasgow Exhibition of 1901) at Gilmorehill, saw further heartbreak. Sandy struggled with an injury to his knee, sustained in the semi-final and aggravated in the first game of the Final against Third Lanark. He was out of the replay, and it was perhaps no coincidence that the team folded to a miserable 0–3 defeat from Third Lanark, aided by a few more goalkeeping howlers by the once very reliable Dan McArthur.

An unpleasant development in Glasgow's football history must be recorded in the context of the game against Rangers at Gilmorehill in the first round. The first game was a draw – no real surprise there – but the replay the following night, which attracted fewer spectators saw Celtic win 1–0 with a goal from Johnny Hodge. But some of the Rangers fans did not take kindly to this. Cries of "Papist!" "Catholic" and "Fenian" were heard, emanating from those who possibly did not know what the words meant! Then both McMahon and Campbell were spat upon as they left the field. Sandy was "fain to retaliate" (a man of his size and physique would have made an awful mess of some of these undernourished, illiterate, ignorant youths) but was persuaded not to, and content himself with a remark that Celtic had won 1–0. "It was as well that there were no members of the Irish community in the vicinity of the incident," the Press adds sagely.

Religious prejudice against Celtic was by no means uncommon in the 1890s and early 20th century, but it was a shame, says *The Glasgow Observer* to see members of the Rangers persuasion involved. The Rangers team and the Celtic team had always got along very well, but one of the consequences of Rangers success (they had now won the Scottish League for three times in a row) was that they attracted the sort of following who embarrassed them and who, "had no place in any sporting arena and who simply shamed their club and its establishment".

This did not however hide that fact that 1900–01 ended a trophyless season for Celtic – something that the fans always find hard to take. In that era Celtic usually ended up winning something. Dan McArthur himself accepted blame and said, "it was the unluckiest year I have ever had in football". McMahon felt likewise, but he was also aware that now he was 30, the clock was beginning to tick rather loudly on his footballing career at this high level. Yet, give or take the odd twinge from his knee, he was fit enough, and Maley and the Celtic fans seemed in no doubt that he was still the main man at the Celtic club. Any revival next year would depend to a very large extent on Sandy McMahon.

12.

1901–1902 – INJUSTICE

Season 1901–02 was another difficult one for Celtic and their followers. McMahon was out for a spell at the beginning and at the end of the season, and in the middle of the season there was one astonishing miscarriage of justice, which did nothing at all to dispel the feelings of paranoia and persecution which, even at this early stage of history, pervaded Celtic circles. It was beginning to be clear however that some of Celtic's old guard, McMahon included, would need to make way for younger players if there was to be any progress made. Yet 1901–02 was a remarkable and unique, if ultimately rather disappointing, season with a final sting in the tail.

This season, in addition to the other competitions, there was the Glasgow Exhibition Trophy. The Glasgow Exhibition, much trumpeted in *The Glasgow Herald* and elsewhere, was a celebration of Glasgow, now commonly regarded as "the second city of the Empire". It was also called "the engine room of the British Empire" or the "boiler house", and Glasgow had grown at a phenomenal rate over the past century. There had however been a cost.

There was a certain amount of criticism from ever-growing radical sources that the glorification of Glasgow tended to ignore the appalling problems of poverty and health, which affected large swathes of the city, not least among the Celtic-supporting Irish. An astonishing amount of young men, for example, who had tried to enlist for the Boer War were prevented from doing so because they did not reach the basic standards of health and fitness! There had been in Glasgow in 1900 an outbreak of an illness with all the appearances of medieval plague! Nevertheless, it was argued that this Glasgow Exhibition, attended by royalty and dignitaries, would have a great effect in making Glaswegians feel good about themselves. The cynics must also record however that it made money!

In the first of these Glasgow Exhibition Trophy games, Sandy McMahon sustained a bad injury to his knee. Both knees had been giving him trouble for some time, and the slightest knock was liable to make things worse. Celtic won this game at the Exhibition Centre at Gilmorehill on 22 August, beating Hibs 1–0, but McMahon was seen to limp off at the end, and by the time that he returned in mid-September, the Exhibition Trophy had been lost to Rangers.

Rangers also won the Glasgow Cup but in circumstances which seem bereft of logic or common sense. Very impressively Celtic, with McMahon back in form and scoring two goals, had beaten Third Lanark 5–1 to reach the Glasgow Cup Final to be played against Rangers at Ibrox on 26 October. The two clubs agreed, privately, to toss a coin for venue. Rangers won. At a meeting of the Glasgow FA, both Celtic and Rangers therefore voted for Ibrox as distinct from the neutral Hampden, a stadium, which was now in a state of some disrepair and already plans were in place to build a new one.

The game was a good one before 40,000 people (which Hampden in 1901 could never have come close to containing) on a fine autumn afternoon. All the goals in the 2–2 draw came in the first half, and although Celtic felt that their defence let them down, everyone agreed that the forward line of McOustra, Livingstone, Campbell, McMahon and Quinn was "a fine combination". As the crowd dispersed, there were the usual cries about "fix" after a draw, but everyone agreed that it had been great entertainment and everyone looked forward to the replay to be held at a venue and place to be decided by the Glasgow FA on Monday night.

The meeting was held with Mr J. Livingston of Third Lanark in the chair. Celtic felt not unnaturally that Celtic Park should be the venue for the replay, but Rangers argued that, Celtic having agreed to toss a coin for the first game, the ground chosen should also be used for the replay. A long discussion took place, and eventually Rangers won by a single vote. Those who suggested Hampden or Cathkin or even the Exhibition Centre at Gilmorehill, (all of which would have been possible, but less desirable venues) were defeated by the undeniable fact that each of these grounds would struggle to hold the expected massive crowd, and the argument was that Ibrox had been chosen, so Ibrox should remain the venue. Mr O'Hara of Celtic then said that Celtic were withdrawing from the competition. The Glasgow FA then agreed that the Cup and the medals would be handed over to Rangers.

There are at least two amazing things about this story. One was that it was surely logical that Celtic Park should be used for the replay. This was of course what happened in the Scottish Cup and in other rounds of the Glasgow Cup, and Celtic are clearly at fault for not insisting on that at the time that they tossed the coin for choice of venue. But the other bizarre thing is that Celtic should "take the huff" in a way that punished themselves and their supporters and did themselves out of another 40,000 gate! So the cries that football was all about making money, were not totally justified! Pride, even misguided pride, seemed to come into it as well!

Be that as it may, Celtic had now lost yet another Glasgow Cup to Rangers. There is a certain indication that not all players, McMahon included perhaps, were 100% behind the kneejerk and rather emotional decision to withdraw from the competition, when a more rational and thought-out analysis of the situation would have indicated that playing the game, even at Ibrox and perhaps under protest, might have been better. As it was, the common perception in Glasgow was that Celtic had "run away" from Rangers, and one does recall the events of spring 1968 when the circumstances were reversed. Rangers withdrew from the same Glasgow Cup, alleging fixture congestion, but the perceived Glasgow wisdom was of "cowardice".

Certainly for a spell, Celtic's League form suffered with defeats to Hearts, Queen's Park and a miserable draw with Hibs – a run of form that would be significant in the loss of the Scottish League – but Rangers too had dropped points, and a fine 4–1 win for Celtic over Kilmarnock at Parkhead on an awful day between Christmas and the New Year meant that Celtic supporters looked forward to the New Year's Day fixture against Rangers with a great deal of relish.

There was a clear chance that Celtic could win the Scottish League that day. Celtic had played 17 games and had 26 points whereas Rangers had 20 points for their 14 games. As there were only two points for a win and as this was Celtic's last League fixture, it was clear that a win would give them 28 points and Rangers could then only reach 26. A draw would keep everything open, but a win for Rangers would certainly give them the advantage for their fourth successive League championship. (There would be 77 years later an astonishingly similar situation in the run-up to Celtic's last game on 21 May 1979 against Rangers at Celtic Park. Sadly, 1902 did not have such a happy outcome).

Although Celtic had had a few bad performances of late, and indeed should have tied up the League Championship long before it came to their last game, their supporters enjoyed their New Year revelling and approached Celtic Park that fine day of Wednesday 1 January 1902 with a confident spring in their step.

This game is so significant in the life of Sandy McMahon, and has astonishingly been so little dealt with by Celtic historians that it is worth looking at in a degree of detail. The normally reliable and informative *Glasgow Herald* disappoints on this occasion, not going into any details other than a few remarks about the game being full of fouls and the players not respecting the referee's decisions. It prefers to talk about the Second Test Match in Australia – it was indeed an interesting day's play in which 25 wickets went down!

The Evening Times talks of a huge crowd – at least 30,000 – and how the gates were opened at 12.00 for a 2.00 pm start, but even before then, "thousands were outside clamouring for admission". Very soon the ground was filled and the atmosphere was tense. It was the sort of game that players like McMahon looked forward to. He knew that, however friendly he was with Rangers players (with whom he played in Scotland games and charity matches), today's game would be played in grim earnest.

He did not know quite how grim. The referee was a tall man from Cowdenbeath called Mr Nisbet. Celtic had had him before, although not very often, and there had been no bother at the games in which he officiated. Someone, however, thought that there might have been a smell of drink on his breath before the start of the game, but that was dismissed as simply daft. Referees, even on New Year's Day, did not drink before a game. Did they?

New Year had of course been celebrated with gusto the night before, and quite a few of the spectators looked as if they had not seen their beds overnight. But the atmosphere, although tense, was not particularly nasty. The game being at Parkhead, Celtic fans predominated, singing their songs about Ireland and the "wearing o' the green", but showing a certain tolerance to those of the other persuasion. Crowd segregation did not happen in 1902, and handshakes and drinks out of each other's bottles to celebrate the arrival of 1902, in which the new King would be crowned and hopefully that South African war could at last be finished, were commonplace in the crowd. Alcohol was, of course, allowed at football grounds until the 1980s.

It would be wrong to suggest that everyone was full of good cheer and happiness, but most were. In any case the police were on hand in strength to make sure that things did not get out of hand, for alcohol, everyone knew, could have its bad effect as well on behaviour. But it is important to realise, in view of what happened in this game, that the poisonous atmosphere of hatred that would later prevail at subsequent Celtic v Rangers games, was not present here. Indeed a large percentage of the crowd would happily describe themselves as "football fans" and would decide on a whim who they were going to support, and even then would appreciate the good play of the opposition as well. There was less of the fierce, uncompromising commitment to one side or other that one gets today.

After two minutes Barney Battles tackled John Wilkie who had to be assisted off the field. Then without giving names, "One player attempted to lay out another," according to *The Evening Times*, and after about 20 minutes, the referee stopped the game, called together all 22 players and "lectured everyone for two minutes". In spite of that, fierce tackles kept going in, but there was some fine football as well, not least when Sandy McMahon converted a free-kick by heading cleverly ("a fine angular header" according to "Bedouin" of the *Daily Record and Mail)* past Matt Dickie in the Rangers goal.

It was a great moment for the Celtic fans, but the game continued with fierce tackles and eccentric and histrionic refereeing from Mr Nisbet who pointed theatrically, threatened players with ordering off (pointing clearly in the direction of the pavilion to several players, particularly the innocent Celtic right-winger John Hodge). But the game, although rough, was still under control until Rangers equalizer, which was not so much controversial as sheer wrong.

Virtually on the stroke of half-time, Rangers were awarded a free kick on the edge of the penalty area. In 1902 there was no distinction between a direct free-kick and an indirect free-kick, for all free-kicks were indirect. One simply could not score a goal from a free-kick unless someone else got a touch on the ball. So when Nick Smith took the free-kick and the well-drilled Celtic defence stood back to allow the ball to sail innocuously and almost apologetically into the net, the crowd expected a goal-kick to be awarded to Celtic. But there was more to it than that, for goalkeeper Rab McFarlane, even if he had wanted to touch the ball, was clearly baulked from doing so by Bob Hamilton of Rangers, and so the correct decision should have been a free-kick to Celtic.

For a brief spell, Mr Nisbet gave no decision, then shook all of Parkhead to its core by awarding a goal to Rangers. Even the Rangers players gawped in astonishment, the crowd were beside themselves in anger and bewilderment at such an outrageously bad decision, and Celtic players, even mild mannered men like Sandy McMahon and Johnny Campbell surrounded Mr Nisbet with someone taking hold of his jacket. *The Daily Record and Mail* says that, "Mr Nisbet is of commanding height. He wrenched himself free at the expense of torn cloth". Manhandling the referee was of course out of order, but no action was taken against whoever did it.

Mr Nisbet then signalled for half-time, and left the field to a chorus of boos and catcalls with several members of the Directors of both teams getting together over their half-time cup of tea in the Celtic Park pavilion and wondering if Mr Nisbet was fit enough to be in charge of such an important fixture. Outside, the crowd were in stunned and unnatural silence at what had just happened. No player of either side was within a yard of the ball as it entered the net. It was not so much that the referee had made a mistake; it was that he didn't seem to know the rules of the game!

And worse was to come, particularly for Sandy McMahon. Rangers scored within a couple of minutes of the restart, but there were at least two things wrong with the "goal". Rab McFarlane was once again impeded by a Rangers forward, the ball was quite clearly handled by John Campbell of Rangers, and there was a certain amount of doubt about whether the ball had actually crossed the line or not before it was hooked clear. Once again, the ground erupted in a mixture of rage and consternation, and the Celtic players once more surrounded the referee while the Rangers players stood back in a little embarrassment.

The Daily Record and Mail now says, "McMahon, in turning, tripped the referee who partially stumbled. In the belief that the incident was intentional, Mr Nisbet promptly ordered off the veteran Celt. McMahon seemed more than amazed and the club supporters made the air ring with their shouts. The Celtic team did not relish the unexpected ordering off of one of the fairest of players".

Celtic almost refused to play. George Livingstone, reputed to be a Rangers supporter in the past but now a fiercely committed Celt, "banged the ball among the straw beyond the touchline," in frustration and anger, as the rest of his teammates watched the tearful McMahon disappear into the pavilion and stood in an angry circle, debating whether they should continue the game. They "were waiting for a lead. (Johnny) Campbell gave it and like the sportsman that he is, his influence told", and play resumed with an incredulous Rangers side now 2–1 ahead.

Celtic fought hard and if McMahon had still been on the field, they would have clearly won. Both teams scored again, (Jack Robertson for Rangers and Henry Marshall for Celtic, both good legitimate goals) Celtic shot past the post on one occasion and over the bar on another, more fierce tackles flew in, some ignored by Mr Nisbet, some not, George Livingstone was booked for foul language, and then Mr Nisbet capped it all by allowing Rangers fourth goal by Bob Hamilton to stand when he was many yards offside. *The Glasgow Observer*, admittedly a biased source, claims rather improbably that Hamilton was "30 yards offside", but the other papers agree that he was "clearly" and "blatantly" offside. This made the score 4–2 and any chance that Celtic might have had of reducing the leeway disappeared when Mr Nisbet capped it all by blowing for time some three minutes early!

To say that this game was the talk of Glasgow and Scotland for most of January 1902 was no exaggeration. *The Glasgow Observer* explodes in fury and sarcasm, but it is worth also reading the words of the *Daily Record and Mail,* a paper with no known affiliations or sympathies with either side. "Bedouin" is outraged at what was done to McMahon, "the most skilful and sporting player of the age," and quotes what people said about the game. James McIntyre of the Rangers committee admits that, "The game was worth a draw," and at the close, Councillor John Ure Primrose, well known for his Rangers sympathies and connections but also for his sporting demeanour sought out Sandy McMahon and said, "You are the last man in the world that should be put off a football field," Such were the consoling words of the popular ex-Baillie, and James Welford, now of Hamilton Academical but who in his time had played both for and against Celtic said, "McMahon is the fairest player I ever opposed, and it is nonsense to say he merited being sent off the field. The sympathy of all those I have spoken to is entirely with him".

"Bedouin" also said that, after the game, Campbell, Smith and Drummond of Rangers declined to say anything that they could allow to be printed but "shook their heads when talking about the referee". We thus have the rare situation of Rangers being embarrassed by a victory over Celtic! Not only that, but Mr Kirkwood of the SFA was seen to walk out of the Celtic Park gallery before the end of the game in apparent disgust with that he had seen.

"Man In The Know" in the *Glasgow Observer* writes in a fine mixture of outrage and bewilderment. "I don't think that Mr Nisbet meant to be unfair, but dissatisfaction, not to say disgust, followed his every action from the time he threatened Hodge till the last minutes of the game when he presented Rangers with their fourth goal!...yet he puts me in a fix when he says the Light Blues were scrupulously fair in all they did". Warming to his theme, he splutters "...in (Johnnie) Campbell, they (Celtic) had the finest forward on the field – a player who showed pure football from start to finish. And what was his reward? Why he was played more foully than any other there! He was tripped up at least a dozen times, twice when about to shoot and at other times he was kicked and hacked disgracefully. And yet it was McMahon who was sent off! Please don't laugh at Scotland's most scientific forward being run off the ground for anything shady. Fancy a man like McMahon – a player in a class all by himself; a forward whose unrivalled touches have never been approached by any other player in the kingdom – being ordered off by a referee whose decisions would have tried the temper of a saint!"

"Man In The Know" then states, with tongue in cheek and in language and imagery that his readers would understand that, "McMahon assisted at the UIL (United Irish League) Convention in Dublin last Wednesday, but it is not true that he has engaged The McDermott QC (the most famous barrister of the day) on the advice of Mr Redmond (the leader of the Irish Nationalist Party), but I believe he has spent much of his time in rehearsing some famous passages from *Speeches From The Dock*"

By this time, however, serious questions were beginning to be asked about Mr Nisbet of Cowdenbeath. Rumours that he may indeed have had a drink problem were now freely circulated. Apparently after the game, he had said that Celtic's goal had been scored by "Drummond" (the left-back of Rangers!) and his report about the sending off of McMahon was several days late. He claimed that he had sent it on 4 January, but in fact the postmark said 6 January (*The Glasgow Observer* says acidly, "they do things different in Edinburgh" ignoring, incidentally, the fact that Cowdenbeath is many miles from Edinburgh and separated by the River Forth!).

Nisbet was then struck off the list at the Scottish League Committee for, "refusing to answer a civil question", and at the SFA meeting to discuss the alleged misconduct of Sandy McMahon and George Livingstone, President Kirkwood exonerated the two men without even a censure, not only on the legal technicality of the report being late, but also (by implication) that the referee was incompetent. In this he was backed up by Mr Morgan of Renfrewshire and Mr Rooney of Lanarkshire, but according to *The Glasgow Observer* (never slow to see persecution, whether real or imaginary) Mr Kirkwood had to fight off some opposition. But the "bigots were baulked".

There the matter closed. McMahon continued playing without any suspension, but the sad fact for Celtic was that the Scottish League Championship had been lost, for Rangers won their games in hand and claimed the crown for the fourth year in a row. "Man In The Know" reflects sadly however that it was all Celtic's fault for not tying things up earlier. This was, of course, true that Celtic had lost to both Hearts and Queen's Park in the last few weeks of 1901, so it is perhaps unfair to blame everything on the events of New Year's Day 1902. But he is delighted that justice had been done as far as McMahon was concerned especially in view of Sandy having had the misfortune to encounter a referee who was, "as autocratic as the Czar and as infallible as the Pope" – somewhat strange language for a Roman Catholic newspaper to be using!

Possibly traumatised by these events, McMahon did not return until an Inter City League game on 18 January against Hibs. He came on to a great reception from a crowd that had clearly not lost any affection for him. The following week, 25 January, saw Celtic at Gay-field, Arbroath in the Scottish Cup. It being Burns Day, the weather was appropriate with a biting East wind, and snow, which according to some reports, "fell in pancakes". Whether it was the conditions or the fanatical home support on a small ground, Arbroath twice led before half-time, but Celtic equalized and then with a goal which was remembered all over the locality for decades, McMahon scored with a brilliant shot from a distance.

It was the first time that a £100 gate had been registered at Arbroath, and the Arbroath players were visibly disappointed, not that they had not defeated Celtic, but more that they had not drawn and therefore had the chance to play a game at Celtic Park. A letter to the local paper from a Celtic supporting Arbroath man claims illogically that, "I am disgusted with the modern Celtic. The Irish in Arbroath are ashamed of them. Don't they shoot anymore? It's the high wages that did it." He then goes on to exonerate McMahon from such criticism.

Celtic then spent the whole of February of 1902 playing no one but Hearts! There was an Inter-City League match, a Scottish Cup game played as a friendly because of a frozen pitch, the real Scottish Cup game which finished a 1–1 draw before in the replay at Celtic Park on 22 February, the Duke scored twice to give Celtic a 2–1 victory after Hearts had gone ahead. The victory was ascribed to Celtic having been at Rothesay the week before with, "some solid training interspersed with loads of table tennis and billiards," and the usual evening soirees when they entertained the other guests with songs and recitations, something at which the erudite and urbane McMahon continued to be a great success.

A crowd of 26,000 were there at Celtic Park that day to see Hearts in the replay. Hearts would claim that the absence of the excellent Bobby Walker (because of a family bereavement) was crucial to their cause, but the truth was that this was an inspired McMahon performance. His first goal came from a free-kick, and his second was a brilliant cross-cum-shot which deceived the otherwise excellent goalkeeper George McWattie who kept the score down to 2–1 when a higher score would not have been unjustified. Last year's Scottish Cup Final had been avenged, and McMahon had been, yet again, the main man.

Such fine form earned McMahon another Scottish cap when he was invited to play for Scotland against Wales at Cappielow on 15 March. Funnily enough, this was the first time that he had ever played against the men from the Principality. *The Glasgow Observer* is predictably delighted and equally predictably, perhaps, snipes churlishly at Bob Hamilton of Rangers being picked as well. "Hamilton is being rushed for the position, but we won't mind his inclusion so much if room is to be found for Sandy McMahon, still the cleverest forward of the day". Hamilton, apparently has "friends in high places" and is likened to "Methuen", a word, which clearly meant something to the readers in 1902, but nothing to us today.

McMahon on the other hand, according to *The Glasgow Observer* is still a great player. "At Cathkin last Saturday, McMahon shone with great brilliancy (sic) and his singlehanded runs through the Third defence proved him still a power in the land, despite boycotting and purblind selectors". They were not however so "boycotting and purblind" as to omit him from the team against Wales, and the forward line of Campbell (Celtic), Walker (Hearts), Hamilton (Rangers) McMahon (Celtic) and Smith (Rangers) simply ran riot at Cappielow as Scotland won handsomely 5–1.

This was significant for McMahon's collection of momentoes, for he now had the full set, adding the cap against Wales to those he had had won against England, Ireland, Canada the English League and Irish League. He had also, of course, won the four domestic competitions of the Scottish Cup, the Scottish League, the Glasgow Cup and the Glasgow Charity Cup. Very few other players of the time could claim that.

The Press predicts that he and Campbell might even find themselves in the side for the "big" International against England at Ibrox on 5 April. McMahon's partnership with Alex "Cutty" Smith of Rangers was described as "classy and productive" and indeed Smith scored a hat-trick. McMahon himself now lived in hopes that he might yet be selected. He had played well enough against Wales, but crucially didn't score, and when the Selectors sat down after that game at Cappielow to choose the team for the Home Scots v Anglo Scots on 10 March (generally regarded as being the final trial for the "big" game), McMahon's name was conspicuous by its absence. It was as well for McMahon, however, as it turned out, that he wasn't chosen to play in that fateful game against England at Ibrox.

22 March saw the Scottish Cup semi-final against St Mirren at Love Street, the scene of many battles between players and fans in the past. This time, there was a strong referee, Mr Simpson from Aberdeen, who agreed with Celtic's protest that the black and white vertical of St Mirren was too similar to the green and white vertical of Celtic. St Mirren, the home team, therefore, had to change into light blue. (It was the rule in 1902 that the home team had to change). Celtic then scored in the first minute and remained on top in a tight contest, which finished 3–2. McMahon did not score but had a hand in all three goals scored by Livingstone, Campbell and McDermott.

Hibs met Rangers at Ibrox in the other semi-final in a game refereed by no less a person than Mr J Nisbet of Cowdenbeath who may have been struck off the list of Scottish League referees but was still, it would seem, on the SFA list and thus available for Cup ties! Nothing untoward seems to have happened, but Hibs won 2–0 and thus we had an all green Cup Final for the first time between Hibs and Celtic. It was due to be played at Ibrox on 12 April.

In some ways this brought things full circle as far as Scotland's two Irish teams were concerned. Hibs had won the Scottish Cup in 1887, and it had been said that it was this victory that persuaded the Glasgow Irish to try to form their own football team. Celtic had reached great heights, partly because they had allegedly denuded Hibs of star men like McMahon, but since then, Hibs had fought back and now we had the "Irish Cup Final" as it was commonly referred to.

But before that could happen, there occurred the disaster at Ibrox that would dominate the thinking of football for many years. It was at the Scotland versus England game held at Ibrox (Celtic Park might have been a better choice, but it lost the vote on the grounds that Ibrox was newer, the same reason that, presumably, had influenced the Glasgow FA committee in their strange decision last autumn concerning the Glasgow Cup Final), and McMahon might have been playing but for the quixotic inconsistencies of Scotland's selectors. He had played well against Wales, but found himself out of the team for Ibrox, although his friend Johnny Campbell was chosen at inside-left.

When Campbell reported injured and withdrew, the selectors turned not to McMahon who would have been the supporters' choice but to another Celtic man George Livingstone, a good player certainly, but not as good as McMahon. Any disappointment that McMahon may have felt, however, was swamped in the sheer horror of what happened at the game itself.

The collapse of a stand at the Broomloan Road end of the ground (the Celtic end in modern times) caused the death of 26 spectators and injuries to countless others. The "stand", made of wood, in which the spectators actually stood to watch the game, simply gave way and spectators plunged to their death or were crushed by other spectators or debris falling on top of them. It was said to be caused by the swaying of spectators to watch future Celt Bobby Templeton, "the Blue Streak" as he was called, charging down the wing. The game was played to a finish, and was a 2–2 draw, but very few people were concerned about that. It was an awful catastrophe.

Blame was of course thrown around at Rangers and their architects, there were immediate calls for all football to be stopped indefinitely, and of course the wilder lunatic fringe of religious movements claimed that God had caused it all because he objected to "atheistic and pagan" demonstrations at football grounds. More serious people did now begin to realise that there might be a problem with large crowds in stadia that were not particularly well designed, and belonged to clubs which, frankly, showed all signs of being interested in cramming spectators in with not very much concern for their welfare. Questions now began to be asked by politicians and newspaper editors.

There was one immediate consequence for Celtic and McMahon, and that was the postponement of the Scottish Cup Final, due to be played at the same ground the following week, a day on which virtually all football was now postponed to show respect to the dead. Not only that, but Ibrox was out of commission for some time, and a new venue had to be found for the Final. Hampden was now considered to be too small, the new Hampden would not be opened until October 1903, so the only venue left that could contain the large crowd was Celtic Park itself. Hibs were clearly unhappy about this, but after a certain half-hearted period of protest, moaning and unhappiness about, "Glasgow, as always, ruling the roost," saw the logic of it all (and the possible financial benefits), acquiesced and accepted the SFA decision.

"Milo" in *The Evening Times* is glad that the Scottish Cup Final is at last to be played, wherever it is to be. There had even been suggestions that the whole Scottish Cup should be abandoned but "Milo" affirms that, "Paralysis prolonged is nothing less than weakness and the eventual moping is nothing less than the surrender of common sense. We must arise and pull ourselves together and finish the season with something like enthusiasm". This is good advice for dealing with adversity but he also thinks, without giving any convincing reasons, that the delay will favour Celtic.

In going through the teams, "Milo" is convinced that McMahon will be a key player. "He has a style of his own and is without doubt the most marvellous footballer of our time. This is his eighth Scottish Cup Final (in fact, "Milo" is wrong here for it is only his seventh – 1892, 1893, 1894, 1899, 1900, 1901 and now 1902) yet he has been practising new tricks to baffle Breslin and delight the crowd."

The rabidly pro-Celtic *The Glasgow Observer* has a few doubts, however, and is sceptical about the attitude of some of the Celtic players who had "…not the slightest apprehension. I will not go so far as the use the word 'cocksure' but something very near it describes the feelings of the Celtic players…I trust the final will not prove another object lesson for the Celtic". Sadly, no one at Parkhead seemed to heed the Cassandra-type predictions of the newspaper, which loved them. The teams for the 4.00 pm kick-off on 26 April were:

Hibs: Rennie; Gray and Glen; Breslin, Harrower and Robertson; McCall, McGeachan, Divers, Callaghan and Atherton.

Celtic: McFarlane; Watson and Battles, Loney, Marshall and Orr; McCafferty, McDermott, McMahon, Livingstone and Quinn.

Referee: Mr R.T. Murray, Stenhousemuir.

McMahon would not have been one of the super-confident Celts that *The Glasgow Observer* warns about. He must have approached this game with a few qualms and doubts, and not without a few internal traumas of his own. A sensitive man like Sandy was clearly upset about the Ibrox disaster of three weeks previously, but there was also the fact that Hibs, to a certain extent, remained his team. Some of his friends and family still lived in Edinburgh and district and were Hibs supporters, however much they were proud of what he had done for Celtic.

In spite of Hibs own reservations, the game itself turned out to be one of the few highlights of the impoverished Easter Road history. For Celtic it was a huge anti-climax. The crowd was a meagre 15,000 on a dry, albeit cold day of 26 April. The paucity of the crowd was put down to the increased admission charges once again, genuine fears for their own safety of potential spectators, and the widespread (and possibly justified) perception that football clubs were interested in little other than their own profits even if it meant exposing spectators to unnecessary risks. There was also a rumour going around that the game itself was a bogey, for Hibs were bound to protest once again about the choice of venue and that the game would be declared a friendly. In addition, it was widely believed that the game would be a draw for another lucrative replay!

Be that as it may, the poor crowd turned up to pay the exorbitant price of one shilling, and those who came from Edinburgh departed the happier. It was a Scottish Cup Final, which never really got going. Hibs scored through Andy McGeachan with a back-heel half way through the second half of a dull game, and hard though McMahon tried, he simply could not get past the excellent Jimmy Harrower and Celtic did not get back into the game. It was an unhappy experience for McMahon who had now lost four Scottish Cup Finals and won only three.

Little is said about McMahon's performance in contemporary newspapers – the implication being that he did not do particularly well. *The Glasgow Observer* talks about "The Woeful Final", but then gives every impression of having changed sides with fulsome praise for the Hibs men. For Celtic, it says, the defence did quite well, but Johnny Campbell was out of the side and badly missed. But "Even Campbell cannot make stars out of duffers" – a reference to the other members of the forward line which included McMahon. It also asks the legitimate question why, when things were beginning to go badly for Celtic, did Livingstone and McMahon not change places? McMahon, presumably might have done better at inside-left alongside his young protégée Jimmy Quinn.

Years after this game, in the tribute paid to Sandy McMahon after his death in 1916, *The Evening Times* makes an odd comment about this game, and one which reflects little credit on a former colleague of Sandy's. In the context of how good Sandy was at scoring headed goals, the anonymous writer tells a story about John Divers in this

Cup Final. "Divers, the old Celt, now a Hibernian, saw a corner-kick coming straight to McMahon and just as the latter jumped up to make the flag kick a goal, he was gently pulled down by his old comrade, unnoticed by the referee and Celtic were deprived of an equalizing goal."

If this story is true, then it is to McMahon's credit that he did not make a fuss of this. Indeed, there may have been a certain feeling of stoical happiness for Hibs in McMahon as he sat at the meal at the Alexandra Hotel in Bath Street where the Cup was to be presented. Hibs had been the team that gave him his start in football and he still had many friends among the Irish community in Edinburgh, and indeed among the Hibs players that day. He would have been glad to see them back in the business of winning honours, even though the relationship between Scotland's two "Irish" clubs was not always good, certainly not in the minds of the supporters.

One hopes, in passing, that Hibs enjoyed their Scottish Cup triumph of 1902. There was a certain amount of insecure triumphalism about Hibs celebrations with the Scottish Cup being paraded along Princess Street. The team got off the train at Haymarket, thereby disappointing a large crowd of people who had been waiting at Waverley! Sneers about Celtic dominated proceedings. The players apparently sang, to the tune of the Boer War song *Goodbye Dolly Gray;*

Goodbye Celtic we must leave you
And you must reflect upon your woe
For we are off to Embra'
The Scottish Cup to show!

For a long time the Scottish Cup and Hibs have been strangers. Many times Hibs fans have emerged from the grim Leith tenements to face Celtic in Scottish Cup Finals, but Patsy Gallacher in 1914, Joe Cassidy in 1923, Dixie Deans in 1972, Henrik Larsson in 2001 and Gary Hooper in 2013 have broken their hearts. (And talking about Hearts, there was also, was there not, 2012?) Even in their great days of the early 1950s and early 1970s, Hibs never lifted the Scottish Cup.

And just to prove how wrong some writers can be, "Milo" in *The Evening Times* quotes an English writer as saying that, "the Scottish Cup may remain in Edinburgh for some time, for neither Rangers nor Celtic seem to be the teams they were". The next three Scottish Cups were in fact won by Rangers, Celtic and Third Lanark!

As far as McMahon was concerned in 1902, brave words about Hibs were about as good as it got. He was now more and more susceptible to injuries particularly in both his knees. He played on the Wednesday after that in the semi-final of the British League Competition (sometimes called the Exhibition Trophy, sometimes the Coronation Cup) when Celtic showed another meagre crowd of supporters what they could and should have done on the Saturday. McMahon was in fine form at inside-left organising the fine play of Tommy McDermott, Johnny Campbell and Jimmy Quinn as Celtic beat English League champions Sunderland 5–1. It was a pity that only 5,000 were there to see a fine exhibition of football, in what was, for all anyone knew, the swan song of Sandy McMahon. He knew that at the age of 32 and with knee problems, his days were numbered.

Apart from a few friendlies, he missed the games at the end of the season, in which Celtic's form was a mixture of terrific and appalling. They went down 6–2 in the rain and wind to Hibs (again!) in the Glasgow Charity Cup Final, but then won the British League Cup in glorious fashion with a Jimmy Quinn hat-trick after extra-time against Rangers. Sandy, injured and now contemplating a career other than professional football, watched these events from the touchline, genuinely happy for the success of the introverted young Quinn, whom the more prescient of Celtic supporters and commentators kept marking out as Sandy's successor.

Summer 1902 was a remarkable one in other respects. The Boer War ("no end of a lesson" according to Rudyard Kipling) at last came to an end in May 1902 after a fair amount of internal criticism from within Britain itself, particularly from the Liberals and the nascent Labour Party, and growing opposition to this seemingly pointless conflict. King Edward VII was crowned – but not before a serious health scare, which necessitated an operation for something similar to appendicitis, very risky and dangerous in 1902, and the postponement of the actual Coronation from June until August. On the sporting front, a great deal of attention focussed on the Australians winning of the Ashes in England. This series was indeed memorable, including as it did the infamous "Fred Tate's Match" and a famous innings in a lost cause by Gilbert Jessop, "the Croucher", as he was called, of Gloucestershire and England.

McMahon watched these events, still a Celtic player, but naturally wondering for how long. Realistically, he must have known that he could not go on at this level for ever, but he was still enjoying his football, and he still loved the club he played for, although he was aware that the four League Championships in a row won by Rangers had allowed supremacy to pass, temporarily at least, to the Ibrox side. In addition, losing two Scottish Cup Finals in a row to the Edinburgh teams had been hard for Celtic and their loyal supporters to swallow. The events of the New Year still vexed him as well. He knew that if he had stayed on the field that day, Celtic would have won the Scottish League, even with a mad or intoxicated referee.

B. Battles   N. Marshall   A. M'Mahon   J. Campbell   A. M'Pherson   P. Somers

W. Lonie   J. Moir   N. Watson   W. Orr   D. M'Leod

AGNEW & SON, PHOTO.

J. Quin   J. M'Menemy   W. M'Cafferty   W. Maley   A. Crawford   T. M'Dermott   J. Hamilton
(Manager)

CELTIC FOOTBALL CLUB, 1902-1903.
HOLDERS OF THE GLASGOW EXHIBITION FOOTBALL TROPHY.

*Celtic in 1902. It is a fair guess that the image of
McMahon (at back) was a later insertion!*

Yet Sandy retained faith in Willie Maley who was forever looking
for further talent to supplement what was already there in Jimmy
Quinn, Willie Loney, Willie Orr and Peter Somers. A couple of
youngsters from Rutherglen Glencairn, for example, James McMenemy and Alexander Bennett had recently been given trials. It was
clear that Celtic were going to fight back, but it was even clearer that
for the veteran McMahon, it would not be easy to find a way back
into that team. He also knew that, in any case, his days as a professional footballer were numbered. But, then again, nothing remains
forever.

13.

THE TWILIGHT OF A GOD

It is generally agreed that 1902–03 was not a good year in the history of the Celtic club. The injured McMahon was out for the early part of the season, leading to the belief that he was finished. He had played in a game against St Mirren on 23 August at Parkhead – a tough, rough game in the tradition of Celtic versus St Mirren, and one which had led a correspondent to one of the sporting papers to complain that, "the modern game has degenerated into a hard, bashing, ungraceful and reckless display of sheer animalism". The crowd was a poor one of less than 5,000 and the poor attendance was believed to have been caused by the counter-attraction at nearby Bothwell Castle Policies, where the great Gilbert Jessop, who had recently scored a century for England against Australia in record time at the Oval was doing likewise for Gloucestershire on tour against Uddingston!

Sandy played in the game against St Mirren, an unlucky 2–2 draw, but seemed out of sorts and aggravated his knee injury and thus ruled himself out until early December. The Glasgow Cup had gone yet again in a dreadful performance against Third Lanark in the Final, and points had been dropped in the Scottish League. Nor did things improve immediately on the return of McMahon. Form was dismal with a goalless draw at Partick Thistle, a defeat at St Mirren and an insipid draw with Morton at Parkhead on 20 December before a poor crowd. On that same day, Hibs won at Meadowside, the then home of Partick Thistle, and thus became the Scottish League champions for the first time to break Rangers stranglehold of the competition.

McMahon of course would have been glad to see this, for in spite of jealousy inside the Irish community; there was a certain residual happiness for this team. In particular, it was nice to see a monopoly of Rangers winning the League being broken. Indeed some Celtic supporters, although by no means all, were happy to say that they supported Hibs as well. It was often said 50 years later that Celtic supporters, disappointed and frustrated by the repeated failures and inadequacies of their own team in the late 1940s and early 1950s would express some happiness about the successes of the great Hibs team with their forward line of Smith, Johnstone, Reilly, Turnbull and Ormond. They may come from the strange city called Edinburgh, but the still wore green and white, and if Hibs were winning the League as they did in 1948, 1951 and 1952, at least it was not Rangers!

Hibs players in 1902 had not done themselves very many favours in the Celtic community by their triumphalism after the Scottish Cup Final last year, but there was still a curious relationship between the two teams – something that would last for the next hundred years and more. They were like brothers, kith and kin, but like most families, when there was a falling out, it was a spectacular one. But they were still (in 1902) undeniably Irish – possibly even more so than Celtic – and the supporters sang the same songs. Yet who can explain why it was Hibs (yes, Hibs!) who were the leaders in the campaign to have the Irish tricolour removed from Celtic Park in 1952? Perhaps even more difficult for some to get their heads round was why Rangers supported Celtic in this stance! Aye, there are things that, "a fella just can't understand," as Sam Weller used to say in *The Pickwick Papers*!

That Hibs were worthy champions was proved on 2 January 1903 when they came to Parkhead and won 4–0. This sort of form seemed to betoken a long period of success for the Easter Road men but the large Glasgow crowd of 18,000 were all the more disappointed in this lacklustre Celtic performance because the previous day had seen a tremendous 3–3 draw at Ibrox in which McMahon had scored twice. Against Hibs on the other hand, McMahon seemed lethargic, uninterested and clearly very slow, as if his injuries were now beginning to take on a permanent character. The second game in two days seemed to be too much for him.

There then followed a Scottish Cup tie against St Mirren, which incredibly took six weeks to complete. Two postponements because of weather, two draws, and an abandonment meant that it was 14 February before Celtic made everyone wonder what the fuss had been about as they beat St Mirren 4-0 at Parkhead before a massive crowd of 35,000 with McMahon scoring a wonder goal at the start of the second half. No one however realised that this was the last that he would score for the club.

Port Glasgow were then despatched in stormy conditions the following week to set up a prospectively thrilling Scottish Cup third round tie against Rangers at Celtic Park on the last day of February. In fact it was anything but. The weather was dreadful, but 40,000 were still enticed to watch a very one-sided 3–0 win for Rangers, with large sections of the crowd disappearing during the second half as their team, three goals down before half-time, failing to mount any sort of fight back in the second half.

"Man In The Know" in *The Glasgow Observer* is quite scathing in his criticism of the Celtic team. "Those who went out to Parkhead on Saturday with the expectation of seeing a close game in the Cup tie must have felt grievously disappointed at the runaway nature of the Rangers win…The Rangers have never played better and the Celtic have never played worse". He then goes on to stress that "new blood" is required and, although McMahon's name is never mentioned, he repeatedly talks about the failure of "Celtic's veterans". Everyone knew who he meant, but it was almost as if he felt it would be some kind of sacrilege to point the finger and to name and shame the man who had been Celtic's talisman for so long, Sandy McMahon.

The Daily Record and Mail is of the same opinion, with the added criticism that the team had been done no favours by being taken to their new "home from home" at Seamill Hydro. They were "stiff, slow, lethargic and short-winded". Yet on the day before "Milo" in the same newspaper had said that "there was not a brass farthing between the two teams". He was clearly very disappointed in Celtic.

The forward play was dreadful, and most of the crowd left convinced that changes would have to be made with fingers now pointed in particular at the old guard Johnny Campbell and Sandy McMahon. *The Glasgow Herald* agreed, saying quite unequivocally that, "McMahon and Campbell were lost on the heavy ground," and when Sandy was not picked for the following week's game, he must have realised that his days at Parkhead were over, as Maley began to take to heart the need for "new blood".

In truth, he had lost his place to some fine players in Jimmy McMenemy, Peter Somers and Jimmy Quinn. This was the new emerging generation, the ones that would become, without a shadow of a doubt, the best in the world in a few years' time. The problem was that the building of a team takes a great deal of effort, but Maley was painstaking in his efforts to do so. McMahon accepted that his great days were past, and not being a jealous man, helped the youngsters all he could, supplying advice to Maley when asked. Sandy being a centre-forward himself could see that this was the best position for the muscular, stocky but occasionally gauche Jimmy Quinn, but it took a while for the penny to drop with Maley on that issue.

Although he was still nominally a Celtic player until the summer of 1903 when he and Johnny Campbell were put on the "open to transfer list", he became far more interested in his bar at 209 Great Eastern Road, a job in which he excelled for he was efficient, sociable, welcoming and still very popular among the Celtic fans, who recalled his great days and did not blame him for the disasters of the 1902–03 season. In any case, there was a pleasant end to the season because the club, without McMahon but with a brawny youngster from Bristol Rovers called James Young, won the Glasgow Charity Cup, a harbinger of things to come as a new Celtic began to emerge. It took the sting from the pain, which had now lasted several seasons.

There was a small postscript to McMahon's career when he played a few games for Partick Thistle in the 1903–04 season on an amateur basis, (he was also offered a game on a match-to-match basis for Clyde) including one at Cathkin Park against Queen's Park who were at that time "between grounds" as their new and mighty stadium (also to be called Hampden) had yet to be opened. The new stadium would indeed open on Hallowe'en 1903 when Celtic came. McMahon's appearances for Partick Thistle were few and far between, and by the end of the season suffering from ankle and knee pains and even the occasional touch of lumbago, he gave up the game and concentrated entirely on his public house which was now called, unofficially at least "The Duke's".

His good friend Johnny Campbell was not quite finished with football yet though, and Sandy would have been delighted to see that. The manager of Third Lanark, a character with the unlikely name of Frank Heaven, was delighted to pick up the veteran Campbell, and Campbell had a marvellous season for the Thirds winning the Scottish League and the Glasgow Cup with them. It was Campbell who scored Thirds' only goal in the Glasgow Cup Final to beat Celtic on 28 November 1903, and he played consistently well in the forward line throughout the season teaming up with Hugh Wilson, Willie Wardrope and Tom McKenzie to play his part in winning Third Lanark's only Scottish League Championship in their sadly impoverished history.

McMahon would have cheered Johnny from the side lines, one feels, in this respect, but Campbell was less fortunate with Thirds in the Scottish Cup, for they lost to Celtic in the semi-final in 1904, this time Johnny finding the eager young half-back line of Young, Loney and Hay just a little too hot to handle. Campbell also played on until season 1904–05 when Thirds won the Scottish Cup – but the Cup Final was won without the now veteran Johnny Campbell. Campbell remained a loyal friend to Sandy, and Campbell himself reached a rare longevity for professional football players by living until 1947.

It was perhaps appropriate that the Celtic team changed its jersey to the horizontal hoops rather than the vertical stripes at the start of the 1903–04 season as the new Celtic began to take shape. Thus McMahon never wore the hoops, but he had certainly worn the stripes. He, as well as Maley and others, certainly laid the foundation for the new Celtic but it is sad to reflect that he never wore the famous hoops, not did he ever play at the new huge Hampden Park.

His bar flourished. McMahon had the advantage as well of being a well-read man, who recited Shakespeare and Burns at Celtic soirees. Like so many great men and great Celts, he was not snobby, conceited or bigheaded. He was proud of his achievements, but he also relished the glory of his successors, delighting for example in the goal scoring exploits of Jimmy Quinn, (especially the hat-trick in the 1904 Scottish Cup Final) the wiles of Jimmy McMenemy and the continuing managerial success of his old colleague and friend Willie Maley.

The Celtic community sustained a bad blow in the very early death of Sandy's friend Barney Battles in early 1905. He had just turned 30. McMahon and Battles were men of a totally different character, but both shared the same passionate love for the Celtic, even though Battles had taken a wayward path with disastrous consequences at one stage. But McMahon had welcomed him back, and the pair remained firm friends with McMahon remaining very supportive for Barney's widow and children after Barney died of gastric flu at such a young age. Barney's wife was pregnant at the time of his death, and the posthumous child was also called Bernard and grew up to be the Hearts legend called Barney Battles junior.

Time and time again, Sandy would be asked about his great games. In particular the headed goal of the 1899 Scottish Cup Final was a constant topic of conversation in the bar with Sandy being asked to show how he did it. He always of course maintained that football is in essence a simple game – just get to the ball first and put it where you want it! Either pass it to a teammate, or score!

Things began to go wrong when he lost his wife, Annie, in March 1908 in the most tragic of circumstances, in childbirth, of "puerperal septicaemia", something that simply would not have happened a hundred years later with the improvements in medical care and the National Health Service. But 1908, although a modest beginning to welfare reforms had been begun with the Liberal Government of Campbell Bannerman, Lloyd George, Herbert Asquith and Winston Churchill, was very much the dark ages as far as medicine and social welfare was concerned.

She was only 33, and he had been totally devoted to her, and she to him. From then on, Sandy's own life and health (and that of his children) went downhill. We now enter upon a dark phase of Sandy's life, for like many a man, however successful in other respects, he found domestic life too much for him. Too old for war service in 1914, (he was now almost 44) but still compelled by regulations to do some war-related work, Sandy found employment in the munitions industry as an iron-borer, a job he tried to combine with his interests in the licensing trade, but this did not last long before his health broke down completely.

He suffered from nephritis, a chronic complaint of the kidneys, a condition, which compelled his removal to the Glasgow Royal Infirmary in late 1915. It was left to Willie Maley, who had attended him assiduously, to tell the story of what happened a few days before his old friend's death on 25 January 1916. One Sunday night at the height of that dreadful war saw the great Willie Maley in tears as Sandy rolled back the bedclothes, pointed to his emaciated legs, bruised and scarred by many injuries sustained on the playing field. "Willie", he said, "at least these two legs have done their bit for the Celtic".

One has to be careful about that story because it is also told about Dan Doyle who died a couple of years later, but it is certainly in character with the man. Like many an early Celt, he died young, at the age of 45. "Man In The Know" of *The Glasgow Observer* pays him an eloquent tribute calling him the "Bayard" of Scottish football. Bayard was a medieval French horse famous for its magical powers, and it is difficult to imagine a more eloquent tribute to the man, even though the writer at one point seems to confuse the Ibrox Disaster of 1902 with a heavy Scottish defeat sustained some 10 years earlier in 1892, and which was indeed called the Ibrox Disaster in footballing terms, until the Disaster in another sense rendered this description in bad taste.

THE BAYARD OF FOOTBALL.

A TRIBUTE TO SANDY M'MAHON. (BY "MAN IN THE KNOW.")

There passed away on Tuesday afternoon the greatest player Association football has ever known. That is not a personal opinion, but it would be the unanimous verdict if a vote were taken of those who were fortunate enough to see the late Alexander M'Mahon—Alexander the Great, I might term him—in the prime of his football career. Fortunately I do not require to labour the point. The spectator of twenty years ago can better tell the story of Sandy's greatness than I or any other writer, even if a whole page of this journal were taken up. "I will let the old hands explain to the younger generation what manner of player he was, for it is beyond me to put on record his mystifying gift that amounted to, genius. I can only repeat there never was such a wonderful player in all the history of the game, nor are we ever likely to see his equal. He was unique, unapproachable, literally and figuratively, the last word in scientific football, the delight of spectators, the despair of opponents. To analyse his play, to describe his subtle methods, would take up a good deal of space, even if one were able to explain the incomprehensible.

Born in the Border district 45 years ago, Sandy removed to Edinburgh, and when quite a lad attracted the notice of senior clubs by his play in a junior club, the Woodburn. A short term followed at Easter Road, and then he came to Parkhead at the close of 1890. His first match was against Dumbarton on the New Year's Day of 1891, and he had the pleasure of seeing his future partner on the left wing score the equalising goal. But not until the season 1891-2 did

M'Mahon and Campbell

begin that career as the great left-wing of all time. Sandy had come to Parkhead as a centre-forward, and filled this position for nearly three months. About the middle of March the Celts set out on their first Lancashire trip—they had already crossed the Border and met the Corinthians at the Oval in 1889—and it was then that the M'Mahon-Campbell partnership began, to last several seasons, and astonish the football world by its brilliancy. The first match was at Bolton and ended in a draw—2 goals each. Sandy went clean through the Bolton defence to score the equalising goal, and at the finish 2,000 spectators waited outside and accompanied him to the hotel, cheering him all the way. Such football they had never thought possible as Sandy showed all through the game. Next day the Celts met Ardwick, won by 7—2, and the left-wing later found the boys at Blackburn on top by 2 goals to 0, with M'Mahon fooling Dewar, Barton, and Brandon to such an extent that Geordie Dewar spoke to Campbell on the field and asked him who in thunder was the unknown player who could do as he liked with the mighty Rovers. Then on to Sheffield, to win by 3—1, and home again, tired out but happy, though they had to go down to Paisley at the week-end, where they lost to the Saints in a League match by 1—0, and lost the League Championship as well. However, if the championship was lost, the three cups were won next season, and the championship lost by only 2 points; Dumbarton gaining 37 points to Celts' 35. The season of 1891-2 was the Celts' first great season, and the first in which M'Mahon and Campbell played together from start to finish. Sandy was capped against England that season and was one of the eleven

Associated with the Dreadful Ibrox Disaster.

Next season Scotland claimed both Celtic wingers, and if we were beaten at 'Richmond the fault lay not with the Celtic contingent — M'Mahon, Campbell, W. Maley, and Kelly. Three times was M'Mahon capped against England, and other international honours were showered upon him, he and Willie Maley also figuring against the Canadians in 1891. (Continued on Page 5.)

(Continued on Page 5.)

FAMOUS CELT'S DEATH

(Continued from Page 3.)

Unfortunately he had first one knee and then the other put out, to say nothing of an ankle, but that long before his time he had to drop out of the game, leaving behind him a reputation such as no other player is ever likely to gain. Had it not been for the accident that befel him I feel certain he would have beaten Alec. Smith in point of years of service, for his was the style which required neither speed nor virility for success. He could get through a game on one leg, I might say, and that he had to do many a time; indeed, it seems but yesterday that he hirpled through a Cup Final on Old Cathkin, and helped to beat Rangers. To reprint an old saying, I may add that as a footballer and a gentleman-footballer, we shall never look upon his like again.

On and off the field he was the same good-natured, philosophic, kindly fellow, taking the frowns and smiles of fortune like the man he was. He was as difficult to upset temperamentally as physically, and was never known to grumble. I never betraying no confidence when I state that his last words to the clergyman who attended him on his deathbed were words of gratitude. He thanked the reverend gentleman for all he had done for him, and near the finish, when speech was denied him, he smiled and gently pressed the visitors' hands when told that Willie Maley, Michael Dunbar, Johnnie Campbell, and other old friends, were standing over him. That was Sandy; smiling and grateful, kind and affectionate, facing death without fear, leaving life void of regret. So passed away the Bayard of football, without fear, without reproach—the type of a perfect gentleman—R.I.P.

The funeral to Dalbeth Cemetery took place on Thursday afternoon from the residence of his brother, Mr James M'Mahon, 28 Slatefield Street, Glasgow. The mourners included:—Messrs T. White, J. Kelly, J.P., J. Colgan, M. Dunbar, J. Shaughnessy, W. Maley, P. M. Rogers, A. Murphy, J. Cruden, etc.

The funeral arrangements were efficiently carried out by Mr F. M'Cabe, 71 London Street, Glasgow.

So many bad things were happening in January 1916 – and would continue to happen for some time – that there might have been a danger of people forgetting Sandy. It might have happened with a lesser man, but this was Sandy McMahon, a man whose contribution to the very early Celts, frankly, is incalculable. He is one of the truly great Celts whose name deserves to be venerated and adored.

His death was reported in *The Southern Reporter* a Borders newspaper in the context of his family, and we are told that his cousin, also called Sandy McMahon is the famous Galashiels cricketer. *The Evening Times* of 26 January 1916 even admits him to its leader column with a glowing tribute to his literary achievements, "Showing that the professional footballer has thoughts higher than the kick-game, I may mentions that the late Sandy McMahon was a keen Shakespearian student, and could quote the Bard of Avon as freely as he and many of his patriots can quote the Bard of Ayr."

The same newspaper then pays a fulsome tribute to Sandy McMahon, calling him a, "source of inspiration to all young players who sought to excel by more forceful methods than those skilful movements so peculiar to the Celts". He did not indulge in, "heavy charging, tripping or hacking". It being in the middle of a war, and military imagery being the order of the day he is described as a, "Field Marshall in those tactics and high strategy which go to win battles, and no player ever left his mark on Association Football to the same extent as the dead Celt."

As for his interests off the field, *The Evening Times* then goes on to remind readers about his love of Shakespeare and to state that, "he was never so happy as when witnessing one of the master's plays". Unusual for footballers he had a "philosophic turn of mind", showed great "equanimity" and as for other sporting interests, he was a proper "Edward Diggle". Edward Diggle being a great snooker and billiards player of the day, and a man to whom McMahon bore a slight physical resemblance.

The Daily Record and Mail agrees with most of this and adds that McMahon was a, "well-read man who might have adorned a higher walk in life than that in which he earned his living. He was the soul of good nature, possessed of a pretty wit and was a first class story teller". Very few folk had a bad word to say about him, and it was generally agreed by all sources that a real injustice was done to him on New Year's Day 1902 when he was so cruelly sent off for what was a pure accident.

Naturally people talk romantically about football players after their death, but in Sandy's case, "facts are chiels that winnae ding," in the words of Sandy's hero from Ayrshire. His record speaks for itself, and there is the undeniable fact that Celtic had two bad seasons in the 1890s – 1895 and, in particular, 1897. In both these seasons, Sandy McMahon was out for long spells, and that is surely significant.

As for what he was like off the field, there is enough for us to form a judgement that he was a human being of the first order. Kindly, good-natured, never one to harbour a grudge – even against those who deliberately set out to crock him on the field – and a man who showed the greatest humanity to all. He was aware that he was lucky in his gifts as a footballer and he was proud of what he could do to make his supporters happy. Those who lived in Glasgow at that time would have had loads of evidence to see just how impoverished and miserable so many of the supporters were. Sandy was happy that he gave them something to cheer about.

Years after his death, he was still remembered by those who saw him play. Celtic in the mid 1930s went through a really bad patch with little being won, and Maley and others would frequently upbraid those who wore the green in 1934 and 1935 comparing them unfavourably with "the Celts of Old". By this he meant, mainly his own great team of 1907 and 1908, but he would also talk romantically about Sandy McMahon. Another person who saw Sandy in action is clearly sorry for the present generation, "You who did not see Sandy McMahon play know nothing about the weaving artistry of our football game; all ease and grace, as if born to make a football answer his will".

Those who saw him play have now long gone, but it is all the more incumbent upon the new generation of Celtic supporters and historians to remember him. He was one of the very many men who in the own way laid the foundations for the Celtic that we have today. There can be no greater tribute than that.

Sandy's grave in Dalbeth Cemetery after the service organised by the Celtic Graves Society

HONOURS WON

3 Scottish Cup medals

4 Scottish League medals

4 Glasgow Cup medals

4 Glasgow Charity Cup medals

6 caps for Scotland

8 caps for Scottish League

1891–92	Scottish Cup	Glasgow Cup	Glasgow Charity Cup
	v. England	v. English League	
1892–93	Scottish League	Glasgow Cup	
	v. Ireland	v. England	v. English League
1893–94	Scottish League		
	v. England	v. Irish League	v. English League
1894–95	Glasgow Cup	Glasgow Charity Cup	
	v. English League		
1895–96	Scottish League	Glasgow Cup	Glasgow Charity Cup
	v. Irish League		
1897–98	Scottish League		
1898–99	Scottish Cup	Glasgow Charity Cup	
	v. Irish League		
1899–00	Scottish Cup		
	v. Irish League		
1900–01	v. Ireland		
1901–02	v. Wales		